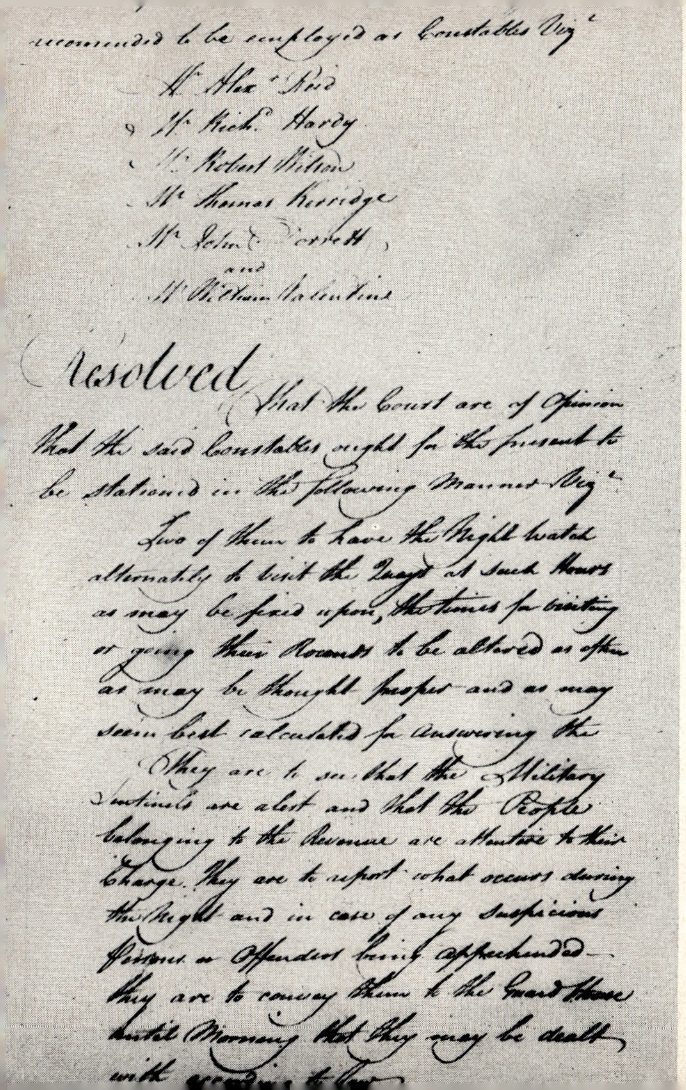
recommended to be employed as Constables Viz^t

Mr Alex^r Reid
Mr Richd Hardy
Mr Robert Wilson
Mr Thomas Kerridge
Mr John Dorrett
and
Mr William Valentine

Resolved That the Court are of Opinion that the said Constables ought for the present to be stationed in the following Manner Viz^t

Two of them to have the Night watch alternately to visit the Quays at such Hours as may be fixed upon, the times for visiting or going their Rounds to be altered as often as may be thought proper and as may seem best calculated for answering the

They are to see that the Military Sentinels are alert and that the People belonging to the Revenue are attentive to their Charge. They are to report what occurs during the Night and in case of any Suspicious Persons or Offenders being apprehended they are to convey them to the Guard House until Morning that they may be dealt with

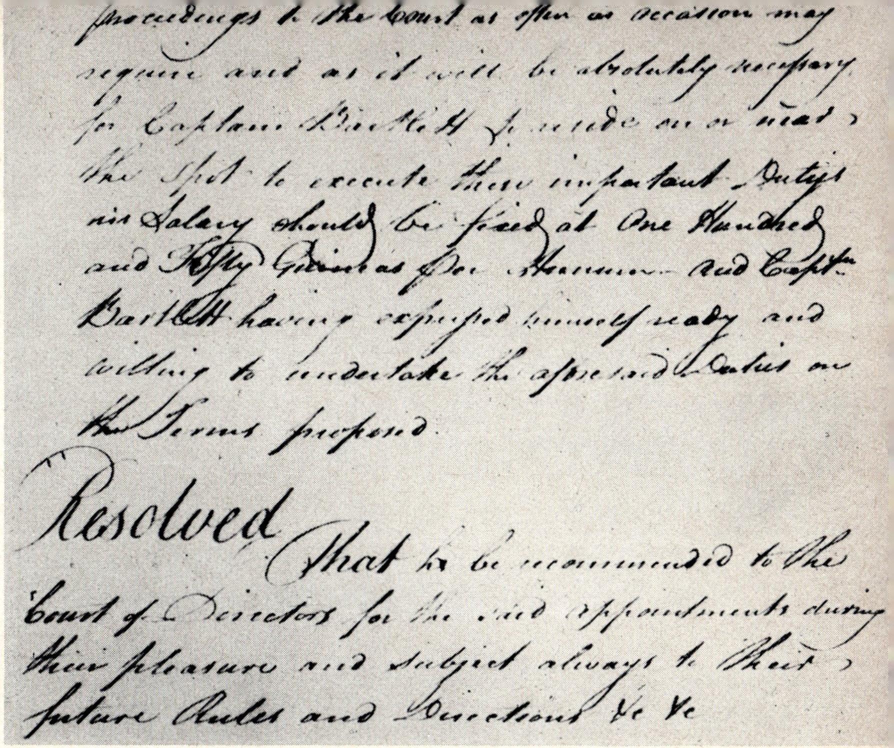
proceedings to the Court as often as occasion may require and as it will be absolutely necessary for Captain Bartlett to reside on or near the Spot to execute these important Duties his Salary should be fixed at One Hundred and Fifty Guineas per Annum and Captn Bartlett having expressed himself ready and willing to undertake the aforesaid Duties on the Terms proposed.

Resolved That it be recommended to the Court of Directors for the said appointments during their pleasure and subject always to their future Rules and Directions &c &c

Left: West India Dock Co. Minute, 5th November, 1802, showing the first constables and operating instructions.

Above: West India Dock Co. Minute, 26th October, 1802, showing appointment of Capt. Robert Bartlett.

DEPARTMENTAL LIST, OCT. 31, 1888.

POLICE DEPARTMENT.

Sheet **94.**

NAME	Age in years and months on 30th June, 1888		Appointment or Employment	Date of Appointment or Employment		Nature and extent of Duties	Length of Service in years and months on 30th June, 1888		Rate of Pay or Wages				Amount of Superannuation Allowance on 31st Dec., 1888	OBSERVATIONS
				First	Present				On 30th June, 1888	Rising to	Date of Maximum	Date when last raised		
	YRS.	MTHS.					YRS.	MTHS.	PER YEAR £	PER YEAR £			PENSION £	
CAHILL, J. Z.	38	3	Superintendent of Police ...	21 Jan. 1875	1 Aug. 1888	Responsible for security of docks and premises, both by day and night, as to fire and depredation, and for the strict observance of the law, and Company's Bye Laws. Maintain a vigilant supervision of the Dock Police, inspect and keep efficient the fire engines, hydraulics and gear connected therewith, inquire into accidents, and take depositions of witnesses	19	2*	245	250	1889	1 Jan. 1888	90	*Service to date 26 April, 1869. House rent free.
WEST, W.	58	11	Chief Inspector (Western Dock)	31 Dec. 1849	15 Sept. 1871	Instruct the Sergeants, Constables and Watchmen as to their duty, and visit them on their stations at uncertain hours. Superintend the search of labourers at cessation of business, and be responsible for the general behaviour of the men under their control	38	6	130	...	1876	1 Jan. 1876	104	House rent free.
CAMP, J.	54	9	Inspector (Eastern Dock) ...	31 May, 1852	27 April, 1881	Ditto ditto ditto	36	1	130	...	1884	1 Jan. 1884	96	Ditto
FRENCH, W.	51	3	Inspector (Town Warehouses) ...	26 Aug. 1867	5 Jan. 1886	Ditto ditto ditto	20	10	119	...	1890	1 Jan. 1888	52	Ditto
ROSE, R. T.	40	8	Inspector (Tilbury Dock) ...	31 July, 1875	8 Feb. 1887	Ditto ditto ditto	12	11	107 10/	...	1891	1 Jan. 1888	29	Paid 10s. a week in lieu of house.
WELLS, W.	57	4	Sergeant	24 Nov. 1854	28 July, 1875	Assist the Inspectors, prevent the use of fires, caulking, repairs and plumbers' work on the Quays without permission, attend tide at dock entrances with sufficient men to preserve order, and keep persons out of danger, and vigilantly supervise the Constables and Watchmen of their reliefs	33	7	PER WEEK s. d. 42 6	...	1878	1 Jan. 1878	74	Sergeants perform 12 hours' duty per diem. House rent free.
McLEOD, C.	60	8	Sergeant	6 May, 1862	18 April, 1877	Ditto ditto ditto	26	1	42 6	...	1880	1 Jan. 1880	57	Ditto
BLATCH, F.	57	10	Sergeant	27 Sept. 1867	11 July, 1877	Ditto ditto ditto	20	9	42 6	...	1881	1 Jan. 1881	46	Ditto
SORTWELL, C.	47	6	Sergeant	1 Jan. 1864	21 Aug. 1878	Ditto ditto ditto	24	6	42 6	...	1882	1 Jan. 1882	52	Ditto

Top:
London Dock Division, P.L.A. Police—Summe
1915. (*Taken on retirement of Insp. Beech*
CENTRE BACK: Police Electric Ambulanc
with P.C. Lewis and Attendant. BACK ROW
Firemen Palmer, Simmons (later Ch. Con.) an
Hobbins. Barg.-Searchers Marshall, Edgar an
Billings. CENTRE ROW: Office P.C., 3 Sgt.
unidentified, Sgts. Richards, Wheatley, Jone.
Knolls, Hyams, Chambers and Cotteril
SEATED: Det. Ch. Insp. Pyke, Insps. Berr
White and Meacham, Insp. Beech, Mr. Stua
Baker (Ch. Pol. Off.), Supt. Seaton, Ins
Matthews, Insp. Trumble, Det. Sgt. Damer,
Det. Insp.

Above:
London Dock Division, P.L.A. Police, c.1935.

Left:
Two stalwarts on duty, West India Dock Ma
Gate, c.1899. (*Photo courtesy Donald Rumbelow*

Above: Group of Mr. Stuart Baker's Shipping Police, c.1 925.

Left: Police-manned Ambulance, Royal Docks, c. 1925.

Above: *Opening of King George V Dock*, 8*th July*, 1921. *S.S. "Demosthenes" entering from lock.*

Left and below: London Do Main Gate — ancient a modern. "Plus ça change, pl c'est la même chose!"

Above: Lord Ritchie of Dundee (Chairman P.L.A., 1928-41) at Annual Parade, 1930

Below: London Dock contingent ready for visit by H.M. The Queen, 1959.

Left: Mr. Gannon and his Deputy Mr. Ellen with Lady Ellerman.

Above: Mr. Oliver's last parade—March, 1972.

KEEPERS OF THE DOOR

The History of the

PORT OF LONDON AUTHORITY POLICE

— by —

GLYN HARDWICKE

Published privately by Peel Press on behalf of the Port of London Authority Police.

A

Printed in England by Adams & Sons (Printers) Ltd., East Street, Hereford

ACKNOWLEDGMENTS

Over the many years involved in the writing of this story, my wife (of whose work I write in the Introduction) and I have received a wealth of help and goodwill from many sources. Of those not obvious and named in the text, we would particularly like to mention Sgt. Vic Hardy, and we both owe a notable debt to Frank Marsh, lately P.L.A. Librarian, and to his successor Dick Brown. But many good friends and ex-colleagues at all levels of the Authority, with whom it was always such a pleasure to work, may know that their assistance and goodwill neither has been nor will be forgotten. I would also record my profound gratitude for his most generous help and advice to Colin Simpson, "but for whom . . . ", as they say.

One important acknowledgment remains. While one hopes that the interest of its subject may ultimately bring a readership wider than merely those directly concerned in it, yet for all the goodwill, without the assistance of a most material kind this book simply could not have achieved publication. Were its contents not already dedicated to the men of the Force it concerns, may I say merely that it would without a moment's doubt or hesitation be laid at the feet of the distinguished and gracious lady to whom it owes, in a very real sense, its existence—Lady Ellerman.

GLYN HARDWICKE

"The Port of London is the front door of the Kingdom – and the Port of London Authority Police are the keepers of that door."

The late Sir GERALD DODSON, when Recorder of London, in a trial at the Central Criminal Court, Old Bailey.

KEEPERS OF THE DOOR

ILLUSTRATIONS

All the photographs are by courtesy of Port of London Authority with the exception of Page II (c) which is by courtesy of Donald Rumbelow.

INTRODUCTION

The scope of the Port of London Authority, even now that the up-river groups of enclosed docks are successively closed down, is yet vast enough for there to be ample interest in the history of any of the aspects which make up the whole. In my case, from my work for more than a decade as the Authority's Prosecuting Solicitor, that aspect is naturally law enforcement. Gratification of the slightest curiosity will reveal that the initial source of the P.L.A. Police lies much further back in history than 1909, when the Authority itself was created – and much further back than is generally realised.

The arrogant young lorry-driver visiting the Docks for the first time who takes offence at a routine patiently and courteously carried out by the uniformed man at the gate, and who snaps, "Oh – f . . . off and get a real copper!" realises little – and no doubt cares less – that the officer on whom he vents his coarse spleen is a member of the second oldest police force in the world – a force founded in 1802, some 27 years before Sir Robert Peel inaugurated the Metropolitan Police.

Not that this history is directed at the arrogant young lorry-driver. In one sense, though it is a story worth telling for its own sake, it is but the communication of my intense pride in the Force with which it was my privilege to work. For the Port of London Authority Police is a corps of specialists, second to none in efficiency and integrity, effecting in the highest traditions of the British Police Service, of which it is a small part, the enforcement of the criminal law in the thousands of acres for which it is responsible. Some measure of its effectiveness may be judged by the respect in which it is held by members of all other forces whose work brings them into professional contact with it.

Personally, I am aware that when I joined the P.L.A. in 1961, it was less an organisation than a family, sticking proudly to Winston Churchill's initial definition of it – "a public trust for public service". Even as I continued in its service, I saw it renounce that definition and set out to become a commercial colossus in its own right (or wrong?), standing on its own feet. Those of us who knew it as it once was may now deem it inadvisable to recollect that in its original conception this public trust used to make a quiet million or two each year, every penny of which was ploughed back into services and amenities for the port's users. Remembering which, I recall faces of men who would once almost have sold their souls for the Authority, each assume a faintly smiling mask. But perhaps at the back of their memories may ring a sentence pronounced long ago by a great historian – "It is only by the light of the past that we may hope to penetrate the infinite darkness of the future." And perhaps, as the story of their police is told, there may be found deep within it some element, some secret based upon which there will return, one day, the pride and glory that the Authority once knew and the importance and prestige of its police whose history, never before written, I now set out to tell.

But I would first like briefly to mention that it was the vision of the man who first brought me into P.L.A. which was the initial inspiration for this project. It was he who directed my chance discovery of Colquhoun's Treatise of 1800 into a determination to tell this story. Dudley Perkins will be remembered justly for achievements far more significant than this, but by me for this above all.

Many years have passed since I first began this gigantic labour of love – too many, I confess, for there have been long periods when it has been laid perforce aside, later to be revived and resumed. During these years I have left the service of the Authority, accepting "professional vasectomy", as Voluntary Severance was once wittily described.

I have spent an immensely happy period as Assistant City Solicitor at Guildhall. And now I have been retired and have left London – to live, by a happy coincidence, in the Cotswolds, only a few miles from the geographical source of the Thames whose lower reaches form the "front door of the kingdom" of which the P.L.A. Police are the "keepers" of the title.

I should like to add a few words of explanation regarding the position of my wife. Through my interest in the history of law enforcement generally, she developed an interest of her own in it, no less strong. When I undertook the task of writing this history and had completed the first two Parts of this book, I came to know that the third and longest part of it lay hidden within the uncharted Minute Books of the original Dock Companies which lay, literally by the hundred, in the cellars beneath that proud and endearing Head Office building affectionately referred to by the police as "Trap One" – and which those who came to run the Port of London Authority deemed it ultimately proper to dispose of for cash.

The task I faced was to read every page of every one of those 420 books in sequence, extracting from them every reference to the Dock Company Forces which, after many amalgamations, finally came together in 1909 under their present title. Each of those ancient books is some 500 pages long, every page covered in spidery handwriting in faded ink on dusty paper often almost like vellum. The magnitude of the project was nothing less than daunting. As far as we could ascertain, no-one had ever before tackled the entire sequence, for any purpose. It was this task which my wife undertook to shoulder.

For months – for years – she stuck to this formidable loom. Eventually, the work completed, she set about the selection of the extracts she had made, uniquely able to see the whole picture and thus to instruct me so that the true perspective was retained. She has spent literally hundreds of hours in the Authority's library and elsewhere, being involved in this history as wholly as I have been.

If the work of any historian were to be defined as the final writing of a factual narrative and no more, then I would truly be the sole author of this book. Since it most clearly is not, then my wife is quite as much the author of this history as I – in many respects, indeed, more so. It was my intention that she should be named as what in truth she is – its co-author. She has however insisted on having no more than a researcher's credit. I have with reluctance capitulated.

Therefore – on behalf of my researcher and myself – to the PORT OF LONDON AUTHORITY POLICE, from the Chief Constable to the most junior man on the gate, whether of 1802 or of today or of any time between – I beg with respect and affection to dedicate this history.

GLYN HARDWICKE

PART ONE—THE SOURCE

The origins of Police in Britain — Saxon systems of law enforcement — Norman systems — The English Constabulary — London in 1796.

PART ONE—THE SOURCE

Nothing can be seen in perspective save against its true background. To consider the historical development of the Port of London Authority Police is to consider a great landscape through which it winds like a river from its source. And just as the Thames, London's neglected highway, has travelled far from its source in the Cotswold Hills before it enters, at Teddington, the control of the Port of London Authority to become, in the late Recorder's words, "the front door of the kingdom" – so the history of the P.L.A. Police must be traced back to and past its source and followed through many years before its members may justly and properly be seen to be keepers of that door.

Of all the facets of the English sociological system which make up life as we know it today, there is certainly none about which the ordinary citizen is less informed than its police system. The late Charles Reith called this ignorance "the blind eye of history". Yet not only may a study of it provide us with many useful lessons, but in the story of its development lie the seeds of comfort and of confidence. Nobody who has studied the English police system which, save for those deriving directly from it, is unique in the world, could retain any fears about the possibility of this country ever becoming a 'Police State' – the parrot-cry of the anarchist and agitator. This makes it a study worth making even apart from our present purposes.

When England as we knew it was centuries younger than she is today, there grew among its inhabitants the realisation that civilization is valueless and governments impotent unless there is observance of law. Man – from his earliest development a gregarious animal, cannot live alone. He will always collect into communities. For reason of collective security, each community must have rules – or laws. And since there have always been and will always be, a small minority who will not keep the rules – who will try to take advantage of others for their selfish ends, some means must be found, if society is to continue at all, of compelling these to conform – to enforce not uniformity but conformity.

The whole conception of law enforcement in a free country is but a balancing act. Against the liberty of the individual must be weighed the sanctity of life and property that belongs to him as a member of a community. Complete freedom is not, nor ever has been, the prerogative of the individual. It cannot be. If it were, it would include freedom to steal, to rape, to kill. If society is to exist at all, then the individual within it must or should be free to act as he wishes provided he does no injury to his fellows.

Indeed, as has been wisely written, so naturally is society free that only by its failure to secure and maintain observance of its rules – its laws – can it destroy itself. But should it prove itself unable, then it cannot escape self-destruction.

Now from the earliest history of mankind, there have been but two contrasting methods of law enforcement open to him. "Yer pays yer money and yer takes yer choice" runs the old fairground maxim. So with the roots of the plant that is the hemlock or the rose in the garden of society today. Which will you have – enforcement imposed from above, or enforcement exercised from below? There is no other way.

In the darkness of law enforcement history glow two tiny star-points of light. Enforcement from above, entailing the use of military or para-military power – that is one star to follow. The other involves the placing of social responsibility upon the community – inducing and developing in its members the realisation that they are interdependent – that if the weak are not to be imposed upon by the strong, then it is the community itself which must prevent the evil which lies somewhere within the hearts of all men.

Of all the nations in all the history of all the world, it is remarkable but true that none save our own (and those whose methods derive directly from us) has ever followed that second star.

Turning their backs upon the easier, the more obvious method of law-enforcement, involving the power of the military and the fear of punishment, our earliest rulers devised the alternative way – the creation of the whole-time citizen, to deal with the law-breaker not as representative of the ruler, but on behalf of the people of which the law-breaker is himself one.

The earliest known community organisations in England were those of the Danish and the Anglo-Saxons. Basically, they devised three systems of law-enforcement for England. One was *gegildan*. The population was divided into units or *gilds* – not guilds – upon each of which was imposed the personal responsibility for the good behaviour of the members of that group. If a gild-member did anything unlawful, then the gild had to pay the penalty due.

There followed a development of this system which was known as *bohr*, a word which means surety. It was really the pledge of good behaviour of not only oneself but of all the other members of the community of which one was part, – a wider concept than that of the local gild, or brotherhood.

The third system outlasted both these – indeed, in certain of its aspects it exists today, enshrined, if fossilized, deep down in the strata of the common law. This is *tything*. From this really sprang the origins of the British police service. It began – as most things in England began, and still begin – in the City of London, in the reign of one, Athelstan. Everybody in London was recorded as being a unit in a *ten*. Each group of ten had a leader, who was responsible for the behaviour of himself and the other nine. Each ten of these groups formed a *hundred*, and the ten primary leaders freely elected one from among themselves to be their leader, he being responsible for himself and all the leaders and, through them, for every member of the hundred. And all that the national leader did was to direct that every single person should belong to a "ten." What one may ask, could be simpler?

Now these tens and hundreds were charged with the duty, under their elected leader, of catching and punishing thieves from among their number – and also, be it noted, reimbursing the victims to the extent of the loss sustained. Thus the leader of the "tithe" (Saxon for "ten") became an official of the peace. So, above him, was the "hundred-man".

From tything there grew the more complicated and sophisticated system known as *frankpledge*. The population increased, and the hundreds had to become enlarged. The new, larger unit was the *shire*, which elected a leader from among the "hundred-men". His duty included attending and giving judgment at all the courts wherein all disputes in the shire were settled. And when these courts so multiplied as to prevent his seeing to each one, he was allowed to appoint a representative – known as the *shire reeve* whose name was eventually elided into *sheriff*. Here was the foundation of today's Justice of the Peace, as we shall see.

There followed a period of development difficult to outline, much of it being obscured by the mists of time. But what happened was that the original groups of ten became groups of twelve, their leader becoming responsible for the production of any one of his group at the court held by the sheriff. If he did not appear, the maximum penalty was thereupon imposed on the group as a whole. Here lie the origins of policing by mutual responsibility.

In due course, the Normans came, changing the ways, the customs, even the language of the conquered. The sheriff became the *vice-come*. And above him came the first identifiable demonstration of that evil which, centuries later, Lord Acton was to immortalise in one of the greatest truisms in our language (so often misquoted to boot!) – 'Power tends to corrupt, and absolute power absolutely'. Central government tasted power and became intoxicated with it. Frankpledge, not eliminated, was changed and exploited. The *courts leet* became the means of collecting unjust and tyrannous fines and taxes. And yet, far below in the hierarchy, the original leader of ten survived – he was now the *headborough* – responsible for the arrests of criminals in the name of the people. And as such, he was too useful to those who had tasted power to remain himself wholly uncorrupted. By the 13th century, he was a mere executive officer of the sheriff (the name which had somehow crept back into common usage).

The next development was swift and dramatic. Under the King stood now the Barons. Beneath them, the sheriff had sadly declined in power. Between them stepped the Knights – winning power at first by force in order to check that of the Barons. And to administer the localities in their control, the Knights used the ancient headboroughs, who recovered something of their original integrity. And from the Knights in due course sprang the centre-piece of English justice – the Justice of the Peace.

Below them, the headborough now became a junior Peace Officer. By the time of Elizabeth I, he had acquired a new title – "Petty Constable",* – in which basic capacity he was not finally extinguished in office until the industrial revolution of the 19th Century.

In due course, the shires were divided by central government into parishes. To each Parish there was a single Constable. He was elected or appointed at the local Court Leet. All fit men were liable to serve in this capacity, whether they liked it or not. The position, by the way, was unpaid. Towns followed a similar pattern, their constabulary officials being known as the Watch. The night watch used often to be provided by the Craft Guilds.

Meanwhile, the general political development of the nation was scarcely as serene as the outline above might make it seem. Above all – upon the political history of England lies, even in retrospect, one awful and ugly blot – the only period during which England in all her history lay under military and personal dictatorship – the sentence England served under a renegade Welshman named Williams, who called himself

*There are many and varied suggestions proffered by police writers of the past and present as to the etymological derivation of "constable". The true explanation is both simple and obvious. It makes nonsense of *comes stabuli* (an inexplicable combination of one Norman and one Saxon word!) and varieties of *cuninge* (a wholly Saxon source for a word unknown until long after the Saxons had been evicted by the Normans!). For the answer, one has but to appreciate that "able" as a suffix has been known for centuries, bearing the same meaning as it does today – and then one must consider the modern word *connâitre* in French – in particular the *circumflex* accent. This accent indicates the absence of a once-present "s". Thus the Norman equivalent of *connâitre* was *connaistre*, or possibly *connestre*, the meaning being "to know" in the sense of recognising or identifying. Thus we have a Norman official who was able to be known to everyone in a small locality – one who was *connâitre-able* or, as it would more probably have been written, *connestrable*. Now allow for the normal elision of the "r" and we have, in essence, the name and definition of the "constable" – in the language existing at the time of his first appearance.

Cromwell. Arrogantly this mistaken man tried to abolish the "kin police" system (as it was sometimes known) and to substitute for it sheer military power. This was a sad, if temporary, resort to that other system which England alone of every civilized nation on earth had chosen wisely to ignore – law enforcement imposed from above by fear and naked power.

Cromwell divided the country into twelve districts, placing each under the personal autocracy of a Major General, each of whom had a force of some 6,500 armed and mounted troops with which to impose his, and his ruler's, personal will – a figure which, by the way, does not take into account the collection of spies which are the essential adjunct to any totalitarian system.

In a few short shameful years, all this enforced structure simply fell apart. Seeking the reason, not even the most ardent monarchist could claim it was the personal quality of that charming philogynist, Charles II. Happily, it seems that there is something in the English people which renders them able to do almost anything they are asked and almost nothing they are told. Cromwell could not last because he was practising a system to which the English people simply will not respond.

Speaking of Charles II, one item for which the merry monarch is perhaps given too little credit is the institution of a body he intended should be known as Bell Men but who were very soon, from their founder's affectionate diminutive, popularly called Charlies. In essence, they were set up to combat the criminal tyranny of the highwaymen – and indeed, had not most of them been decrepit, they might have succeeded, but the Government for its part inaugurated a series of rewards and pardons for those who informed. The result, certainly with the benefit of hindsight, was all too inevitable, as the ill-served population metamorphosed itself into a veritable army of blackmailers, rendering the constabulary impotent.

The office of constable itself became progressively more unpopular. The duty galled. A policeman's lot was emphatically not an 'appy one. Understandably, the Parishes chose the wrong solution. Constables on their appointment were now permitted to pay deputies to act for them – a privilege which created another army of professional scum, otherwise unemployable, who became almost at once a subsidiary branch of the enormous industry of crime.

Meanwhile in London, the main source of these evils, the early 18th Century saw the slide into total breakdown of the parish constable system, and the start of a cancer which spread remorselessly through the Home Counties and into the Provinces, reaching its nadir in riot and uncontrollable crime.

As early as 1691, however, there had arisen in London the Society for the Reformation of Manners. There was a large number of these – one of which, astonishingly, was composed of constables! Some of them had been formed from desperation, some from less worthy motives, but all were really private armies, vigilante groups, taking the law into their own hands. In 1694 were published the infamous Black Rolls, listing all who had been prosecuted by these private societies during the preceding year. Indeed, in 1738, when they were discontinued, they were sufficiently detailed to be regarded as criminal statistics.

Behind these self-styled guardians of morality toiled a laggard and reluctant legislature. Actors were the first to be singled out – in 1713, 'all players of interludes' were deemed in law to be rogues and vagabonds and in 1737, this was extended to all thespians save those expressly licensed by the King – this was recognised as a measure attributable to Sir Robert Walpole, and his personal reprisal for the satires of Henry Fielding.

There is on this topic the interesting case of *R. v Handy* in which tumbling was found to be permissible since no copy of a script was available for the authorities – a legal circumstance later to be paralleled exactly by the epidemic of strip clubs in the West End of London before the Lord Chamberlain's office in this respect was abolished.

In their passion for reform, these private societies became at best 'a kind of voluntary police', as Radzinowicz describes them. Their methods of operation were not without interest. Their agents carried blank warrant forms. The informers trotted round to the nearest society agent, collected from him a blank warrant, filled it in, and appeared hastily and formally before a magistrate, who signed it. Back went the informer to the agent, where the warrant was passed to a Constable by whom it was served. Such was the level to which that ancient and once honourable office had deteriorated – a mere civil process-server.

A measure of considerable importance at this time was the Receivers' Act of 1702. Before that date, receivers of stolen goods had been no more than accessories after the fact. Under the Act, for the first time the receiver could be convicted even without the thief being first identified and then prosecuted to conviction. (Shades of Fuschillo!). But without effective policing, the cuckoo of corruption reared its head in this nest also, and there grew up the practice of owners coming to agreements with receivers, such as the infamous Jonathan Wild, which amounted to – 'Give us part of the goods back and we will refuse to prosecute' – a practice not made strictly illegal, by the way, until s.23 of the Theft Act, 1968! But tragically, it was the active participation of Constables in the original scheme which made it both safe and profitable for all concerned.

In course of time, it began to be realised that one of the essential elements in effective law enforcement was the honest and willing assistance of the ordinary member of the public. But the appointment of more constables, which the occasion demanded, was rendered of small value by the establishment of professional deputies.

In 1735, it was the Hue and Cry Act which was mainly relied on to catch villains, with its penalty (of £5, at that time really worth something) for any who declined to join in the chase. But a pamphlet of 1738 really declaimed the need of the age and the attitude of the citizen. Summarised, it said "We don't want more laws – we want more order!" And a letter traced by Sir Leon Radzinowicz dated 1751 is not only on the point but contains an amazing forecast of what was to become the second of the nine principles established in 1829 by Rowan and Mayne. Having stated that the natural force of the people was the best instrument for the control of disorder, it ran: 'Its strength will be found to be proportionate to the people's respect for the laws'. This remarkable foresight will stand out with a greater significance hereafter.

In fact, the letter goes on to recommend that greater attention should be paid to the ancient office of Sheriff, suggesting that he might be given *posse comitatus* – power to conscript anyone between 15 and 50 to his assistance in defence of the law. But there was no identifiable response from the legislature.

Indeed, the law had made an even more serious blunder in deciding to bring into operation the Rewards Act, which though passed in 1692 had remained without any appreciable effect. Worse than that – and again to cite Sir Leon Radzinowicz – "although the institution of a standing army continued to be regarded as incompatible with the constitutional freedom enjoyed by the people of England, the practice of calling out troops, and more particularly the militia, to act in lieu of the police whenever public order seemed to be in danger, was becoming a regular tactic of the civil power".* The shade of Cromwell, it seemed, had not been exorcised.

At all events, one sees at this point the legislators of England taking, for better or worse, a fresh course – a new tack. They decided to commit the country wholly to the reward system, this being in their mistaken view the only effective weapon against crime. Suddenly the world – or at least the underworld – was thrumming with the magic of "incentives", in the form of immunity, impunity, relief from services, and ordinary filthy lucre. Statutory rewards having proved inadequate, private ones were encouraged. Rewards became so much routine that the lack of them was regarded as injustice. In 1753 one, John Poulter, arrested for robbery, wrote almost in the shadow of the gallows an account of his last five years of activity, which set out the names and particulars of all his criminal associates and included everything down to a glossary of criminal argot. When by some mistake he was hanged as originally sentenced, there was a public outcry!

If a man were convicted on the information of an accomplice under any of fourteen main statutes, pardon for the informer became claimable as a statutory right. This was often used to set a receiver against the thief and vice versa. But more and more incentives now seemed to be required – such was the basic fault of the system.

Pardons became the established price of important information, even being advertised by the Home Office! It took a little-known reformer writer named Edward Sayer, to sum up the decline in 1784, condemning the system in his 'Observations' as "rotten to the core, but necessary to some extent for lack of a preventive police". Then, prefacing uncannily the wise words of Lord Gardiner and others of our time, Sayer remarked "The one security in punishment lay not in its severity but in its certainty". It seems, indeed, that beneath a veritable cess-pit of injustice and corruption, minds that could think were active. Voices could be heard to cry for some entirely fresh alternative to the reward system.

But for the time being, no action was taken. Transportees came flooding back to homes and families because there was no police to prevent them. One could get up to £25 reward for smuggler-catching even if one happened to be a smuggler's mate! Armed gangs arose, bringing rewards for their apprehension of up to £500 plus a share of the goods seized from them. One legislative development is interesting today when our Criminal Injuries Compensation Board is active – the Waltham Black Act of 1772, under which up to £50 could be claimed by anyone losing an eye or a limb while trying to arrest offenders.

As for the parish constabulary – while they disclaimed receipt of such rewards, official records show that between 1786 and 1797, no less than £94,000 was paid out to law officers for services in obtaining convictions of offenders.

And still, understandably, the volume of crime in London increased. A reduction by Parliament in the rewards payable, served only to make prosecutors more reluctant. The public were now responding directly to Government bribery, and yet the Government seemed unable to see it. One far-sighted M.P., a Mr. Bennett, seeking a fresh start, did propose the total abolition of the reward system. In the end a Bill was allowed

*An obvious parallel with the activities of the late and unlamented "B" Specials in Northern Ireland, is struck here, those regrettable armed paramilitary chaps having nothing to do with Special Police at all. It will be happily remembered that one of the first actions of the Committee sent there under Sir Arthur Young was to dis-arm and abolish the whole institution.

through to this effect, though only in 1798, and then it was so mashed by amendments that it proved useless, and Peel had it abolished in 1826.

Thus, public rewards continued to be advertised and accepted as incentives to private treachery by local authorities, as indeed by the Home Office itself. Many were the examples cited to support the theory that the system was the best that could be devised. Yet it was not until 1800 that Government rewards became payable only in respect of offences against the Government.

The system was not only deep-rooted – it was infectious. H.M. Customs followed the Government's lead and municipalities were not far behind. Even parishes took part – often, from impecuniosity, restricting themselves to supplementing private rewards. Magistrates took the same wayward course, and encouraged the wealthy to do likewise.

From as far back as 1716, Insurance Companies had advertised rewards – this really being the germ which set going the whole disease. It will not go unnoticed that they continue to do this today, the contemporary standard being 10% of the total value of the goods recovered. One day it may be examined officially whether this practice, so beneficial, commercially, and not without occasional limited advantage to the local C.I.D., may not have the effect of subsidising crime. Of course the Insurance Companies of today would never be willing parties to such failings, but there are many today who are gravely concerned that their contemporary 10% might have just such an unintended effect. Cerainly the history of the 17th and early 18th centuries serves to show that it is, as a system of justice, perilous in the extreme.

Another blight on the health of society had long been the Common Informer, whose motive was never justice but strictly personal gain. This excrescence was one who started private prosecutions for certain crimes and offences without being either personally or even vicariously aggrieved. Yet he was, in law, entitled to claim a part of any resulting fine imposed on the person convicted. Those who seek to justify the accusatorial system against the 'enquiry into truth' which the English criminal trial does not even pretend to be, may here in the Common Informer see the devastating example of the 'vested interest' in conviction and penalty far more than even the weakest police could be said to have today.

Of course, not only was the Common Informer indefensible, he was never regarded with other than wholesome contempt. History contains several splendid examples of proper vituperation – notably 'viperous vermin' (by Coke, no less!) through 'unprincipled pettifoggers' to 'practisers of extortion through caprice and moral tyranny'. The title itself became one of abuse. The one strange thing is that they were allowed to continue, with statute after statute recognising their existence as if they were necessary.

We can see a variation in the late 16th century, with the statutory appointment of an official Government Informer in the drapery trade. This was followed by the creation of similar offices in the world of coal, silk and lead. As will be anticipated, corruption at once increased and the Long Parliament, to its credit, abolished all of these officials. Behind their slimy trail, the Common Informer re-emerged, slug-like, from the undergrowth of the underworld.

There followed next a period in which Parliament's intention seemed to parallel that curious contemporary deterrent to integrity enshrined in the adage 'if you can't beat 'em, join 'em!' It was as if Parliament, having found the Common Informer ineradicable, tried next to have him used for the benefit of society, at least in the case of lesser offences. They let his obtainable gains range between a few shillings and a hundred pounds. (In passing – under one act of George III, up to fifty shillings could be diverted from fines to the Common Informer whose proceedings saw the conviction of anyone for having in his possession any materials stolen from a ship in the Thames).

It was suggested that at his best the Common Informer was almost a voluntary policeman, – but the theory becomes untenable as soon as it is realised that payment was on results. Even today, time and energy has to be spent in combating the recurrent slander that promotion from the beat depends on the number of convictions obtained. (A very great Flying Squad friend of mine, now long dead, used to say, "Mate – if promotions depended on arrests, I would have been the Commissioner bloody years ago!"). Radzinowicz observes with unaccustomed gentleness, "The result was a social situation which relied upon the Common Informer to act as a protector of the community against a vast mass of delinquency. These hopes were unfulfilled". With the benefit of hindsight – small wonder!

This whole septic state of affairs came to its suppurating head when the 18th Century was but one third past. We who are so cynical, even if correct, in tracing modern criminality in America and, later, Europe directly to the ill-starred imposition of Prohibition after World War I, would do well to recall that the English Parliament made a similar and equally ill-starred error in 1736, when a statute was passed imposing a total ban on the consumption of alcohol in Britain. This provided the Common Informer with a veritable riot of fun and games, and blackmail, perjury and a free trade in informations directly followed.

Indeed, by 1738, they became so universally hated that, with 12,000 informations under the 1736 Act alone under their belts, Common Informers had to be given some degree of protection! Assaults on their persons was made a felony, punishable by transportation for seven years. And yet this, which marked for practical purposes the summit of their personal power, marked also the start of its decline. By 1816, their doing of evil for personal gain was universally condemned. When the Metropolitan Police was founded in 1829, its first Joint Commissioners, Rowan and Mayne, publicly and vehemently opposed the continuing existence of the Common Informer. By 1839, the Magistracy was given power to reduce or even refuse their cut. Yet it is astonishing but true that 48 Statutes which included Common Informers' rights were repealed only in 1951 – and twelve of that 48 were passed into law after 1825 – one even in our present century!

Still – while it was never less than evil that a man should be permitted to execute justice for motives of personal greed, it would nonetheless be wrong to condemn all forms of incentive to a reluctant criminal – or even a reformed one – to come clean. One such incentive had been created as long ago as 1699 and lasted for almost 150 years. This was the Tyburn Ticket. Its definition shows its title to be misleading. It never was a certificate of immunity to the attentions of the hangman. Under the 1699 Act, anyone who brought to justice a burglar, shop-breaker or a horse-thief was entitled, upon the latter's conviction, to a certificate – but of exemption from compulsory service as a parish constable. This became known as a Tyburn Ticket only because the specified crimes were all carrying the death penalty, with its concomitant trek to the foot of the Edgeware Road and its resultant sobriquet.

Some interesing legal arguments are recorded as to the limits of exemption gained. In 1761, a protracted trial established that it was limited only to the parish in which the felony was committed. Even so, it was extremely saleable, and was often sold for up to £40 cash. The system was abolished in 1826. It may have done some good, and its harm was small when compared to that wreaked by the Common Informer.

The lot of the Parish Constable itself was scarcely "'appy" – as mentioned – if he did fail to pay a deputy to do his job, or if there was negligence in its performance by such deputy, he could be fined up to £20.

Looking now in greater perspective at the principle of collective responsibility – we have seen that its foundation lay in the Danish and Saxon systems. It was the Statute of Winchester in 1285 which established the compound result in law. It was 1585 when actions for damages against the hundred were recognised in part of an Act of Elizabeth I. In 1735, formalities such as 'notice' were imposed to limit such actions, and 14 years later, there was a top limit of £200 on the recovery against the hundred unless the action had included proper corroborative evidence. In 1766, the same system was extended to looting from shipwrecks. And not until 1827, under Peel, was the hundred, and the rights against it, formally abolished. And despite the examples we have seen (the Common Informer and the Tyburn Ticket) of incentive by personal gain, there were repeated instances of attempts to stimulate the ordinary citizen to recognise his civic obligation to ensure that the peace of his locality was kept.

At which point, and against that briefly sketched background of the English system of law enforcement – it is time to take a short but close look at the state of England as she was in 1796. For it is that year which forms the springboard from which we may leap into the years of history that lie ahead of it.

London in 1796 had a population of 870,000. (It was to increase by a full third in the following 35 years). Within the metropolis, then as now, the City within the city functioned under a system derived from ancient charters and Acts of Common Council. Indeed, the City was the only part of London which had any properly organised system of local government. All around it lay this vast urban sprawl – Cobbett's "great wen" – without legal being – a huge collection of townships, manors and parishes which had, as Maitland wrote in 1885, "no common ruler at all save King and Parliament".

The City comprised but 12% of the total population of London. And yet 40% of the effective constabulary lived and worked and had their being within the square mile. Outside the City, there were but 3,500 constables and watchmen and similar functionaries split up into independent local units and without unifying control.

Peering at this unco-ordinated muddle, we may see still retained the High Constable, the original unpaid conservator of the peace appointed by the ancient 'Hundred' – now sworn in before the Magistracy and the one remaining link between the Magistracy and the Petty (Parish) Constable.

The Petty Constable was elected or appointed annually by the Magistrates but was responsible not to the population of which he was a part, but to the High Constable on their behalf, by a curious twist of events. The Petty Constable was unpaid and usually mainly or wholly illiterate, socially as well as literarily. (Blackstone observed that perhaps this was just as well!). The office was still compulsory, but the hiring of 'substitutes' was now de rigueur.

Separately from the Petty Constables, the parish appointed and paid several lesser types of peace officer – beadles, night-watchmen and the like. To find details of their appointment and their employment generally, one has to turn to Local Acts. Again, the perspicacious Edward Sayer sums up the whole: "The peace officers were either orderly without power or powerful but disorderly". Then there was that isolated private army – that group of men, mostly villainous to some degree, controlled by the Metropolitan Magistrate at Bow Street since Henry Fielding and his fraternal successor – soon to be a mere venerable relic and never a 'police' force in the 'preventive' sense of that term – the Bow Street Runners.

For in 1792, an Act had created seven official police offices, in addition to the one at Bow Street which had grown haphazardly from the high morality and blind integrity of Fielding. Now it was to serve as an example. The Act of 1792 created 21 Metropolitan Stipendiaries, three attaching to each of the seven new Offices. To these was to be added, as we shall later see, in 1800, an eighth, of far greater importance than any – the Thames Police Office at Wapping.

The Stipendiaries were appointed from barristers of three or more years standing. They received from the Home Office a salary of £400 per year, later progressively raised to a final £800 plus pension. Each had its specified area of jurisdiction, Bow Street overlapping all in this respect. The Stipendiaries were more than magistrates – they administered and personally directed the men under their control, being literally "guardians of public order". Each had his establishment of gaolers, messengers and the like, and each had power to appoint precisely six constables. (In 1821 this number was altered to "a sufficient number"). To this ruling the Thames Police Office, upon its creation in 1800, was the sole exception, having a force of eighty-six constables. Indeed – creation there might mislead, for this was really but a statutory recognition of the Marine Police Institution – of which more shortly.

But it is vital to appreciate that these police were in no sense preventive police, which is the meaning of the term that we know and take fully for granted. These police were but executive officers of the Stipendiaries. For the ordinary parish constable, however, they had understandable contempt. One Stipendiary, Allen, said, "The police constable and the parish constable are animals of the same genus, the one being the natural enemy of the other!"

Thus we have two types of police, neither being police as we understand that term. But that was not all. For, superimposed upon and intermingling with these two bodies were a number of forces of independent police. Expensive to set up and to maintain, private security forces were yet perfectly legal at this time. They were usually restricted to a small personal area, comparable in many respects to the security companies that we know today. And of these, several were established and maintained by various Merchant Companies. Even so – and we shall return to them shortly – they were less 'police' in any sense than salaried watchmen.

There was another form still of incidental police, to be found in the emergency units set up ad hoc and specifically to quell riots and similar public disturbances. The outstanding example of their activity relates to the Gordon Riots of 1780. Another was an association of gentlemen elaling themselves "The London Military Foot Association", which in 1781 reconstituted itself into "The Honourable Artillery Company", whose long and glorious history since its foundation is far beyond the scope of this volume. For our purposes, it must be stated that the very existence of such bodies evidences the parlous state into which the constabulary system had sunk.

One final example of incidental police which must be touched upon is to be found in the institution of the Special Constable. His foundation dates originally from a statute of Charles II in 1662, misleadingly entitled "An Act For The Better Relief Of The Poor". Special Constables were appointed for a specific emergency, acting under the immediate direction of the Metropolitan Magistrates, though sometimes in conjunction with other bodies. Their enlistment whenever public order seemed in danger became routine. They were technically mobilised by the Home Office. Since the creation of the Metropolitan Police in 1829, they have held a place not without honour in the police service of this country, being currently appointed by a Chief Constable under s.19 of the Police Act, 1964. The first Act mentioning them was passed in 1831, and their work during the Chartist Riots of 1848 has never ceased to be recognised as invaluable.

Under the Act of 1792 which created the Police Offices, the constable's salary was twelve shillings per week. Though this was progressively raised, it may be noted that in 1829, the constable was paid less than the average ordinary unskilled labourer of the day. He received neither pension nor compensation if injured on duty. But they were permitted to receive rewards and to earn private fees for warrant-serving and the like. A form of overtime grew up, under which the occasional bonus was obtainable. There were also means less reputable by which the constable could increase his income and several of those who had won themselves some name would hire themselves out for private service at rates which showed a handsome profit. Several of the Bow Street group retired in due course and set up as private enquiry agents – but Bow Street was always exceptional, and when the runners were finally abolished by the Act of 1839, they were working almost wholly on the incentive system, choosing their duties and even their employers to suit themselves, some of them not even above suspicion of conivance in crime.

Still, in 1796, the idea of policemen as full time servants of the state was not thought of. The Runners were fundamentally executives of local magistrates' courts, concerned with the enforcement of the Stipendiary's decisions. Some became Clerks of those courts. A few even became practising solicitors! But long before 1829, neglect of duty was almost endemic among the British constabulary. High Constables were often no more than petty tyrants, and Parish Constables feeble and contemptible.

For example, we have Colquhoun's Treatise of 1796 to inform us that there were in that year 43 official gaming houses in London, which attracted between them over 8,000 regular gamblers, whose bets totalled well over seven and a quarter million pounds! Lower down the social scale were to be found an almost infinite number of brothels and taverns which, since vice was no more than a common nuisance, became the bases for the criminal fraternity. Corruption was everywhere. Whores paid the local police regular fees for the right not only to walk their beats but to be protected from rivals! Worst of all were the flash houses, of which there were over 200 in London alone. Here thieves resorted, robberies were planned and robbers were hidden when on the run. Police officers not infrequently dropped in for drinks "on the house" – thus ensuring the continuance of the business of the house without molestation. Complete impunity for such places was universal. The bigger ones had secret exits, departments for receivers, and "schools of crime".

By now, incentives were indistinguishable from temptations. Rather than put such places down, the watchmen relied on them for a large proportion of their income. Even in the City, it was the fact that the Billingsgate Fish Market lost thousands of pounds to another unofficial market nearby expressly existing for stolen fish, and materially underselling its provider!

It is of course true that information cannot be purchased, save at the price of at least retrospective connivance. But the principle had been enlarged so as to increase by far the bounds of propriety and the public interest. Compounding a felony – refraining from prosecuting in consideration of a reward, – had been a serious offence since Saxon times, where it was known as *theft-bote*. But it had become so overlaid by statute and by case law that its operation had eventually become wholly obscure.

Under what was known as Jonathan Wild's Act in 1717, it had become a felony punishable by death to take a reward under the pretext of helping an owner recover stolen goods. (Wild had commanded a veritable army of criminals, selecting victims, planning the thefts, indexing the loot and selling the goods back to the owners for half their value). In 1752, another Act had stopped anyone advertising a reward for the return of stolen goods "with no questions asked", under penalty of a £50 fine, which makes an interesting comparison with s.23 of the Theft Act, 1968. These two Acts were not repealed until 1827, under Peel. And yet more than a century before, an acute City Marshal named Hitchin had observed "The Thief-taker is a thief-maker". For the system was useless, devoid of some organisation of preventive police.

It is one of the pitfalls of history that time has a habit of fore-shortening itself unless deliberately stopped from so doing. But if today's reforms seem slow to us, it is worthy of remembering that the basic change which was about to be launched in 1796 by Colquhoun had been voiced, without effective accompanying action, continually for three quarters of a century.

But during the final increased vocal agitation for reform, one landmark had taken its place in 1755 in the form of the Thief-Takers' Trial. Its full story is too long even to be summarised here as fully as one would wish. But it had started on a summer evening in 1754 in Deptford, with the robbery of a tailor by two youths named Kelly and Ellis. They were in due course convicted, mainly on the evidence of two men – Eagan (who had bought some of the goods in an inn) and McDaniel (who had arrested them) but behind these two were signs of a sinister figure, a professional thief-taker named Berry. And even as the Deptford court pronounced Kelly and Ellis guilty, the High Constable of Blackheath – a giant of integrity named Joseph Cox – stepped smartly in by arresting Eagan, McDaniel and Berry – together with the robbed tailor – for conspiring together to effect the robbery. Their trial took place at the Old Bailey in March, 1755, and brought a "special verdict" – the jury seeking legal direction as to whether the accused could be guilty when a court had earlier found that Ellis and Kelly had robbed the tailor with no suggestion of conspiracy. Legal argument went on with intervals until the following December. Finally, the slimy four were acquitted, only to be re-arrested by Joseph Cox and convicted early in 1756 for conspiring to procure rewards by falsely obtaining convictions of Kelly and Ellis, who were at the same time pardoned and their initial robbery convictions erased.

Nor was that all. For the trials of McDaniel and Berry in particular had brought to light the fact that several innocent people had been wrongly convicted in the same way. Altogether, between 1754 and 1759, McDaniel and Berry stood in the Old Bailey dock no less than seven times, although in the end, they were convicted only on the original Deptford conspiracy. Eagan, in passing, had been stoned to death by a furious populace during an earlier period in the pillory!

The only redeeming feature of this appalling series of disclosures is that at least no official police officers were involved. But the five years during which the affair remained a cause celebre served to demonstrate to every literate citizen in the land the shocking degradation to which the administration of justice in England had descended. Many years later – in 1816, after a series of parallel disclosures, John Townsend, a noted commentator of his day, was to refer back to it, emphasising the generally overlooked but wholly admirable integrity of Joseph Cox, summing the matter up by saying, "The system which placed personal gain in direct opposition to moral duty was perhaps even more to blame than the creatures who slithered about under it".

But Townsend was looking back fully twenty years after one man had contented himself not with speech but with action. This was Patrick Colquhoun. For him, the cess-pool which London had become stank now too much for silence. At first alone, and later supported by John Harriott – a man if not as brilliant, then as brave – Colquhoun had spared no efforts to put into operation and into law his certain conviction that the only answer to the depths of corruption was the creation of a force of preventive police.

Within two years, Colquhoun had established the "Marine Police Institution", (today the Thames Division of the Metropolitan Police) and within six, a second and similar force of preventive police – the force that is today the Port of London Authority Police.

PART TWO—THE STREAM

Colquhoun's theories and projects — The "Honourable Companies" — The Marine Police Institution — The Treatise of 1800 — The first enclosed docks — Colquhoun's second force.

PART TWO—THE STREAM

History is generally regarded as a chronicle of events, of facts, of action. While undeniably true, this conveys an impression which distorts more than it reveals. For history is more than all else the story of people, of their actions and reactions, and of the events that resulted. Having briefly looked at the development of the police system in Britain, and having seen the rough state of the country in 1796, we shall find ourselves from this point onwards concerned exclusively with the Port of London. But while it is necessary to show the state of the kingdom's "front door" at this point in history, not least because it was the launching pad from which two men, Colquhoun and Harriott, leaped blindly into the future, in the confidence of their beliefs, it is right, if people are to be regarded as more important than events, to become acquainted with these two leading actors before we consider the stage on to which they strode and what they did upon that stage.

First, then, let us consider Patrick Colquhoun – for even if we allow no derogation from the bold and colourful Harriott, Colquhoun remains our primary hero. He was a Scot from Dumbarton, full of all the resolution but little of the dourness of his people. Born in 1745 and educated at the local Grammar School, he was off across the Atlantic before he was out of his teens to learn commerce and to practice it. Within a few years, these ambitions fulfilled, he returned, successful and wealthy, to Scotland.

Perhaps his absence had given him sufficient of an outsider's eye to be able to appreciate the dreadful state of the Scottish economy, its industries depressed, its morale abysmally low. At all events, nothing satisfied Colquhoun but that he should journey to London and explain Scotland's desperate plight to the Government of the day. Once there, nothing satisfied him short of complete success. He returned, armed with the promise of Government assistance, to Glasgow, which great city, with a proper appreciation of his service, promptly elected him Provost. He was precisely 37 years old.

He had already founded the Glasgow Regiment. Now, as Provost, he visualised and created the Glasgow Chamber of Commerce. Then he set off again southwards, where he undertook the complete reform of the Lancashire cotton trade, presenting William Pitt with detailed measures for its reorganisation. Then in 1792, with a progress that in retrospect seems inevitable, he moved to London. His reputation had preceded him. Men of vision were too rare for him not to find himself immediately and totally occupied. Within a year, he had become a Magistrate and had turned the arc-lamp of his vision upon the wave of crime which was turning whole areas of London (the Port in particular) into putrefying compost heaps of moral and physical filth. His Scots persistence, allied to his breadth of outlook and his genius for organisation, were placed at London's disposal.

Having first appreciated the problem, his first task was to ensure that others appreciated it. He assembled the most comprehensive set of criminal statistics which a bewildered Britain had ever seen. These he then published, bombarding the wealthy and the influential with their message.

He was by now not entirely alone. John Harriott, his exact contemporary, was a man of Essex, brilliant in several respects. Having joined the Navy as a midshipman, he had seen service around the world. Then, switching from Navy to Army, he served outstandingly until wounded in action near Madras. He was sent home, fuming at his ill luck, and cast around for some outlet for his tremendous drive. He tried Insurance and then the Wine Trade, before becoming a farmer. He reclaimed vast areas of land, he invented farming implements, he became a road surveyor and a local Magistrate.

Then one night a fire destroyed his home, his land, his living. Facing disaster, he called his creditors together, won them over to faith in him, and set out for America. When he returned, some years later, to London every one was fully paid off. There is a story, which cannot be fully authenticated, that his sailing by ship up the Thames gave him his first experience of water-borne criminals when a band of them held up the ship. Harriott immediately conscripted a party of the crew, lowered a small boat, and beat the pants off them!

Unaware that Colquhoun was already working along similar lines, Harriott approached the City about the need for some security force on and around the River. The City indicated it didn't give a fig for him or his problems! Harriott turned at once to harry the Government. Lord Portland, the Home Secretary of the day, was personally not unsympathetic, but there was insufficient support in Parliament, and he knew it. However, having heard of Colquhoun's efforts, his Lordship providentially put Harriott on the track of his fellow pioneer.

Alas, there is no record of the first meeting of these two outstanding minds. It might have stood out quite as vividly as the first meeting, a century later, of those two fictional (and less equal) partners in detection and crime prevention, Holmes and Watson, in the Long Bar of the Criterion. It must have struck immediate sparks. Colquhoun had completed the assembly of his statistics and was trying to convey them to a distressingly uninterested public. When the two first met, Colquhoun was busy trying to bend the ear of the influential West India Company.

It must be remembered that there was up to this time no police force as we know the term in this country. The old Parish Constable system had completely failed – the Watch was mainly corrupt and helpless to stem the persistent and increasing waves of crime. Emergencies, as they arose, had to be dealt with by military assistance. It was Colquhoun's and Harriott's vision which showed them a system of preventive police made up not of representatives of executive government, but representatives of the people – whole-time professional citizens in a sense, policing the land on behalf of the people themselves. This had been the theme of tything and frankpledge. Now it was to be dared once more.

For Colquhoun had discovered that no less than one quarter of the annual financial loss through crime in the Metropolitan area occurred in the Port. More than half a million pounds worth of goods were stolen on the river and around the festering quays. And of that half-million, nearly half belonged to the Honourable West India Company. Colquhoun felt that some response must be obtainable. For London in 1796 was the greatest port in the world. Two thirds of all trade in the United Kingdom entered or left through the arms of the Thames Estuary. The wealth and power of the City itself had sprung from that source alone. £18 million worth of Imports, £24 million worth of Exports – that was London's trade during 1796 – two thirds that of the nation's, bringing nearly 7,000 ships into the port.

It is easy to imagine the chaos that could easily – and did clearly – occur. There being no controlling body for the River itself, there was much silting-up. In one reach not more than 2½ miles long, 3,419 craft were trying to move. About 2,000 of these were barges, half of which were used literally as warehouses. Often the resulting obstruction was so great that ships had to wait a full week before they could attain the Pool. And there – the Upper Pool had been designed to hold 550 ships, and there were often 750 trying to make use of it. Goods were discharged overside into barges, which took them to quays no larger in 1796 than in 1666, for examination by Customs. Further delays ensued. There was an open black market in goods awaiting Customs examination.

At last Colquhoun seemed to be making headway. True, the usual volume of irrelevant legislation dribbled from the maw of Parliament, but there was genuine public concern now in evidence. Slowly it was realised that the seething mass of ships and men in the Port of London had become a hot-bed, a breeding-ground of crime and criminals.

Against such malefactors there was no organised body of authority. The Customs service could manage no more than street-keepers armed occasionally with cutlasses. These men earned between five and ten shillings a week and those of them who were not ineffective were largely corrupt. In 1797 this useless organisation appealed to the Treasury for military aid. They did not of course get it.

Of all the commercial interests to suffer from crime, the greatest, the most rich and powerful and the best organised, was the Honourable West India Company. As far back as 1749 they had tried to create some security force, but the embryo was smothered by the rewards system. Naturally every Captain and crewman of the Company was subject to rules and standing orders, but this was nothing like enough.

It was this murky scene that Colquhoun had flood-lit with his statistics. His 1796 Treatise on the Commerce and Police of the River Thames exposed the scabrous state of the Port and pointed to the only workable solution. Nine-tenths of all the crime was committed, he showed, by port workers, the watchmen, and the Customs service. Of these, the most alarming was the last category. Some Revenue Men were receiving as much as thirty guineas a night – they had what was virtually a licence to plunder.

The vividness of Colquhoun's descriptions demonstrates his flair. He spoke of "the river pirates – the most desperate and depraved class of the great fraternity of nautical vagabonds". He spoke of "the Night Plunderers – river pirates in league with receivers – who got their information from the watchmen, and would swoop, pillage and then disappear into the murky darkness loaded with spoils, knowing the markets through which they could dispose of the loot".

He defined the Light Horsemen, who concentrated mainly on the West India Company's ships, boarding them in the river at night with tools to open casks, extract items such as sugar and re-seal the casks, carrying off their gains in a black strap – a bag large enough to carry 100 lbs., dyed to make it invisible. A lesser organisation was that of the Mudlarks, who would wade about in the ooze, transporting loot from Horsemen to the Receivers waiting on the shore.

Dealing with Receivers, Colquhoun divided them into twelve classes. He detailed their operations and methods and cited their personal argot – sugar was 'sand', spirits were 'vinegar' for example. Stealing and receiving in the Port had almost the status of a trade.

Finally, with a flourish which at this time was more than radical – it was revolutionary – the author reached his convincing conclusion. To use it may seem obvious and mild. To the West India Company and the Merchants with whom they dealt, it was neither. "Something," he thundered, "is wanted in addition to the letter of the law which shall operate effectually to the relief and security of society. As in war an enemy is intimidated by the power and the superior position of the army, so in seeking to conquer delinquency, impressions must be excited indicating the efficient design and vigilance of the forces of good."

He mentioned the Bumboat Act, which dealt with the supply boats used by the ships, which the Act had compelled to be registered. They were registered all right – registered traders in stolen goods! Then he propounded his grand solution. "Where property is exposed at all," he winds up this part of the Treatise, "a Preventive Police must be resorted to."

The Treatise can be obtained and read in full. What is of marked interest, however, is its effect. In June, 1798, the West India Company issued the following Notice which they posted all over the Port of London from the Pool to Greenwich:

MARINE POLICE ESTABLISHMENT,
259 Wapping New Stairs,
sanctioned by Government and at the earnest desire
of Merchant and Ship Owners.

"For the express purpose of rescuing the Port of London from the great injury and disgrace which has arisen from the enormous Pillage and Plunder which has heretofore prevailed on board West India and other ships and in lighters conveying cargoes on shore, as well as upon Legal Quays where goods are landed – a MARINE POLICE OFFICE has been established to which are attached more than six hundred Lumpers for working our Ships and two hundred Constables, armed with the authority of the law, to act as guardians on board each discharging ship, together with a number of boats commanded by Police Surveyors and navigated by Officers of Justice, with power to seize, search and apprehend all persons whatsoever, suspected of taking or having in their possession Sugar, Rum, Coffee, Cotton, Ginger, Pimento, Indigo or any article whatsoever comprising cargo, stores or materials of any vessel in the River Thames and to bring all offenders to justice without respect of persons. It is therefore hoped that this early caution will prevent every description of persons, whether working or acting in any capacity on board ships being discharged, and all persons whatsoever, from making free with even the smallest quantity of Sugar or other such articles as above – as in the case of detection (which will be certain) nothing can prevent the ignominy of Prosecution for Felony and punishment upon conviction."

One may guess whose hand was responsible for the grandiose wording! But it is interesting to note the marked similarity between the exposition of the power to seize, search and detain and the words of s.66 of the Metropolitan Police Act, 1829 – which in due course was applied by the Port of London Act, 1917 to all P.L.A. precincts.

While on the topic of comparison, one may see in the employment of 600 registered lumpers the essence of decasualisation which P.L.A. effected in 1967. The statement implying, correctly, that deterrence rests not in punishment but in the certainty of conviction, is in spirit almost identical with recent political pronouncements.

The Marine Police Establishment was made up of four separate Departments. There was first the Judicial Department, having a superintendent magistrate residing at the Wapping headquarters, with two judicial clerks, one chief constable and seven constables, their individual duties being set out in detail. The cost of this Department is set out as £980 per annum which, we may see from the West India Company's report to their members on June 26th, 1798, had received Government sanction and would be paid from public funds.

Then there was the Accounts Department, responsible for the general administration of the Office. (One item refers to the Office's Solicitor for Prosecutions. But who he was, how he lived, what he did and so forth – are all insoluble mysteries!).

The third Department was the Preventive Department. The inclusion of police in the judicial Department was of course normal, referring to their duties as 'executive officers of the magistrates'. But it was the Preventive Department which made up the striking force of the Office. For here is the first evidence of the first force of preventive police that the world had ever known, the effect of the vital word preventive being to indicate the very foundation of the police service which we enjoy today.

Its composition must be detailed, so great is its importance to our theme. It had a Chief Clerk/Cashier. It had a House Surveyor. (It was many years before Surveyor as a rank was dropped in favour of that with which we are familiar today – Inspector). The House Surveyor was in command of the Ships' Constables. It had four Boat Surveyors to visit ships, five Perambulating Surveyors for general river duty, eighteen watermen (to row the boats) one Quay Surveyor, two Assistant Surveyors (today's sergeants) and thirty Quay Guards. This force of 62 was supplemented by 220 part-time Ship Constables, enlisted when required from a central pool of selected, uncorrupt and trained men available to ship-owners for special individual duties.

The cost of this Preventive Department was borne entirely by the private funds of the West India Merchants, who also bore between them (acting through a Committee) the cost of the Accounts and Labour Departments. It is this whole business of private financing which has misled several historians, insofar as it causes a confusion between the control of functions and the control of geographical jurisdiction. Here lies the link which we shall see in due course between not this Force but Colquhoun's second force and the Port of London Authority Police.

The fourth and last of the Departments was the Labour Department. Under its auspices, the West India Company would allow no-one to touch its cargoes save that he was first registered on an approved list of workers and handlers. These were enrolled and paid by the Office. There were 820 Lumpers listed and 80 Master-Lumpers to act as Foremen. Colquhoun set down most precise directions for their employment, governing every stage of the work. The men were sworn to their duties by an oath. There were special Registers to record meritorious conduct on the one hand and dismissals on the other. The Office imposed a levy of 5% from all Merchants whom it served, to defray the cost of this Labour Department. (The parallel between this and the National Dock Labour Board as Ernest Bevin conceived it and applied it, centuries later, is striking).

Turning back now to the Preventive Department as that which directly concerns our subject, the duties of this unique force were set out in most remarkable detail. There were disciplinary measures and penalties but there were also incentives for good work. If a theft took place on any ship on which they were working, the Magistrate could (and frequently did, in the early years) stop the wages of the policemen engaged thereon. Punishment for any policeman actually engaged in criminal activities was intended to be exemplary. A shift system of general police work was applied, not unlike the three "turns" which we know today.

The continuing statistics showing the effects of the new force indicate the same cardinal error which afflicts those of today! We all know that beneath the figures of recorded crime lies a dark figure of undiscovered or unreported crime. It cannot be estimated, but it is regularly, and rightly, advanced in all Reports. It seems never to be recognised that at the other end of the same scale there is a light figure of crime which never took place because a patrolling uniformed policeman happened along ta a given moment. True, this is sometimes crime postponed, occasionally crime re-placed, but it is very often crime prevented. Though impossible to estimate, it is as entitled to mention in criminal statistics as is the dark figure which Colquhoun was the first criminal statistician to record in his figures.

It must further be realised that this force of preventive police was more than a collection of private preventors and detectors of criminal activity. One of the signs of today's policeman is that he is a public servant. It is thus a joy to see the scrupulous instruction given to all men of the Marine Police Office that they were to give immediate and disinterested assistance to any vessel or any person who might require their help. Drifting vessels were their greatest concern, particularly in bad weather. They dealt with them irrespective of any criminal activity which might or might not have taken place in or on them.

The police were forbidden to delegate, or even to accept assistance from anyone save their colleagues. Towards the Revenue men they were warned to be courteous but "on no account to accept their offers to watch as this indicates strong suspicion that it is with no good design".

They were furnished each with a cutlass "which, however, is never to be shown or used but in your own defence, and a prudent officer has seldom occasion, in seizing offenders, to have recourse to anything but the authority of the Law, manifested by exhibiting his staff of office. Arms are to be used as a final extremity only". The same principle has since been immortalised by Rowan and Mayne in the Nine Principles upon which the police service of today is founded. Radzinowicz, with benefit of hindsight, writes – "Every effort was made to build up a Force proud of its vocation and fortified by the tradition of honourable police service".

Harriott's part in all this must not be forgotten. From July 2nd, 1798, when the Marine Police Institution had begun its activities, he had acted as Colquhoun's deputy throughout. On Page 161 of the Treatise on the Commerce and Police written by Colquhoun in 1800 (a copy of which lies before me as I write) there is the following handsome personal tribute which I quote in full:

"Mr. Harriott has for several years acted as a Magistrate for the County of Essex, where his talents, integrity and public spirit had justly procured him one of the most handsome public testimonies of intrinsic worth that ever fell to the lot of any individual to receive. His indefatigable attention to the public interest since he had presided at the Marine Police Office, his zeal for the public good, his prudence, discretion and humanity in execution of the law and the important trust committed to his charge, joined to the extensive local and nautical knowledge which he possesses, and which he employs, with the assistance of an acute and discriminating mind, in carrying to effect systematically the plan of a Police Service which has been adopted for the protection of commercial property, is best explained by the success which has attended this important design in diminishing in so great a degree (without resorting to acts of severity) the delinquency which had so long affected the trade of the River Thames".

Considering two such men, it would have been surprising if they had failed. Even so, their success, and its immediacy, were whole-hearted and all-embracing.

If I may be permitted further to digress for a moment – one of the very influential persons with whom Colquhoun and Harriott had had occasion to negotiate – one of the most hearty supporters of their enterprise and whose correspondence is referred to by Colquhoun in his 1800 Treatise (See footnote on Page 229, quoting a letter of

December 18th, 1798) was one, Mr. Edward Ogle. Mr. Ogle was at that time Chairman of the River Wharfingers, and one of the most important people whose life was bound up with the Thames in its middle reaches. Now there happens to be a fascinating mystery as to just how and why the men of the Thames Division of the Metropolitan Police (the direct successor to the Marine Police Institution) are known to and by the watermen and river-workers as *Ogglers*. There are several theories as to how this name grew up. None even claim to be satisfactory. It is my view that the nick-name derives from Mr. Ogle whose activities, as recorded by Colquhoun and others, place him as one of the brave spirits directly responsible for the creation of the Force from which today's Thames Division derives its birth.

Some concrete measure of the success of the whole enterprise may more clearly be judged by the terms of a resolution by the Committee of West India Merchants of January 4th, 1799. This reads as follows:

"THAT this Committee are deeply impressed with a high sense of the singular advantages which have resulted amid the commerce of the Port of London in general and the West India Merchants in particular, in the protection afforded to their property by the exertions of the Marine Police Institution as well as by the general system for the prevention of pillage and plunder arising out of the measures for detection pursued by Magistrates presiding at the Marine Police Office by which great and extensive benefits have also resulted to His Majesty's Revenue."

In the following June, Lord Penrhyn conveyed on the Committee's behalf a message of appreciation and thanks for the 'zeal, assiduity and perseverance with which they have effected a check on the system of depradation in the Port of London' to Colquhoun and Harriott. This was followed – indeed almost duplicated, by the Navy Commissioners.

And what prompted these felicitous messages? Simply – between July, 1798 and March, 1799, the loss sustained by the West India Company alone was less than one fifth of that suffered in former years. Over £100,000 had been recorded as nett saving. The figures speak for themselves.

It was about this time that Colquhoun's attention was caught by something which he foresaw as something as important as his initial project. In 1799, there was passed through Parliament an Act under the formal and ludicrously incomprehensible title of "39.Geo.3. c. LXIX".* Its ordinary, short and proper title is the West India Dock Act, 1799. Associated with this was a Local Act which empowered the Directors of the new Dock Company to appoint such officers and servants as they consider necessary. Under this authority, the new Company's Directors elected to dispense with the ancient and corrupt system of the watch and to apply, on the advice of Colquhoun and Harriott the principles of preventive police.

It must be emphasised that from the inception of the Marine Police Institution in 1798, the term police took on an entirely new meaning – that of preventive police – the whole-time professional paid citizen.

At which moment, a glimpse ahead, immediately to precede the developments of the system particular to the Dock Companies, may be thought permissible. For the success

*An apt illustration of the esoteric, valueless and now – thank God! – happily discontinued method of statute identification. Let us vary Shakespeare only slightly, by suggesting that the first action of every truly free society is to shoot not lawyers but Parliamentary draftsmen who are responsible for, rather than being able to be proud of, their work, which is to confuse and frighten the ordinary man.

of this new conception of law enforcement was soon recognised by Parliament. On July 8th, 1800, a resolution of the House formally approved the establishment of a Thames Police Office at Wapping "for the more effectual prevention of depradations on the River Thames and in its vicinity". Perhaps more significantly to those most concerned, it went on: "That provision be made out of the Consolidated Fund for defraying the expenses of supporting and maintaining such Police Office".

Three days later, Mr. Henry Dundas, M.P., brought before the Commons a Bill which passed quickly and smoothly through both Houses and received the Royal Assent on July 28th, 1800. It was on lines similar to those which had created the preceding seven Police Offices, and it was not quite as Colquhoun had originally proposed its terms. Nevertheless, as Radzinowicz observes, "it embodied the experience gained by the Marine Police Institution".

Its effect was to convert into a public institution the establishment which had been financed hitherto by the West India Company on the advice of Colquhoun. The Wapping Office contained three resident Justices – Colquhoun, Harriott and one other. Each received £400 per year. Their powers included the appointment and dismissal of the constables under their control. As mentioned, the Government took over the expenses only of the Judicial Department of the Office, the other three being financed, controlled and recruited by the West India Company who had, through Colquhoun, created them.

The provisions for the search and seizure of vessels have been mentioned above. S.14 of the new Act imposed a penalty for 'damaging packages in order to pilfer their contents', adding another offence for letting anything fall from a ship into any other craft with the object of preventing its discovery – and 'the boat itself and all in it could be apprehended and punished'. Justices could issue a warrant for the detailed search of any boat or premises – by force, if necessary – should the presence there of stolen goods be suspected, and if the possessors could not give an acceptable explanation, they were to be punished.

Another provision of the 1800 Act concerned suspected persons. This really dated back to the Act of 1792 which created the Metropolitan Police Offices and was now extended to the Port area. Under it, all suspected persons and reputed thieves found frequenting the River quays or adjoining streets or warehouses with intent to commit a felony, could be arrested and brought before a Magistrate where, upon due proof being given, and if the accused could not give a satisfactory account of himself and his possession of the goods, he was to be 'deemed a rogue and vagabond under the Vagrancy Act' and could be quite heavily punished.

Now the vital importance of the Act of 1800 to our story is that the Dock Constables, when they were later established, had to be sworn in by the Thames Police Office Magistrate. Thus – while they were paid their wages by the Dock Company, they acted, as regards all their powers and duties, under the sole control of the Thames Police Office, thereby acquiring all the powers, and the obligations, created by the 1800 Act and any later Acts which extended or varied it.

There were in fact six such Acts between 1800 and 1829. None limited at all the powers given to the Thames Office and their Force by the Act of 1800 – indeed, some of them specifically enlarged those powers. The Act of 1822, for example, authorised police to enter and search without warrant any vessel where they suspected a felony had been or was about to be committed, as well as to detain anyone they suspected of being implicated, seizing rightfully anything they suspected of being stolen property.

They could in terms "stop search and detain any vessel suspected of having any stolen goods on board it, and anyone on it suspected of concealing such articles".*

These are but a few powers culled from a whole series contained in six Acts of Parliament. But the extent of the powers granted to the Thames Police Office was far wider than that granted to the other Police Offices. And in the Letter-Books extant today at the Thames Magistrates' Court, Arbour Square, may be seen one from the Wapping Magistrates which was written when the Home Office were considering lumping the Thames Police Office with the other seven Metropolitan Police Offices under one fresh Act. It reads:

> "The powers given to the Thames Police Officers are such as can have no application to the general police of the Metropolis and perhaps ought not to be placed in the hands of any officers to whom they are not necessary in the discharge of their duties. We have been enabled by narrowly watching the exercise of these specialised powers – and by making the Surveyors of this force responsible for the conduct of those under them to prevent abuse – but if the proposed consolidation should have the effect of giving those powers indiscriminately to all police officers, we submit that the powers so given would be unnecessary and could not fail, even without undue abuse, to be generally injurious."

Not unnaturally, there was some journalistic criticism of the extent of the special 'stop, search and detain' powers enjoyed only by the Thames Office – but even one of the most outspoken of these critics conceded the necessity for the police engaged wholly in a vast and busy port to possess much specialised summary authority. Apart from the Press, there was the usual lunatic fringe to criticise – cranks of all kinds, as well as criminal organisations resenting the limitation of their profitable activities who advanced their cause in the guise of complaints against the restriction of the liberty of the subject. These things, like the poor, will no doubt always be with us!

A final sentence from Radzinowicz before we leave the general law to examine the documentary records of the Dock Companies in detail – one that is both relevant and, it is submitted, conclusive. "The smooth working of the Thames Police, and the lack of evidence that there was any abuse of the powers vested in its magistrates and officers, knocked the bottom out of these criticisms."

Therefore, let us once more turn the clock back to 1799 and pick up the threads of our individual story from the first inception of the West India Dock Company in that year.

*Vide S. 156, Port of London Act, 1968.

PART THREE—THE WIDENING RIVER

The several Dock Companies and their Police Forces before and after amalgamation — The story as revealed by the Companies' Minute Books.

PART THREE—THE WIDENING RIVER

Section 1. Introductory.

My original plan for presenting this, the most detailed and complicated part of this history, was to extract from the Dock Companies' Minute Books in the archives of the Port of London Authority every reference to Police, and then to fit them together, in a strict chronological order covering the years from 1799 to 1908. As early research went on, however, it became clear that each of the old Dock Company Forces had its own distinct personality and personalities, and that each Force was, as it were, a tributary in its own right to the whole which, at its proper time, as amalgamation followed amalgamation, gradually developed into the widening river of our story. Each positively demanded its own consecutive treatment.

It was therefore decided that the picture most accurate and easiest for the reader to assimilate would be for us to trace each Force separately until its amalgamation. A glance at the diagram on Page 37 will place these developments in perspective in relation to each other. First, however, we must briefly set the scene and establish the background against which our drama will be played.

In 1799, the Marine Police Institution had been running for a full year and Patrick Colquhoun was busy writing his second great Treatise which he was to publish the following year. In the eighth chapter of this most remarkable work, he turned his attention directly to the Docks which the West India Dock Company Act of 1799 had laid down should be created.

The Police, as he had conceived the Service, had now, he insisted, to continue, asserting that posterity would demonstrate the merits and benefits of the plan. "It has been argued speciously that the existence of enclosed Docks will supersede the necessity for any Police," he wrote. "In fact, reasons equally conclusive may be offered as to why the existence of Docks will increase that necessity". He went on to list the principal reasons – and impressive reading they make, even with the benefit of hindsight to show how right he was.

First, dishonest men would not be rendered honest simply by increasing the convenience of the loading and unloading of cargoes. And the more closely these operations were confined, and the smaller the bounds of the operation, the greater would be the danger of dishonesty being practised. It would be impossible, he saw, to use warehouses without the presence in and around them of very many labourers and equally impossible to control that labour's rapacity by taking ordinary precautions.

The Common Watch, he insisted, had no influence and held no awe for men. Their power, compared with preventive police, operated upon delinquents 'in the manner of men without weapons compared with an army of soldiers trained and accoutred for war'. To prevent crime, means had to be employed to bring home repeatedly to offenders the fear of detection and the certainty of being brought before a Magistrate. It is remarkable how accurate this conception has since proved. In 1966, in the course of a debate on crime in the House of Lords, the Lord Chancellor of the day, Lord Gardiner, might almost have been quoting Colquhoun when he said that such little effect as punishment has by way of a deterrent lies in inverse ratio to the seriousness of the crime, there being but one true general criminal deterrent – the certainty of detection. This certainty, said Colquhoun 166 years before, "belongs exclusively to the science of

AMALGAMATIONS WHICH LED TO THE PORT OF LONDON AUTHORITY

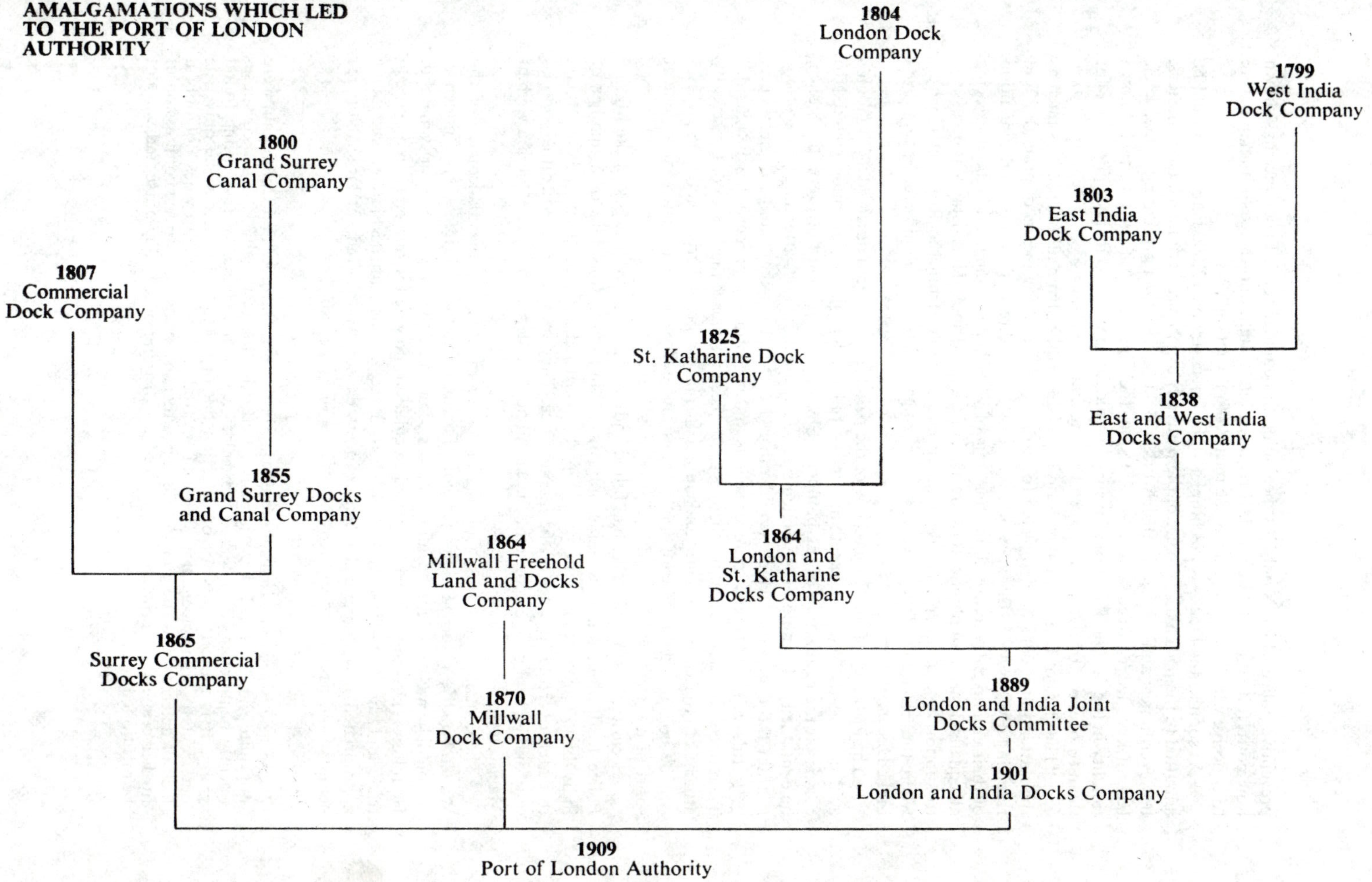

preventive police which is only just beginning to be understood. Experience has shown how powerfully it affects the mind. It required but a slight knowledge of human nature to conceive why it must operate as the means of prevention".*

As soon as the Docks were completed, he forecast, up to 3,000 labourers would be admitted to them each day – many of them already experienced criminals. Dockmasters, however honest and efficient in their work, would be useless in preventing crime. Their lack of knowledge of the science of detection, their ignorance of the law, their known timidity in the face of open rapaciousness, would all combine to make it impossible for them to overawe offenders or to keep them within bounds.

"The class of aquatic labourers on the Thames differ from all others, inasmuch as their attention is constantly directed towards plunder and the means of procuring and receiving it. They are in this view placing themselves in direct opposition to the intention of their employers who are all unconscious of what is happening. The labourers being all equally desirous of plunder they are also, of course, disposed if resistance is necessary, to support one another". He went on to cite examples from the Royal Dockyards, where the selection of labour was able to be much stricter than could ever be employed in the Docks.

The inefficacy of the criminal law of the period received and deserved Colquhoun's acid comment. "When detected in acts of pillage, [criminals] are often suffered to escape on the restoration of the plunder." Short of the existence of preventive police, he continued "the mind of man relents – the teasing difficulties attending prosecutions restrain the disposition which would otherwise exist to make examples, and hence, petty thieves have become more audacious and numerous as property has increased." Then once more he repeated his theme's centrepiece. "Deprive the Docks of the security attached to the science of police and enforced by its power, and crimes and like excesses will be committed in spite of locks, gates and every other preventive arrangement short of a system which overawes."

Security, he stressed, as he had found and proved through the work of the Marine Police Institution, was obtainable only by making it the sole duty of a number of individuals – professional citizens – properly instructed, relieved at intervals by others, to watch over the conduct of the labour force. They must be trained to their special duty and be kept pure by constant checks, all being under the basic control of a vigilant Magistracy.

Then, in flowing terms, Colquhoun set about attacking the inadequacy of the Watch. Finally, he turned to the question of finance with the same infectious confidence. It would, he was confident, be infinitely more economical than any other security method. He follows this statement with detailed calculation showing the burden shared between trade and shipping – it comes to £10,000 at most. This sum he planned should be appropriated by Commercial Commissioners chosen by the trade at large. Not one penny would be devoted to the remuneration of Magistrates!

*To be strictly accurate, it is submitted that both Lord Gardiner and Colquhoun were not quite right! It is a fallacy to assume that detection of the guilty, and their subsequently being charged, indicates more than a sporting chance of their being found guilty. It is the certainty not of detection but of conviction which is the only true deterrent to crime. Detection followed by trial and acquittal, provides not only a lack of deterrence to the guilty – it is a positive encouragement to the commission of further crime. This principle is, I concede, something of a hobby-horse and will not be mentioned again!

The expense proportion was related to the degree of benefit enjoyed by each branch, and calculated on the extent of the tonnage carried, the value of the property dealt with, and the degree of risk. He emphasised that the operations of his Marine Police had in two short years reduced the losses of the river traders to less than half what they had been before 1798. He ended with his system for collection of dues through Custom House. He had forgotten no detail.

His peroration, however, is worthy of quotation in full. He asserts that his scheme "will prove a treasure which can never be sufficiently estimated. The good effects which it will produce will develop themselves every year in the removal of evils and pressures in a manner hitherto thought impracticable because the labour would be Herculean and therefore unlikely to be undertaken. The ground, however, has now at last been cleared. The evils have been brought within a focus capable of being contemplated, in mass and in detail. Their extent and magnitude have at last been understood and such remedies have been suggested as, when fairly applied, will without question be successful."

Section 2. West India Dock Company, 1799-1838.

The short title of the 1799 Act which created this first of the great Dock Companies, was The Wet Dock Act. Its full preamble ran as follows: "That the ships in the West India trade frequently arrive at the Port of London in large fleets and occasion great crowding, confusion and damage therein. That great obstructions and delays arise from their cargoes being carried by lighters to the Legal Quays, and that in the passage thither, such cargoes are subjected to pilfering and fraud, whereby the owners sustain great loss and the Revenue is much injured, and that if wet docks were made in the Isle of Dogs, with Legal Quays, wharfs and warehouses attached thereto for the reception and discharge of vessels in the West India trade, much additional room would be given to the rest of the shipping using the Port, and that the West India produce might be effectually secured from loss by theft and other causes and the public Revenue greatly benefited. That it is therefore expedient that such docks, quays, wharfs and warehouses, etc., should forthwith be made. That several persons have agreed to form a Company for this purpose and have entered into a subscription for the purpose of raising £500,000 as capital, for carrying the works into execution."

The first minutes are those of The Committee for Carrying Into Execution the 1799 Act, and it is some little time before the Court of Directors meet and record their activities.* Even then, they are naturally unconcerned at that stage with security. It is therefore not until March, 1802, that we find the first minute relevant to our story. But it is not without its dramatic moment, speaking of "the dread with which the works at the Isle of Dogs are regarded by those classes at present engaged in a system of plundering upon the River, and the threats which have, on good authority, been communicated to the Company of attempts to destroy by fire or otherwise the works whenever in a state of sufficient forwardness".

Six able men from the Company's staff were selected to act as watchmen to guard the warehouse at night, and stringent regulations against the use of fire and candle were promulgated at once. Meanwhile a military guard was urgently requested of the

*Court of Directors is the correct term, but is apt to cause confusion with a court of justice. The term Board will therefore be used in future text.

Government. The matter was passed to Lord Pelham, Home Secretary, who wrote to the Company on March 12th saying that the guard requested would be supplied just as soon as accommodation for its members was constructed or converted. One officer and thirty men needed somewhere fairly substantial and the major contractors, Messrs. Gwilt, were asked to see to the conversion of a large house and workshop previously occupied by a Mr. Liney. Either the work was less than had been supposed or the speed with which it was done was exemplary, for on May 11th, the Directors received a letter from Gwilts announcing completion by the 15th. The object of the Guard, stated in a later Minute, was 'to protect the warehouses under construction and prevent any person whatever from approaching them by night'. Sentry boxes were to be provided.

The conception of a police force was not yet appreciated by the Board but, though their contents are not cited verbatim, it is easy to deduce the subject of correspondence between the Board and Mr. Patrick Colquhoun, Thames Police Office, Wapping.

The Minutes also contain references to letters from John Harriott, but these concern not security, for he was an energetic inventor and fairly peppered the Directors with details of new machinery, his requests being accompanied by plans, etc. Each was courteously acknowledged. Not a single one was ever used. Poor Harriott's letters became more and more appealing and pathetic and finally dwindle to nothing. The brilliant Magistrate was not so brilliant an Inventor!

Friday, August 20th, 1802, saw the formal first opening of the first of the Docks. An additional guard was bespoken from Lord Pelham 'and as the warehouses will from September 1st next contain property and Revenue to an immense amount, the Board trust that his Lordship will see the propriety of ordering the guard appointed for the protection thereof to do duty day and night'.

The great day dawned at last, and the ceremonies seem to have gone without any serious hitch. Among the official guests listed in the Minutes we find Colquhoun, but admission was restricted to few other than the Directors and their personal parties of friends. Nobody without a signed ticket could get near any quay or warehouse.

Henceforward, the Minutes, which remain still relatively and interestingly discursive, take on a slightly more businesslike form. In one on September 3rd the Board promulgated an order to be issued to labourers working out the ships. They had to undress at the start of their shift, wearing special jackets and trousers provided by the Company, and were allowed no access to their own clothes until the day was done, when they had to change back under careful supervision. Anyone detected in trying to conceal or carry off even the smallest amount of any commodity they had been working on would be prosecuted and barred for ever from employment with the Company. Foreman Ship Workers were made responsible for seeing this order carried out, under the direction of Warehouse Captains.

The official opening in August had been of but one dock. The construction of a second was under way, as was an entrance and exit to the River through the Bason (sic) at Blackwall. The instructions to the Military reveal that there were already several ships within the dock. There is also a reference to the Docks estate being surrounded by a ditch – indeed, a sizeable moat, which had to be bridged, as we shall shortly see.

And then, suddenly – here it is – Colquhoun's urging acted upon at last! On Thursday, October 5th, 1802, we find:

"The military having been arranged so as to give the best chance of protection to the property and revenue therein, it was agreed that to render this protection really effectual, a certain number of Peace Officers (Constables) should be selected from the respectable inferior officers of the Company, to perform duty under a Head Constable, who will have entire control of these persons and so to intermix them with the Revenue Watchmen and Military Guard so as to form as complete a check as possible each on the other and on all persons frequenting the Dock. Resolved: That the Chairman be requested to apply to Lord Pelham that he will be pleased to give the necessary directions to the Magistrates to swear-in as Constables such persons as from time to time may be recommended by the Directors as fit and proper persons to be appointed Constables for the purposes aforesaid."

The significance of this resolution is great. It marks first the Company's extreme suspicion of the Revenue Watch and, to a lesser extent, the Military Guard – a suspicion which was to last many years and greatly exacerbate the relationships between them. In fact, the Military soon turned their attention to the defence of the Docks – England being at this time at war with France. The Revenue Watch were known from the start to be corrupt to a man. The greatest significance of all, however, attaches to the swearing-in of the Constables before the Magistracy. To appreciate this, the reader must turn to Halsbury's Laws of England, Volume 30, Page 53 and Paragraph 92 (3rd Edition) which reads:

> "The hall-mark of the constable remains, as in the 18th Century, his attestation as such before a Justice of the Peace. Until he is so attested, a person has not the authority nor status of a constable and, when so attested, he holds the office of constable".

On October 26th, 1802, we find confirmation in the Minutes that the West India Dock Company's Police Force exists in law and in fact – albeit, consisting so far of but one man! I quote:

> "The Directors being of the opinion that Mr. Robert Bartlett is a proper person to be appointed Head Constable to the Company, he has accordingly been sworn-in and, having attended upon the Directors, he was informed that the duties of that situation would be: (1) To see to the opening and shutting of the main entrance when completed and until then to see that no person remain within the ditch or wall of the dock after the time appointed by the Act except such as may be specially authorised by the Directors. (2) That he should attend with his deputy at the main gate for the admission of labourers at the time of their coming to work and check those that are late and also at their exit on leaving off labour and with the assistance of his deputy see that every labourer is searched at the Gate and if any article is found upon any person of which he cannot give a satisfactory account he is to take him immediately into custody and deliver him over to a Magistrate to be prosecuted. (3) That during all hours of business, he is to remain on the quay and have general superintendence of all dock labourers employed so that he may be ready at the shortest notice to take anyone into custody – and he will see that no idle or improper person be suffered to come upon the quay (taking particular care that no liquor be permitted to be brought in) – in short, to aid and assist the Warehouse Captains and other Company Officers in supporting strict order and regularity on the premises always. (4) That as the Warehouse Captains have recommended their Foremen as deputies for the present, he is hereby authorised to appoint them to act as his assistants as regards attendance. (5) That a proper

ensignia of office shall be provided for Capt. Bartlett, to be used ostensibly by him – and in addition to the above duties, it is expected that he will visit the Military Guard and Revenue men pending the arrangements of other assistance, and he is to report his actions to the Directors as often as occasion requires. And as it will be absolutely necessary for Capt. Bartlett to reside on or near the spot, to execute these important duties, his salary should be fixed at 150 guineas per annum. And Capt. Bartlett having expressed himself ready and willing to undertake the duties aforesaid on the proposed terms – IT IS RESOLVED: That Capt. Bartlett be recommended to the Directors for the said appointment during their pleasure and subject to future rules and directions."

It is certain that on a date between the 5th and the 26th of October, 1802, Capt. Robert Bartlett was sworn-in before Colquhoun, Superintendent-Magistrate at Wapping. The actual date of his attestation is not certain but factors short of certainty point to the actual date being Monday, October 25th, 1802.

The mention of Bartlett's ensignia of office is of interest. In the post-war period, it was decided to demolish one of the two block-houses which lay originally outside the military guard-house. Within it were found several items of historical interest, one being a Police Staff – the article which was later to become the truncheon. It is of wood and, as were all early ones, hollow beyond the handle, to hold the Officer's personal warrant of authority. On the silver top of this one is engraved "West India Dock Company No. 1". This beyond a peradventure is the ensignia which Bartlett was directed to useostensibly. It is now held safely in the Museum of London.

Bartlett was no man to let the grass grow under his feet. Three days after his appointment, the Board considered four propositions from him. The first was to get the military sentry box removed from the main Gate "for at present many improper persons are admitted either by bribing the Sentinel or getting in at the west gate." The second was that the men who held the warehouse keys should live near the docks, "for should any accident befall, there is no knowing where they can be found". The third concerned the labourers paid by time, which he asked "should be frequently inspected as numbers of them are constantly absent or idle and this would forward the works and save Company money". The fourth proposition concerned the provision of a floating fire engine.

On November 2nd, Bartlett submitted to the Board the names of the six constables whom he proposed should make up his force. These were Alexander Reid, Richard Hardy, Robert Wilson, John Dorrett, William Valentine and Thomas Kerridge. The Directors duly resolved "That Capt. Bartlett be desired to acquaint these several persons of the nature of the duty expected of them, and that their allowance will be at the rate of 1½ guineas per week each". Moreover, the six were to attend the Directors personally on Friday, November 5th, bearing certificates from their former Warehouse Captains of their past good conduct, together with references from respectable people.

On November 5th, their attendance was recorded and Bartlett was directed to station two to bear the night watch alternately – to visit the quays at times to be fixed – to see that the military sentinels are alert – to see that the Revenue-men are attentive – to report whatever occurs and, if any arrests take place, to convey the malefactors to the guard-house until morning. Two more of the Force were to have the charge of Gates in the daytime, and the remaining two to be used as and where Capt. Bartlett deemed proper. The Directors further resolved that Bartlett wait on the Military Captain on duty, to settle with him the pass-word and counter-sign for every night and so forth. The Minute ends, "And, the said Resolutions having been read to the Constables, they all declared their readiness to accept the office".

Some of the old bad methods still continued awhile. On November 12th, a Notice was ordered by the Board to be posted on the main gates, offering five guineas reward to anyone detecting and bringing to conviction anyone engaged in the theft of sugar, rum, coffee, etc., from the docks. It ends – "N.B. All labourers are to be searched on leaving off work".

On November 23rd a seventh and senior Constable was appointed in the person of Thomas Clapham, ex-Guards Sergeant. And on December 10th, 1802, the seven pioneer constables were sworn in by Colquhoun and Harriott at the Marine Police Office at Wapping. The importance of this date can scarcely be over-emphasised, as it marks the true birth of the second force of preventive police the world had ever seen.

The first instruction to the Force as a whole concerned fire. Even today, this is subject to rigid precautions, its potential disastrous consequences to millions of pounds worth of goods being obvious. Today, the P.L.A. Chief Constable issues special Licences in detailed terms to cover the use within the Docks of any flame, such as the oxy-acetylene burner often needed for minor ship repairs. On December 21st, 1802, the Board informed Capt. Bartlett that no-one was to be suffered to use a lighted candle, even a lantern, on any part of the quays or works on any pretence whatsoever, without an order of the Board in writing.

On Christmas Eve, Bartlett was instructed to station one of his men during all business hours at the Main Gate to prevent improper persons from entering the Docks. No boat or barge was allowed to lie near the wing fences and everyone not engaged in the Docks on work had to produce a pass to obtain admission.

On the following January 14th, 25 copies of the General Orders and extracts from relevant statutes were sent to Bartlett for him to have posted on all Warehouse Doors and other conspicuous places. And Bartlett was told that it was to be his indispensable duty to lock up and open the Main Gate every evening and morning with his own hands. Until he could reside on or near the Docks, he had to lodge the keys with Gwilts' office each evening. Another personal instruction entailed his receiving from the Gate Constable each evening at closing time all the day's admission passes, which he was then to destroy. There was plainly trouble with forgeries, for a new type of pass was issued on February 1st, each signed personally by the Chairman.

A little later, Bartlett was told to arrange for the great Bell to be rung at starting and finishing times – smaller bells to be rung in each warehouse at the same time. After the evening bell, checks had to be made for anyone left inside. Then comes the first criticism – in April. It was noted by the Board that some persons had been admitted without tickets, upon paying monies to the Gate Keepers. Such conduct, if it was ever repeated, would result in immediate permanent discharge, said the Resolution – "since it would entail inevitable disgrace on the Police Establishment".

On April 19th, the Company wrote to the Thames Magistrates asking them to swear-in as Constables Charles Anderson and John George owing to the promotion of A. Reid and R. Wilson. Whether this was promotion to some position outside the Force or to a supervisory rank is not stated. At the same time, a memorandum to Bartlett shows that all the Company's horses were in his care, as were all the Company's guard dogs.

Meanwhile, all was not going well in the war, and for a time, invasion by Napoleon seemed imminent. The Company formed the West India Dock Co. Regiment which disbanded in August, 1806, when the danger was over.

September, 1803, brings an early example of the Minutes being informative but not fully so. Samuel Pett, Clerk to Colquhoun at Wapping, wrote asking for the attendance there of Constable Jenkins to answer a complaint. On October 21st, we read the next step by inference – "Resolved that Pierce be appointed Constable in the room of Walter Jenkins, resigned."

In this case, however, the incident, whatever it was, had some significant repercussions. A Minute of the Law Committee is received by the Board on October 31st, which included the following extract – "The letter from Mr. Bragge, one of the Thames Magistrates, was referred to and it was RESOLVED that the Chairman please inform Mr. Bragge that he (the Chairman) was under a misapprehension when he answered Mr. Pett's letter in supposing that Magistrates within the Docks had power to appoint and direct the Constables therein, and adding that the Board now being fully informed, have asked the Company's solicitor to wait upon the Magistrates at Thames Police Office with Capt. Bartlett, with the object of working out a plan ensuring the necessary co-operation between the Wapping Office and the Dock Police." The identities and activities of Magistrates within the Docks are not recorded, and our certain knowledge is increased only to the extent that the third Magistrate as Wapping was named Bragge. One might assume that one or two of the Company's Directors were themselves Magistrates in jurisdictions where they lived, and had been throwing their weight about a bit. But in any event, it was made abundantly clear that the West India Dock Company Police were not a private security force at all, but Peace Officers of the nation, their functions being limited to the Docks area, and their wages being paid by the Company. That, let it be made clear, is exactly the legal position of the Port of London Authority's Police today.

Another Minute of the time strikes a chord, the echo of which may be heard today. A Warehouse Captain had written to the Board "respecting a place of confinement for persons detected as thieves, until they can be brought before the magistrates". It was decided that a secure place near the entrance gate should be built for this purpose. Pending its completion, the Board directed that 'a room in one of the Constable's houses shall be rendered secure for the purpose', but a note stresses that this is a temporary cell only, and not a place to which a criminal could be sentenced by a court. The modern position – at least prior to 1968, when the Authority had five active groups of Docks, each with a Police Division to police it – was that without there being proper custom-built detention cells constructed in each of the five Divisions, anyone arrested and required to be put in custody would be conveyed immediately after the decision to charge, to the nearest Metropolitan Police Station where he would be formally charged and either detained or bailed. In order to ensure consistency, this basic procedure was directed to be applied even in cases where bail was unopposed in any event. Thus it is that all P.L.A. Police charges come to be laid at Met. Police stations – not through any lack of police powers but simply because of a lack of specially constructed detention cells.

By Spring, 1804, it was clear that there were deficiencies in the Police Establishment. The Board passed warnings to Capt. Bartlett. One goes as far as to say: "The establishment of the West India Docks Police is occasioning a large expense to the Company, and unless very beneficial effects are derived from it, it will be hereafter for the consideration of the Board whether they should be continued. It is expedient that a Constable should be posted on the Bridge at all times to take notice of what passes there and in particular the property being taken out of the Docks."

This general legitimate warning cannot logically be taken much or any further. It is the sort of abolition that cannot exist save on paper or in the mind of an accountant. Once even a relatively efficient preventive police force is abolished, whatever that force cost the Company, its lack would entail a far heavier loss by reason of criminal activity.* It is a fairly common fallacy of modern accounting. Because something is not directly productive in the strict sense, that does not mean it has no value. Money saved from loss is just as valuable as money actually made. In 1970, the Police were costing P.L.A. more than a million pounds per annum. Its absence would have caused to the Authority direct the loss of a sum which could not in all reason be less than twenty million. Thus, the P.L.A. Police, merely by existing, were saving the Authority at least nineteen million a year – scarcely describable as an unreasonable investment!

But we must not unduly digress. A Minute of May, 1804, reveals that the strength of the W.I.D. Police force had risen to ten constables. None were to be admitted if over forty, and each recruit had to be sponsored by a member of the Board of Directors who had first satisfied himself as to the candidate's diligence, sobriety and honesty.

Changes, of less moment if more dramatic, may be seen to take place. In May, 1804, Mr. Gwilt Jr., the effective consultant on all construction and maintenance, was summarily dispensed with – reason unstated. The huge firm are thereafter described in the Minutes as the late Surveyors! Bartlett's salary was raised to £52 – 10 per quarter. And as if to justify this, he put in a major report on the subject of drink in the Docks, which brought a Resolution that there should be no intermission or cessation of dock work during the hours between opening and closing and all liquor was forbidden to be consumed on the Docks save only for porter, which could be brought in between noon and 1 p.m. by one firm only – Rawlins and Oughton.

A trio of Minutes in October, 1804, enable the reader to glimpse something of criminal procedure. On the 5th, a letter was received from William Mason, who had succeeded Sam Pett as Clerk to the Thames Police Magistrates. It stated that Thomas Whiffen, one of the Company's Foremen, "stands committed for felony on board the "Reward" at the Docks and the Magistrates will be glad if someone will please attend his examination". On the 12th, Mr. Tyrrell, the Dock Company's solicitor in this field, was asked to attend and prosecute. His later report revealed that Whiffen had concealed stolen sugar among the ballast of the ship in question, but it should have been discovered before the ship cast off. Searches were ordered to be tightened and only ship's crew allowed on board during discharge of cargo.

A similar examination of two men named Woodcock and Eldridge for theft, two weeks later, led to Tyrrell appearing not only at Wapping but at Quarter Sessions. But while this was going on, the case involving Whiffen unexpectedly brought his acquittal. The Board were furious! Though found 'not guilty', Whiffen was not innocent (acknowledged only by the law of Scotland as by no means necessarily the same thing!) and he was dismissed. On October 30th, Mrs. Whiffen tearfully attended the Board, was received, and informed that there were, despite the acquittal, "circumstances sufficient

*A docker once remarked to a P.L.A. Constable in my time, "You abolish the P.L.A. Police, chum, and I'll work for 'alf a quid a week and all I can carry 'ome!" This is quoted in the Police Federation Newsletter of January, 1968.

to occasion the Board to object to his being re-employed by the Company". But the technical grounds for his dismissal, although not expressly reported at this point, may be deduced from the events which followed, of which we shall be hearing more shortly.

November 22nd, 1804, was a day of great social importance to the West India Dock Company. The Prime Minister (William Pitt the Younger, no less) paid a formal arranged visit to the Docks and was escorted on a full tour of inspection by the Chairman and several Directors. One tenth of the Police Force – in the person of a Constable whom the Board had later not the hard-heartedness to name – was officially appointed to escort the official party. The morning went impressively according to plan, but some sadistic swine either laced the Constable's porter during the pause for lunch, or else persuaded him to try something less legal but more powerful. For the afternoon part of the prodeedings were slightly marred by the entire Police Escort being as tight as the proverbial owl! Bartlett was summoned to the next Board Meeting, and after reporting, was told that the Company considered the incident to have been "highly disgraceful to the general management particularly to the police department". They required Bartlett to make a detailed survey on the efficiency of each of his ten officers at the next meeting. Pitt's reaction is unrecorded, but remembering that he was later to drink himself literally to death, it is surely likely to have combined amusement with understanding, and versions of the incident doubtless regaled many a society dining-table for some time.

Bartlett's report duly appeared and was passed to Capt. Strover, the company's General Docks Superintendent for his independent verdict on the merit and integrity of each man. The result was both dramatic and drastic. "It is expedient," said Strover, "to reduce the constabulary to four, dismissing immediately the following six – A. Farquhar, John Anderson, William Pell, Edward Pearce, Richard Washington and Ed. Anderson. For the present, the Company should retain only the following four persons, Thomas Clapham, James McIntyre, Thomas Yardley and John George. Two of these should do day duty and two night duty, but all four should attend the Main Gate at 4 p.m. daily to examine, under the supervision of Capt. Bartlett, the labourers as they pass through the Gate.

On March 26th, the Board were concerned with structural alterations which is informative to the reader. They directed that "arches be thrown over the great moat, instead of the swing bridges which are in a state of decay" and that several Wall Gates should be constructed. All Gates were then to be locked from evening to morning. Pending this, "Bars" were to be made for the entrances in Commercial Road and Harrow Lane. When the Bars were ready, the Board directed that a Constable should be stationed every day all day at the Commercial Road entrance to take the numbers of all carts going in and going out, with the hour at which they passed.

Three days later, the Board authorised the prosecution of a man named Kilbeaumont for robbery on the "Anderson". And on May 7th, they considered an account from P.C. Yardley in respect of three days attendance at the Old Bailey upon the conviction of Kilbeaumont. The Board decided that Yardley was entitled to nothing more than his normal pay – no expenses for him. One may surmise that the landlord of the Magpie and Stump cared little about the rejection!

On June 28th, the Board approved the zeal of Capt. Bartlett in detecting frauds not immediately connected with the Company – this followed a case which was something of a landmark. There had been criminal activity in the Limehouse Basin which was found to have been the work of a corrupt Exiseman aptly named Crook. Crook was later acquitted at the Old Bailey, which brought a letter from H.M. Customs refusing to allow their men to be searched in future.

The Minutes indicate that Crook was acquitted not at all on merits but on the same technicality which had allowed Whiffen to escape, some time before. Mr. Justice Heath had opined that the count which stated the property as belonging to the Directors of the West India Dock Company was defective in that statute had given them no property at all. The alternative count stating the property as belonging to Captains Strover and Coldstream was likewise defective, they being merely servants of the Company. The second alternative count, stating the property as belonging to persons unknown was also bad, in that the persons comprising the West India Dock Company were known, although it was impossible for them all to be included in an indictment. The Judge expressly stated the position to be absurd and due to a defect in an Act of Parliament – to whom application should be made to remedy it. On September 27th, the Board resolved to apply at once for an Act under which the Company would be able to prosecute effectively those found committing crimes on their premises.*

In the following March, Modifications were made to the Gate routine, whereby a carbon copy of the Constable's records was sent to the warehouses for checking by the respective Captains. Moreover, when crime was revealed concerning goods ex-warehouses, the Formen and labourers at that warehouse were suspended until the guilty person was identified. This reflects directly back to frankpledge, etc. – and not a bad thing, either!

In July, 1806, two more Constables were appointed to cover the Export Dock. Meanwhile, the war went on, for a letter from Bartlett to the Board refers to the improper landing of French prisoners.

In the following October, the Board applied to the Home Office in terms of the greatest significance. These were that a Magistrate should be allowed to sit expressly so that fines recovered by virtue of the Dock Act, 1799, might be applied directly by the Company instead of passing to the Treasury. It was in fact as recently as 1933 that fines were universally directed by law to the Treasury, whatever their source – even local byelaws. Were it not so, any organisation having legally valid byelaws might be tempted to increase its revenue contrary to the interests of justice and the public. The application in this case continued with the information that Rev. Edward Robson, J.P., would oblige, if approval was given, a room for his court being always available at the Mackworth Arms Hotel. It seems as if the application succeeded, for in September, 1807, the Board allotted £50 to Mr. Tyrrell, the solicitor, for him to buy a silver platter for Mr. Robson in token of his active, able and distinguished exertions in applying the Docks Byelaws. The letter of thanks from Robson was emotional and voluminous.

Also not without interest is the action arising from an expense account from P.C. George resulting from service of summonses on behalf of warehouse Captains. "If anything is due," noted the Board, "it must be paid out of the fines and penalties fund.

*In due time the position was cleared up. It stands today as an outstanding monument to the indefensible actions of Parliamentary Draftsmen. Today, under s.5 of the Theft Act, 1968, 'belonging to another' is defined as property 'over which anyone other than oneself has any possession, control or right of interest'. Thus, all property taken from the Docks is the property of, among others, P.L.A. But of course, the Theft Act was drafted, except for ss.15 and 16 (the only ones to give trouble) personally by the Law Reform Revision Committee, which is made up of Judges and lawyers.

Dock Constables, by the way, are not to be employed in anything that interferes with their duties." Later, George was vindicated – his orders had come from Rev. Robson! In deference to the J.P., one Thomas Carter was appointed a Deputy Constable expressly for the service of summonses, etc.

Soon, the Force was increased by one, in the person of James Coleman. P.C. Pearce had done something outstanding, for he was awarded ten guineas in January, 1808, for exceptional diligence. Soon afterwards, Robert Bolton and John Jones were added to the strength and in the same Minute there is a sign of how carefully the Board kept an eye on the Force, off duty as well as on. Bartlett was asked to watch for any of his men keeping lodging-houses. The term at this period was a mere euphemism for brothels or flash-houses, as is clear from the many anonymous letters received by the Board. Bartlett did, shortly after, report that he was taking up a complaint on this score against P.C. George.

The Minutes again and again record the suspension of Constables for intoxication on duty. This seems to have been the sin with which the Force and all the Docks were fairly riddled! In policemen, it had to be taken notice of. From a long list of reports on the point, one may notice one in September, 1808, the culprit being none other than the zealous Edward Pearce! Perhaps he was spending some of his ten guineas. Ten days later, he was fully reinstated.

A letter from Tyrrell in December, 1808, is also of interest. He says, "I attended the examination of John Skerry and James Summers at the Thames Police Office on suspicion of felony committed on board a ship in Limehouse Basin but, the Board having instructed me that it would be improper to prosecute as the ship was not at this time under the protection of the Company, having cast off, I declined to take part in the case. Mr. Colquhoun was much dissatisfied and expressed his astonishment at the Company's refusal to protect its own officers, one of whom had been knocked down with a marlinspike on board the vessel in trying to secure the two prisoners." No doubt Colquhoun was angry at this refusal to accept the universality of the police service as he had conceived it.

It appears clear from a Minute in January, 1809, that the police were not normally armed at this time – a letter requesting the special issue of pistols and cutlasses for the constables on night duty during a time of civil strife being received and the request granted.

The question of legal ownership of the property in the Docks was raised again in June, 1809. Tyrrell sent to the Board a written opinion which he had obtained on their request from Sgt. Gurney, a leading criminal barrister. It said in part, "The difficulties which have occurred in the Company's prosecutions have been unsurmountable since the observations of the Judges on the wording of indictments. The Legislature should be solicited to effect amendments which are as obvious as the need for them. It should be enacted that it shall be sufficient in an Indictment to aver that the property lies in the Dock Company. A clause empowering a magistrate to take cognisance of all cases of persons detected trying to leave the Docks with property concealed about them, should also be enacted."

A week later, a Minute refers to a letter from Rev. Robson, J.P., regarding a man with a bladder concealed under his coat. Robson had thought to proceed summarily under the Bumboat Act, but found this to relate solely to ships in the river. He asked the Board to add to their application to Parliament a request that the Bumboat Act should apply to the Docks and Basins. This was a brief but golden age for thieves!

On April 26th, 1811, Constables Buck and Jones were summarily dismissed from the Force – the record does not say why. The vacancies were filled by Messrs. Pamplin and Eady, two steady, sober and fit men. Three months later, there was the first murder in the Export Dock, and a Minute records that the Board "is quite surprised that such a violent outrage should have been committed on the premises when Capt. Bartlett assisted by twelve Constables are policing them." Such naivety is touching!

Then on January 3rd, 1812, comes a development affecting those who, like the author, have acquired an emotional involvement with the story. "The Board appoint Robert Gibson to be Chief Constable in the room of Capt. Bartlett (retired) at a salary of £210 per year. Mr. Gibson will live near the Docks at his own expense. Capt. Bartlett, in consideration of his services, is awarded an honorarium of 100 guineas in addition to salary then owed him." Gibson's duties are set out at length. On January 18th, he was formally sworn in before Colquhoun at Wapping. I make no secret of the fact that I assumed – wrongly, as will become apparent – that Bartlett had been bought by the rival up-and-coming London Dock Force!

In February, 1812, the plans were passed for the conversion of the Engine House at the entrance to the Import Dock into the new Police Headquarters.

In March, Constables Kettle and Banks were suspended for malpractice. A week later, a fuller report discloses that they had plundered a cask of sugar, which they had concealed beneath the floor of No. 10 Warehouse. 63 lbs. of it was found on them. They were both dismissed, but Kettle only was prosecuted.

Sadder still is the Minute which records the dismissal for repeated intoxication of the good P.C. Pearce. Some men, it seems, then as now, cannot withstand the responsibilities of wealth and praise. He was replaced by one, Thomas Chisholm.

On July 4th, my earlier wrong deduction about Bartlett comes to light. A letter was received by the Board requesting their permission for Bartlett to supply bottled porter for the Import Dock Warehouse Captains. A cold reply, totally rejecting the request, was sent.

Comings and goings have by now become minutiae. Donald McPherson and William Pack were appointed to replace Kettle and Banks. Curtis was dismissed and his warrant withdrawn. Two new constables were appointed. Capt. Gibson was now putting a full report before the Board each month. It is interesting that the Board passed it, after consideration, to the Thames Police Office each month. It shows that the Force was treated as part of the Police Service of the country even though that Service consisted, outside the Docks, only of the Marine Police Institution. It was still 16 years before Peel's New Police were created.

In April, 1813, the Board decided to build three double-houses near the Guard House for occupation by specially selected Policemen. In September, the names of the six Constables suggested were submitted for consideration by the Directors. With the names came a proposal that the ordinary Constable's wage should go up from 25/– to 31/6 per week. This was granted, and the housed allotted to Constables Kinnard, Boulton, Hanover, Eady, Moore and Bradley.

A week later, responding to a bleat by Gibson, the Board sent a very angry letter to the Customs, alleging that Excisemen were obstructing Police searches of vessels in order to shield their own corruption.

In October, two more men were added to the Force and the Board agreed to the building of three more double-houses near Headquarters. Gibson received a bonus of 15 guineas – this being normal for all satisfactory Senior Officers of the Company from time to time. In June, 1814, the houses were completed and the new tenants allocated. At the same time, Gibson's proposal that eight of his men should have cutlasses permanently and other than for special occasion, was agreed to.

Then we begin to see signs of a deterioration in the relationship between Capt. Gibson and his men. P.C. Walker was dismissed after an altercation with him, and Gibson was admonished and told to be "more temperate and guarded in his conduct on any similar future occasion". A little later, Constables Hanover and Latham (shortly to come into dramatic prominence) were suspended by Gibson for neglect of duty but reinstated by the Board on Capt. Strover's recommendation based on promises to mend their ways. But the pressures on Gibson were clearly building up. Even so, he had his annual fifteen guineas bonus – in a Minute which notes that the return of national peace would probably lessen the Company's income and these annual gratuities would probably cease.

In May, 1815, four Constables were dismissed for inefficiency, and one of the replacements was William Fisher. In December, Hanover was caught without his badges of rank as they say, attending a local brothel, and was admonished and suspended for a week!

In the same month, a Minute records the deep concern of the Board at several recent incidents of attempted entry to the Docks by night. The four fierce guard dogs were to be increased to six for ordinary duty, two more still to be used at the Rum Quay. The same Minute speaks of the two Docks Fire Engines being inadequate – "their capabilities hardly going to the extent of extinguishing a Guy Faux (sic) bonfire." The addition of a modern floating engine was ordered.

A month later, Gibson received an increase in salary from £210 to £230, though there were no bonuses at all. Economies were ordered in all Departments. When on January 23rd, the Board confirm the dismissal of William Clark for insubordination, they direct that "his place be not filled and that the Police Forces be reduced by wastage by another four."

In May, 1816, a reference to vacancies in the Force establishes that in total it was then twenty. For Gibson the times were ominous – he suspended Winnall, only to have the Board direct his reinstatement. They questioned Gibson's freeing persons picked up at the Gates on searching, but he was able to assure them that this was known to the Thames Magistrates, who approved of it provided it was done only in cases of very small quantities. This is the much-used Police decision to caution, which, though rarely officially acknowledged, is used wisely in thousands of minor offences every year and all over the country – mostly in the field of motoring, although occasionally even in cases of theft or smuggling.

Another slightly unfortunate incident brings to the fore Constable Latham. In January, 1817, a Lieutenant of the Military contingent who were still in the Docks, though practically inactive, complained about Latham's officiousness and Gibson suspended Latham at once. A later investigation found that the Constable had taken upon himself in an excess of zeal a decision which he should have referred to his superior. He was suspended for two weeks but commended at the same time!

Latham went straight to his cronies, and two weeks later the Board found itself investigating specific allegations by Latham, Fisher and Winnall that Gibson had stolen property in his possession. Upon interrogation, Winnall withdrew his complaint which he agreed was made without foundation. He was suspended, Fisher and Latham being summarily dismissed for insubordination and disrespect. Three days later,

Gibson sent the Board an anonymous letter he had received concerning Winnall, who was summoned to appear before them. The Board put to him allegations that he had acquired some valuable mahogany from ships he was there to protect. Winnall prevaricated and mumbled insinuations against the Chief Constable. He was challenged to say clearly anything he had against Gibson. First Winnall said he had none, then he said he was not ready to give details yet. Pressed further, he produced two sheets of paper covered with detailed charges of theft and corruption against Gibson. Unfortunately for him, there was some reference to a Constable Stevens, for whom the Board at once sent. Stevens emphatically denied that he had ever thought or made the slightest allegation against Gibson. Winnall was summarily dismissed by an anxious Board of Directors.

Two weeks later, Winnall was convicted of stealing lead, outside the Docks and on the same day ex-Constable Fisher sent the Board an affidavit alleging the receiving by Gibson of a box of stolen arrowroot. The Board appointed a Committee to investigate fully at once. In three days, this Committee reported that all charges against Gibson were false and unfounded. The Board accepted the report. Two months later, a Warehouse Captain complained that Gibson had ordered people off the Docks who had some right to be there. The Captain was duly admonished after investigation and Gibson commended. In passing, it is of interest that Gibson was instructed to keep all and disorderly persons out of the Docks. The description presaged exactly the category of undesirable defined in the Vagrancy Act, 1824 – still in use by Police today.

In July, 1817, Gibson put in a long report on the characters of each of his Constables. Several were described as improper to hold such office, and alleged carelessness on duty. P.C. Crump was singled out as addicted to alcohol. The Board directed more care should be taken over recruitment of Constables. Discipline was tightened up. When a matter was raised of a Foreman named Kilby making an error in a document which was insufficiently checked by P.C. Westbrook at the Gate, Kilby was fined 5/–, while Westbrook was fined 10/6.

An interesting illustration of disciplinary procedures occurs in an incident of October, 1817. P.C. Talmedge was assaulted unlawfully by William Whitmore, mate of a barge. The Board resolved the matter by directing Whitmore to pay to a named charity three guineas plus a public apology to Talmedge. Whitmore, now contrite, begged to be let off the publicity of the apology, Talmedge supporting this provided that Whitmore apologised in front of Gibson and before the Thames Magistrates. The Board duly agreed.

The question of fines arose again with the report of the Secretary of the Company that he had failed to convince the Magistrates at Shadwell that fines imposed for Dock Byelaw offences should be retained by the Company as the party aggrieved – although the Thames Magistrate at Wapping had long consented to this being done. No action was taken.

In March, 1818, an interesting point arises. Capt. Parrish brought to the Board a notice saying he had been nominated as Headborough in his home area. The Board authorised the payment of his fine for failing to submit. They also recommended "that the Captain be appointed a J.P., to prevent any recurrance of the event". Following this, it is only by implication that we hear of the death of Capt. Strover, who was in effect the Co-Ordinator of Docks Operations. A Minute of September 18th, 1818 runs "As the late Captain Strover was a Justice, application should be made to the Home Office in the Company's name requesting the appointment to the judicial bench of Capt. Parrish in his place."

On October 20th, 1818, the Board received and considered a long report by the Chairman and his Deputy regarding the reorganisation of the Company's Police Force. This is of great interest but it is too long to be summarised here.

Small personal events in the Police field continue to punctuate the matters set out in the copper-plate writing of Thomas Marsham, the Company's Secretary, and his successors. Names of Constables appointed, commended, reprimanded and discharged flow round like eddies in the main stream of our story. It was, for example, on November 17th, 1818 that poor Crump went the way of all chronically intoxicated. Again and again he had been reported, scolded, fined, suspended. Finally the Board had no option but to discharge him but "in consideration of his kind nature and honesty, he should be paid up to Christmas". Alas poor Yorick!

There was a fuss in the following January arising from vague suggestions that articles seized by Police at Gates were subsequently being converted to the private use of some Constables. Investigation showed the cases to be very few and far between and even in those few there was some reasonable misunderstanding of their privileges by the officers concerned. All was smoothed out satisfactorily. Gibson's salary in the same month was raised to £250.

Then we find two Constables warned that they might lose their jobs if they could not control the drunken conduct of their wives. In this age when screening of the wives of candidates for important posts is acknowledged, if so far mainly disapproved, in England, the insistence in 1819 that the Policeman's wife, like Caesar's, must be above suspicion is not without interest. Another Constable was given notice to vacate his police house but allowed, a week later, to remain "so long as his wife, who has left him, continues to stay away"!

And then suddenly the stream of details is interrupted by police sensation. October 12th, 1821, saw the report of a Special Committee to the Board, urgently recommending the instant dismissal of Robert Gibson, Chief Constable. He is referred to as "totally deficient in the requisites of an efficient head of a Department". Against him were quoted instances of inefficiency, failure to report, partiality and undue severity towards his men. The sorry indictment continues at length. The Committee even went so far as to recommend his successor, John Foy, then employed by the Bank of England, and well known to the Company's solicitor. The Board accepted the report and directed Gibson's dismissal forthwith, directing him to vacate his official house within fourteen days. Foy was appointed to replace him. Gibson's reactions are undisclosed, save that he asked for an extra week to vacate and was granted it. After that, there is only one more Minute on the subject – the grant on March 15th, 1822, of the sum of £300 on account of past services to Robert Gibson. And thus did the seed of discontent sowed years before by Latham, Winnall and Fisher come at last to its unhappy bloom.

This might be a convenient moment to round off the sad story of Robert Bartlett. He had been writing regularly to the Board, openly to solicit grants in aid of his distressed situation. Out of sympathy for a retired servant, the Board were donating on average some £50 a year until 1823. Then the appeals became more and more frequent, and it can all too easily be guessed what the unhappy ex-policeman, ex-porter-salesman was doing with the cash. On November 14th, 1823, he squeezed another 25 guineas out of the Board, though this was accompanied by a note that no further relief could be granted. In the following February, Bartlett again solicited help. The Board refused. Bartlett had not the face to try again. And then in June, 1825, came a letter from a Mrs. Bruce, daughter of the late Capt. Bartlett, asking for some help towards her younger sister's education. The Board replied with a donation of £30 for this purpose in consideration of the long service of the late Capt. Bartlett.

In February, 1822, the Military Guard in the Docks was found by Parliament to be an unwarrantable expense and was disbanded. Special night patrols on horse-back were undertaken by the Police as a passing expedient, and they were given fire-arms – the first reference and the only one to these items the absence of which have so effectively distinguished the Police of Britain from almost all others, save for specific occasion issue. The British police continue to be armed – with their dignity.

By the end of the following June, these armed patrols were able to be dispensed with. Eight constables – unarmed – were to be on duty throughout the night – four between midnight until 7 a.m. and the other four between 7 p.m. and midnight. The remainder covered the twelve hours of the day. Their instructions are set out in full.

In August, 1823, the Board instructed Foy not to take all petty smuggling cases before the Magistrates when there was no suggestion of plunder, but to hand them over to the Customs.

Of the police personalities under Foy, the reader of the Minute Books will follow the steady upward progress of two men, Fairbairns and Talmedge. These had both been appointed Head Constables in 1818. Their salary was now £165 per year, "in consequence of the favourable character they have shown during the five years they have held these positions. The Board hope that they will continue to constitute an excellent example to all those under them".

It was like a cricket commentator remarking that a batsman looks firmly set at the crease, only to see him clean bowled next over. A mere two years after the above remarks, P.C. Talmedge sent to the Board a letter accusing his Chief Constable, Foy, of improper conduct. The Board demanded an immediate reply from Foy, together with an independent report from the Company Secretary. The accusations of Talmedge were wilfully false and entirely without foundation. Talmedge was summarily dismissed. Foy was commended. One may wonder what on earth could have caused this sorry professional suicide by a man of such long and splendid service. It remains one of the mysteries wholly unsolved by the Minutes.

We now reach an important development in our story. In 1829, as has been mentioned, after displaying noteworthy political chicanery and cunning, Peel, using the City of London (who already had the Force on which the New Police were modelled, and had had it atleast since the previous century), founded the Metropolitan Police. It was a hard-won victory – he had been trying and consistently failing ever since 1822! Charles Rowan and Richard Mayne were appointed Joint Commissioners of the new Force. It was much due to their brilliance that the huge success and value of this establishment was within a year recognised by all. Perhaps it was to be expected that in 1830, the Board of Directors of the West India Dock Company set up a special Committee of Enquiry into the expenditure of the Company on its Police Force and to explore the merits and possibilities of the New Police taking over such duties.

On July 13th, 1830, the Board in full considered the report of its Committee. It stated that the creation of the New Police had opened up a useful channel. But even without that, a close look at their own Force revealed that some £850 per year could be saved. The Board decided that some exploration as to whether a Metropolitan Police take-over was viable should be undertaken. Tact was naturally desirable. Meanwhile, the W.I.D.C. Force should have its scales of pay revised and somewhat increased.

In November, 1830, the Minutes reveal that the New Police were already giving some assistance in the Docks, for a report from Parrish indicates that most of them were withdrawn the day before but five men remained active. Apart from this, however, all mention of the New Police and any approaches to it, vanishes.

A year later the Reform Bill Riots of 1831 started. The Home Secretary had directed 100 armed police from Greenwich to guard the Docks against an attack – such is the dramatic first mention. The Company recruited Special Constables from the more reliable of its labour force, in bodies of fifty, each under a Head Constable and armed with cutlasses, the whole to come under Foy.

Most of 1832 is taken up in the Minute Books with wrangling with the London and St. Katharine Dock Company about unfair methods of attracting business, by sending ships down to Gravesend to tout for business, towing ships all the way up river for this purpose at very low prices. Some steps to match these methods were discussed.

Notable in 1833 was a charming bucolic element. Foy had to make arrangements to abate the nuisance of pigs and goats straying through the Docks! A nearby field appropriated for holding them pending discharge. Apart from that, the Minutes contain nothing of moment from a police point of view for some time. In January, 1835, the Board reviewed the work and organisation of the Force and expressed themselves very satisfied.

March, 1836, contains an interesting item, relevant to the Company's Warehouses up in the City. A further one had been bought from the East India Company to store massive quantities of claret, which brought the naming of the covered way past it as French Ordinary Court. (It still exists under that name, running underneath Fenchurch Street Station from Crutched Friars to Fenchurch Street, now being a highly-scented way since the warehouses are nowadays filled with spices!). Twelve men from the Company's Force had to be put to guard this area, although the City Police were asked to give some assistance, and did so.

Then in July, another personal tragedy struck. A letter was received on the 15th from a Clerk with the Company who was also the son of John Foy, stating that the Chief Constable had been attacked by a paralysis (one imagines a stroke) and requesting ten days absence. This was granted of course, but four days later Capt. Parrish reported the Chief Constable's death. Financial aid was at once extended to his widow – the Company's heart was a full and generous one whenever personal tragedy struck.

Almost at once, it seems, an application was received from John Dixon, Superintendent of the New Metropolitan Police which the Board unhesitatingly accepted. (All facetious reference to Dixon of Dock Green will be scrupulously omitted!). He started, with all the energy of a new broom and his first reorganisation placed the whole Force under its Chief Constable, below Capt. Parrish, the Docks Superintendent now so titled. As might be expected, this was less modesty than cunning – all bound up with financial manoeuvring. Another major change was the division of the Force into two separate halves – Divisions – each under a Head Constable. The Specials were to be held in reserve, to give help only in national emergencies. And while they were giving approval to these measures, the Board was arranging to invest £315, the income of which was to be applied for the benefit of Foy's family, who were also to be paid in a lump his salary up to the end of 1836.

Dixon was forging ahead. Three dockers were arrested and charged with armed robbery and were committed to the Old Bailey where they not only received 14, 7 and 7 years transportation respectively but the Judge was constrained to say in open court that "the greatest credit attached to the Dock Company Police who had benefitted society greatly by breaking up so infamous a gang of robbers." By way of further interest, the man who gave the initial information to the Police was within days of the major trial himself arrested and charged with perjury! The Board of Directors of the Company recorded handsome tributes to their new Chief Constable – not least for establishing and using to advantage a cordial relationship with the Metropolitan Police. This, which exists no less today with the P.L.A. Police, remains one of the most vital factors of that Force's operations.

And now we are in 1838. Minutes of February and March of that year are full of the arrangements following the overtures by the East India Dock Company for an amalgamation. From this it is plain that we have traced our course as far as another tributary of the river to which we have likened our story. This, therefore, is where we must turn and trace from its source the new arrival -small in comparison with the West India Dock Company and with less of its pioneering vitality. Yet, it is not without interest.

Section 3. The East India Dock Company (1803-1838).

If there was one concern with an even longer and more honourable record in international commerce than the Honourable West India Company, it was the Honourable East India Company. And they were but a few years behind their rivals in obtaining the necessary parliamentary sanction to open and run a Wet Dock and Basin of their own, which functioned without a break until its closure in 1968. We turn therefore to the Minute Books of the new East India Dock Company to consider the security arrangements contained there.

In fact, the first few books are concerned with the planning and construction of the Dock and Basin, which were to lie at the north-eastern corner of the Isle of Dogs. Naturally they had watchmen during this period. Indeed, though they had not at that date any police at all, the first reference to security in the books is dramatic. On June 19th, 1805, the Board received a report from their Solicitor (Mr. Tyrrell, already familiar to us from his like position with the West India Dock Company) saying that he had, in accordance with their instructions, duly prosecuted Daniel Buckley for robbing and attacking William McDonald during the latter's duty as a watchman at the East India Docks. Buckley had been tried at the Old Bailey, convicted and sentenced to death.

But the start of the East India Dock Company Police lies in 1807. In May of that year, they made application to John Harriott that he should arrange for two men from the Marine Police Institution to attend at the Dock Gates during working hours to examine those leaving, "since plunder and robbery have been taking place". Harriott replied that he could spare no men but would assist the Company in obtaining constabulary powers for two Gatekeepers. After discussion, Harriott was asked to swear-in Richard Over as Gatekeeper and F. Wymer as Principal Constable.

The new Dock Bye-laws as recorded in a Minute of June 26th, 1807, include "(3) The Gatekeepers having been appointed Constables by the Magistrates, all persons are hereby informed that their authority to search and examine may not be resisted by anyone in ignorance."

During 1807 and 1808 the Minutes mention recurring trouble with H.M. Customs, and their corrupt representatives, but no effective steps were taken to resolve this until finally the Company wrote to the Home Office asking that the Thames Police Office Magistrate should be given power to dispatch a Marine Police officer to the Docks regularly in order to search the Revenue men. The Home Office seemed on the point of consenting when political pressure was brought to bear, and they resiled. After much discussion, the Company decided to play the Customs at their own game, and won! Pressure having been applied at high level, the Minute records, a very senior and apparently less corrupt Revenue Officer was appointed to search all his subordinates. Honour was for the moment satisfied.

The next Minute relevant to our quest is significant for the information it gives by implication and deduction. It is dated December 21st, 1810, and it records receipt of a letter from the Chief Clerk at Wapping Office, mentioning that James Murdoch, East India Dock Constable, had formally and correctly applied for the annual renewal of the warrants of himself and three colleagues, Over, Wymer and Sims, but had omitted to attend and reaffirm his oath. Orders were given at once for this formality to be completed. But it may be deduced from this that the Police Warrant at this time – at least as far as the Company were concerned – lasted, without renewal, for only twelve months. This is indeed surprising.

On the following March 1st, a Minute records the Wages of the four Constables being raised from 18/– to 21/– per week.

In April, 1812, the Minutes deal in detail (including the text of several anonymous letters) with a plot which had been discovered, to stage a major robbery in the Dock. Shadwell Magistrates were asked to help with Marine Police constables. A new survey of the security arrangements was directed, the conclusions of which show that the main plunder took place from vessels in transit up the Thames to the Docks. (Some 150 years later, I reached the same conclusion in respect of much theft alleged to take place within the Docks since it is discovered only during discharge).

In June, 1814, the Board recorded the view that the present Force of four men was much too small to guarantee the security of the premises, "men having been discovered under the walls at night with ladders without exciting sufficient attention". Therefore, twelve men of the highest integrity were to be selected as extra Constables, to patrol in groups of three all night armed with musket, bayonet and cartridge as a protection against the violence feared. Each group was to be led by Over, Grubb or Wymer. Their instructions were set out.

On July 1st, 1814, the Board requested John Harriott to meet them at the Docks for a discussion. The result was not satisfactory "as it seems that no sworn statement may be obtained where it might be held to incriminate the maker". Clearly the English right of silence, then as now enjoyed by the criminal, was recognised 150 years ago as a hindrance to justice.

In August it was decided to appoint a Constable to the Force who would be charged with searching all the hoys (small vessels) as they left the Basin for the Thames, and to keep an eye ever wide open on the Revenue men charged with this same duty.

On October 28th, 1814, new Dock Byelaws were issued, of which the most relevant for our purpose is the fourth. This states "All Gatekeepers having been appointed Constables by the Magistrates, their authority to search and examine all persons and vehicles leaving the Dock has legal force, and resistence thereto is an offence". All that was required for search was reasonable suspicion.

A word about punishment at this period. Two men convicted of robbery in the Docks were sentenced to 300 and 100 lashes respectively. This was typical. Punishment was essentially retributive with an element of deterrence. Today's wholly prevailing reformative element was not even present.

The legal questions of ownership were raising their heads again. In December, 1816, the Chief Clerk to Thames Magistrates wrote asking the Company for a list of persons who could give brief, clear, factual evidence as to the location and ownership of all goods in the Dock. The Company demurred, but eventually a list of some sort was sent. This had the effect of several major discussions at Board level, about security generally. The value of goods altogether stored in warehouses was said to be so vast that a Security Department was arranged to be set up. The Police should be much more than Gatekeepers. A Force was to be re-formed which would effect patrols day and night to counter the current criminal tendency of the main walls being scaled and the Sheds plundered. Later Minutes refer to the new Internal Guard as having a night patrol of an Officer and four men based at what has been P.C. Over's house at the Main Gate. They were to make four patrols at irregular hours and cries of 'All's well!' were to ring out from each extremity of the Dock. Should anyone acting criminally be found, the patrol were to fire blunderbusses and spring their rattles. This new section of the Police Force would work from 4 p.m. to 6 a.m. in winter, and from 8 p.m. to 5 a.m. in summer.

A Police scandal appears to have highlighted 1818. The Dock Master reported that P.C. Ingram had been found secreted in one of the rooms near the Main Gate, having broken open the door of the clerks' office and forced the desks within. Mr. Tyrrell was instructed to prosecute and within a week was reporting the successful committal of Ingram to the Old Bailey where, in due course, he was convicted and sentenced to seven years transportation. The miracle was not that the Force had a baddie in it, but that despite inadequate pay and its consequent temptations, there were so few instances of corruptibility.

In June, 1819, a sensational report was received by the Board from the Colonel in charge of troops at the Tower of London, saying that one of the men on sentry duty near the Docks was violently attacked and ill-treated, and that his cries for help were wholly ignored by the Company's police who were standing within earshot. Unless this was a circular to all Companies then existing, it is hard to discover why such a complaint should be made to a Company whose Docks were not less than five miles away to the east. But then there is a reference to the up-Town Warehouses, which extended beyond French Ordinary Court, and the problem lessens. Investigation was made directly, and it emerged in a short time that the idle defaulters were Revenue men. Formal good wishes were sent to the injured soldier with promises of the Company's future co-operation.

The following autumn, a long and major controversy took place which may be summarised as follows: The Company claimed that their Docks were private land and the Police of the Company limited to those Docks. Therefore, if the Company's Police apprehended anyone, it should be the Company who decided whether or not the malefactor should be prosecuted – it was nobody else's business. Counsel's opinion was sought through Tyrrell, and it emerged that the Company's Police had a legal as well as a moral duty to act whenever criminal conduct came to their attention. Granted the discretion to do no more than warn the culprit in minor cases, the Company's Policemen, pursuant to their oath before the Magistrates, had duties far beyond those of a mere private security force of watchmen – just as a private security force could not claim or adopt police powers. The Docks Police are part of the Police Service of the nation. This makes matters abundantly clear, and has its interest in the position being basically exactly the same today. But the remarkable thing is that this pronouncement was made ten years before there was any national police service at all, beyond the Marine Police Institution and the City of London.

In January, 1822, Peel notified the Company that the Military Guard in their Docks would be discontinued forthwith. It points the difference between the East and West India Docks Companies to find the East Company pleading for the retention of the Guard. But Peel proved adamant in any event, bringing the Board to consider at length the enlargement of its own Force. At which point, for some reason quite unfathomable, the Minute Books are wholly silent on both the consideration and the result of it. Nor is this the only example in our survey of all the Dock Companies.

In 1826 there is the record of the putting back of a petition received from an ex-Constable expressing sincere contrition for past misconduct and begging for reinstatement. This, one supposes, could just be Ingram back from Botany Bay, but no identity is disclosed, and the matter is not raised again.

In 1828, H.M. Customs, who had earlier withdrawn some of their men, now informed the Company that they proposed to withdraw wholly from the Docks, leaving the protection of the national revenue to be handled by the Company's Police alone. This meets with an outraged refusal by the Company to assume burdens for which they were never founded and equipped to deal. The Revenue appear to climb down.

As the Minute Books of 1829 are opened in their turn, it was to be expected that the inception of the New Police would obtain a mention – and it does. The nature of the reference is, however, unexpected. On May 20th, 1829, a letter was read to the Board from Mr. Tyrrell, reporting on the confidential instructions previously received to try and secure the introduction of a Parliamentary motion planned to secure an amendment to the Metropolitan Police Bill which would have had the effect of exempting from that proportion of the general rate attributable to Police Services certain areas such as the Docks where those services were already provided and privately financed. Tyrrell says that the clause proposed to be added to the Bill was very strongly objected to by Mr. Peel and the Government and in the end was not passed. It may here be enough to mention that a similar contention was being made during the nineteen-sixties, with a similar lack of success.

In September, 1830, the New Police having been established, a letter was written on behalf of the Company to the Joint Commissioners, Rowan and Mayne, putting the point that too great an assessment for rates had been imposed upon the Company "who receive little or no protection from the Metropolitan Police in the light of having their own Force of Police". There is alas no record of any reply, but it is known that no change resulted in the rating position.

It seems that it was this approach which led to a move which is interesting in that it was the first of very many like it which dot the history of the Port of London Police. The fact that the result was always the same does not seem to have deterred almost every Docks Company from making attempt after attempt. Certainly more than one attempt was made by P.L.A. itself between 1908 and 1970. Its initial appearance comes with the receipt by the Board of a letter from Rowan and Mayne on October 22nd, 1830. "The Commissioners courteously acknowledge the Company's application that all future protection and security for the East India Dock might be provided by the Metropolitan Police, the Company's own Police being disbanded. The question of what charges would be appropriate would not be easy to resolve, and as a preliminary move, the Commissioners would send a Superintendent to view the Docks and to ascertain personally the Company's views and other details."

In a very short time, the Dock Master reported to the Board of Directors the visit of Supt. Smith of the Eastern Division of the Metropolitan Police. The report makes it clear that insofar as the Board had hoped to have the Docks placed in the hands of the New Police, the cause was apparently lost before it had begun. On the other hand, the Superintendent clearly accepted responsibility for the streets and premises outside the Dock Wall which had been thus far policed by a section of the Company's Force. The Met. would at once supply two men by day and five by night for this purpose and a sergeant over them who could be regarded as a Force Liaison Officer between these men and the Company's Force.

In the following January, the Board were disturbed to receive a letter from Lord Melbourne (who had succeeded Peel as Home Secretary) asking for the discharge of accounts relative to the policing of the Metropolis before and after the establishment of the Metropolitan Police. The Board replied that no such details were possible, the Company's Force being applicable only to Dock premises. No figures were mentioned at all. Nevertheless, the Board took the opportunity of expressing "the approbation of the Company of the men allotted to the external area of the Docks by the New Police, which appears well calculated to afford the additional protection necessary for the valuable property contained in their warehouses and docks."

Still, however satisfactory these arrangements appear to have been, all was by no means well with the East India Dock Company as a whole. Cuts were being made in all Departments' finances. A Minute of May 6th, 1835, indicates that the reduction of the Force had left only two Constables, whose duty is consequently very fatiguing. Mention is then made of the West India Dock Company Police Force being large and successful with far higher pay. No doubt it was. But what was fast approaching was an amalgamation which from the East India angle looked very like a take-over by their old rivals. Geographically it was logical that the two Companies should be merged. And as we have already seen, that merger did take place as from July 1st, 1838. Sadly, there is no mention in the Minutes of the new Company for two years of Police. Meanwhile, it is sad to have to record that the last mention of the East India Dock Company's Force as a separate unit takes the form of a report to the Board that Constable James Cook had been dismissed, "he having remained in a state of advanced intoxication for three whole days and refused to surrender his staff of office when ordered so to do."

Our next task will be to trace the existence of the East And West India Dock Company Police.

Section 4. The East And West India Dock Company, (1838-1901).

In charge of the new Joint Force was, as one might expect, James Dixon. And behind him lay one of the Published Rules For All Officers and Servants of the Company. This was headed Obedience to Authority. It began, "The Superintendent of the Docks, the Principal Dock Master, the Superintendent of the Up-Town Warehouses and the Principal of Police shall on all occasions be treated with the greatest respect".

Whether or not it is the influence of the oldest Company, we find as a first item something essentially personal – "As it is important that a Constable should always reside at the Eastern Docks, P.C. Luke should be transferred to the house of the late Constable there". As is now usual late means ex not deceased. In October, 1839, there is a reference which holds considerable historical interest, in that it prefigures the Port of London Shipping Police Force, to which we shall come in due course. The 1839 reference is to a submission to the Board of a proposal that there should be appointed Ship-Keepers, described as "men needed to protect ships in the Docks from being plundered". The Ship-owners were to pay for this specialised Force. The Draft instructions approved included (1) that the new Corps should be entirely under the personal control of the Principal of Police in all respects. (2) That the Ship-keepers' wages should be paid through the Police Department but recorded separately, and that from them, in due course, the Ship Ledger Clerk worked out and charged the appropriate levy on the Shipping Companies.

A meeting of the Board of Directors of the new Joint Company on May 7th, 1841, takes up the first attempt of the Board to abolish its Police entirely, in favour of the Metropolitan Police. First, a Special Committee was set up to consider the whole of the present Police Establishment. The report of this Special Committee is worth a certain amount of quotation in full: "The Committee considered a memorandum and other relevant documents, and reached the conclusion that the system of retaining in the Company's service men long after they have ceased by reason of age to be as efficient as the interests of the Company requires, is highly objectionable. The substitution of the Metropolitan Police would noticeably reduce the Company's expenses, at least by a considerable amount. The Committee request formal authorisation to discuss matters with the Home Secretary – with a view to entirely remodelling the Company's policing". Ignoring the jarring split infinitive (!) the Board approved – and nothing further was ever heard of the result of such approaches. Perhaps the Company Secretary was too tactful to mention abject failure.

On August 5th, 1842, Dixon put in a report that the East India constables were now doing twelve hours at a stretch without relief. The Board granted his request to increase the establishment and to build a Guard-House.

The question of the Up-Town Warehouses was next raised. The labourers there were taking turns at doing a night watch with a very complicated system of reliefs – the general effect being sub-standard. A new system, involving an establishment increase, was approved.

In December, 1843, housing was discussed, especially those houses built expressly for police use which had come to be occupied by others. Dixon stressed the wisdom of having as many Constables as possible living in or near the Docks. The principle was accepted, though action taken, if any, is unmentioned. The only point on record is the Company's decision to pay some £10 per year to cover the rates and taxes of Mr. Dixon's own house – a privilege already accorded to other officers.

With the spring of 1846, we are back to personalities. Constables Alan Wright and John Guy were judged "from age and infirmity to be no longer fit for their appointments. The former has served for 27 years and is 61 – the latter for 30 years and is now 71." It was discussed and eventually decided that Guy should not be replaced while Wright should be replaced by a civilian clerk. This situation still crops up, of course. There is on one hand the strictly economic view which says, unchallengeably, that it is stupid to train a man for special duties and then give him work which anyone without that training could do. On the other hand – where do the flies go in the winter time? Who is more fitted to do police clerical work than a policeman whose health, through the duties he was trained to perform, has deteriorated? If only economics are to be considered, then all culture will disappear. For example – St. Paul's Cathedral, beautiful to the point almost of legend, an historic shrine which has given joy and comfort to the souls of millions over three centuries, is despite its collections and its Son et Lumière, heavily uneconomic. Is it to be threatened?

But the Company callousness as regards its ancient servants was substituted by mercy when it came to minor crime. In 1848, Owen Reading, about whom the Metropolitan Police wrote to the Board, had been pestering the Commissioners with personal and scurrilous letters, demanding arms for the service generally. Investigation disclosed that Reading, a docker, was a harmless crank, not a political tool nor an anarchist, and inspired only by vanity and bad neighbours. He was admonished and allowed to resume work without suspension.

In December, 1849, Head Constable Fairbairns died after long and faithful service, and was replaced in his position by Thomas Gladwill.

Then we find ourselves in 1852, being told that James Dixon, after a long illness and several attacks of paralysis (strokes?) was forced to resign. He was awarded a pension of £200 per year. He was 61 years of age and had been Principal of Police for 16½ years. The Board turned to Rowan and Mayne for help in his successor and were recommended to select an Inspector from the Met. "A" Division, named I. H. Sheppey. The appointment was duly made.

Understandably, Sheppey began by making a long detailed survey of the Force. The Board agreed to his recommendations for pensioning-off some of the oldest and longest-serving constables. The re-arranged Force consisted of Sheppey himself as Principal of Police, two Head Constables, 20 Constables, 24 Day Watchmen for the Docks plus 6 more at the Up-Town Warehouses, and 44 Night Watchmen. Sheppey was most unhappy in that a watchman, not having been sworn in before the Magistrates, had no power in law at all "so that if he made an arrest, the presence of a sworn constable must be summoned, the Watchman in law being no more that a citizen or witness." Sheppey suggested that the Docks Division of Watchmen should be made up of 21 sworn Constables, leaving watchmen to look after the Up-Town Warehouses where the City Police functioned all around. Sheppey also proposed and later initiated a totally fresh system (undefined in the Minutes) of locking Warehouses.

A month later, we see that four more Watchmen were promoted to Constable and sent to be sworn in. Colquhoun and Harriott by this date were both long dead, of course. But the Joint Commissioners were deemed Magistrates for this purpose and were thus empowered to swear-in new members of the Police Service. Today, this exact privilege of being in law a Magistrate, is held by the Metropolitan Police Commissioner and also the City Police Commissioner. The P.L.A. Chief Constable, by contrast, is not so deemed and recruits to the Force are sworn in by the nearest appropriate Justices.

On April 28th, 1854, a Board Resolution directed that a uniform coat be supplied to each Constable to be worn always on duty. Sheppey's request for this had stated, "Passengers through the Gates have so increased in number that it has become essential to put a distinguishing mark on those in authority." For normal uniform, Sheppey suggested a short, dark-blue overcoat with the initials of the Comapny sewn into the collar. These, he estimated, should cost 50/– each. 34 were needed. Their wearing-life should exceed the year. The Board agreed.

On March 23rd, 1855, yet again an enquiry was made "with special attention to cost as compared with that of total use of the Metropolitan Police." (Here we go again!).

In February, 1856, Sheppey reported that four of his men were no longer up to standard – one of them Head Constable Roebuck. All were well on in their sixties. Pensions were awarded, Roebuck's office being filled by P.C. John Shepherd.

In April, 1858, there was an unpleasant incident at the Main Gate when a layabout named Casey assaulted a Day Watchman, and when the Watchman hung on, a gang of thugs stepped in. The Watchman was seriously hurt, and damage was done to several police hats – though just what type of hat is unstated. It may have been a reinforced top-hat, at this period.

In January, 1860, Wilson, the other Head Constable, died and was replaced by P.C. Roberts, aged 45 with 14 years service as a Dock Constable. With the comings and going of the next few years, the Minutes record the arrival for use of 34 police greatcoats at £2 each. The Force consisted now of Sheppey, two Head Constables and 25 P.C.s, with a Corps of Watchmen under it. Sheppey's salary was now £320 per year, which gradually increased to £350.

A strange reminder of the world outside comes with a Minute recording the assassination of Abraham Lincoln and a message of sympathy being sent to the States.

In March, 1867, Sheppey was allotted a new house on Bow Creek, "since his former home at the end of Harrow Lane is certainly no longer a fit residence for himself and his family – being completely encircled by railway lines". (This defies all logical explanation!)

In November of that year, we see an example of happy co-operation with the Met. Police. It seems that 'unauthorised persons and improper characters' (whores?) were coming into the country through the Docks on ships returning from long voyages. The Home Office had arranged that an Inspector and three Met. Constables should board such ships at Gravesend, accompanying the ships to the Docks. There it was arranged that the Company's Police were to be given assistance to maintain order, a need which would continue outside the Docks "where the Company's police have no power to act". As a matter of interest, the P.L.A., by the Port of London Act, 1968, have a jurisdiction over the Authority's property plus anywhere within a mile radius therefrom, together with a pursue and follow clause which, sadly applies not to goods, as it needs to be applied, but solely to persons. But in 1867, the Company's police jurisdiction did not extend beyond the Dock Walls, and if a man escaped therefrom and avoided the Met. Police, he was away with it.

In October, 1868, there appears in the Minutes a suggestion which, however oddly, seems to stem from the Marine Department of the Board of Trade and to have reached the Company through the Marine Police Institution – or rather the Thames Division of the Metropolitan Police which, since 1839, they had been. It appeared that the British Merchant Fleet was suffering badly from crimping. (For the discouragement of the prurient who might read on and find references to crimps luring the seamen to use their houses, a crimp is not at all the same as a pimp. He is a man who decoys merchant sailors and, having first got them drunk, knocks them unconscious, and puts them aboard a new ship, takes a commission from the master and leaves them to recover consciousness at sea). Having investigated the problem, the Company decided that a luggageless sailor would be a less obvious victim of such treatment, and less likely to yield to the false blandishment of the crimps, if a costly luggage-deposit was erected inside the Docks and made compulsory. "He would then emerge free of all natural anxieties about his luggage," ends the report.

Less happily, there were also instances of a clash and non-co-operation between the Docks Police and the Met. Police. The Commissioners told the Company that they regarded it as their duty to enforce the new Licensing Act. The inconvenience was serious – dockers could not be pursuaded to work effectively unless they could have large quantities of beer with their mid-day meal. They therefore applied that their tenants should be allowed to continue selling beer within the Docks. The Home Office said that they had redirected the Met. Police not to interfere with the existing arrangements, but that suppliers within the Docks would issue beer at their peril, as any private individual might lay information against them for infringing the Act. Sheppey, asked to advise, thought this would be a useful opportunity to limit the privilege of sending beer into the Docks from outside, other than to nominated tenants of the Dock Company. The Board however thought that this course of action would make matters worse rather than otherwise. There were no reports of informations being laid when the matter went on as arranged. Plainly the Rechabite docker is – or was – as impossible an animal as the little boy's giraffe.

During 1869, Sheppey reported on the inefficient and wasteful use of manpower in and around the Up-Town Warehouses. It was arranged that one senior policeman should live in a specially converted residence at the back of the Billiter Street Warehouse. The item is of small importance compared with the definition of the individual concerned. Appointed initially as a Head Constable, we see him now referred to as Inspector. In the same Minute as that which first mentions this, it is recorded that Sergeant (formerly First-Class Constable) Gilling should be promoted to Inspector. This is the first mention of this honoured rank, which is so different in effect from the military rank which bears the same name.

Growth and expansion generally continued apace. In January, 1874, Sheppey reported that owing to extensions at the Docks and the opening of a new entrance to South Dock at the end of Robert Street he needed one extra sergeant two new constables and two night watchmen adding to his establishment. The request was immediately granted.

In April of the same year, a series of complaints against the Police Department generally were levelled by an ex-member of the Docks Watchmen. Taking no chances, the Company asked the Secretary to investigate and report. The Secretary duly did, reporting that all the suggestions were groundless, save that night supervision was a little weak. "Night patrolling of the Docks is currently performed by Night Watchmen, whom we pay 21/- per week" ran his report. "At stated intervals, these patrols are visited by Constables on night duty, men not greatly superior in rank to the Watchmen. Dissatisfaction does sometimes arise in consequence. Mr. Sheppey has been consulted and proposes an additional Police Inspector be appointed for night duty, expressly to make all these rounds." The Secretary further proposed that the Watchmen's pay be raised from 21/– to 22/6 per week, the Day Watchmen being given a differential 6d. to 23/–. The Board agreed.

Eight months later, the Police Inspectors were after a pay increase. It was rejected "having regard to the weekly pay given to police of similar rank in the City of London Police". This matching of terms with the City Police is interesting, in that for many years now the P.L.A. Police have been matched with the Metropolitan Police, rather than that of the City, although these two rarely differ much.

In 1875, a Minute basically about Police Offices reveals the information that Sheppey now had a Deputy Principal of Police, to assist him. The existing Offices were directed to be enlarged at a cost not exceeding £300. Their situation was described as the entrance to the West India Import Dock, which puts it pretty well exactly in the big Preston Road house which served it until the St. Katharine Dock House was built and the ground floor of it used for this purpose, in the middle 1960s.

In 1876, the item under consideration by the Board was the Police Box at each Dock Gate. Those which were still of wood (NorthGate of Export Dock, East Gate of South Dock and East Gate of Export Dock) were recognised as being uncomfortable and insecure, particularly as the Gate Constables had much writing to do arising from the heavy horse-traffic pouring in and out of the Docks. The Board directed them all three to be replaced by custom-built brick structures.

Later the same year, smoking on the Docks arises. The Dock Byelaw did not (and still does not!) prohibit smoking, which is generally forbidden on Dock premises, on a ship or barge. Sheppey was asked if he thought one should be made. He said firmly that it would be not at all advisable. "I believe," runs his report, "that many men would continue to smoke on barges only, being now forbidden to do so openly, they would be likely to secrete themselves in ships' holds as well as in Sheds and Warehouses, which would vastly increase the risk of fire." The Board reflected that the Police already had power expressly to prohibit smoking in vessels carrying, for example, explosives, and chose wisely to leave the general smoking matter in abeyance.

A Minute of some mystery is recorded on November 13th, 1877 – the Metropolitan Police had asked the Company about their enforcement of the law with regard to consuming smoke. The period is many decades before the City of London led the world in passing and applying the Clean Air Act. No reply to the Commissioners is recorded.

Early in 1878, there is a reference to the police engaged in the East India Dock taking over new quarters built for them in the archway of the principal entrance.

In the following July, we find Mr. Sheppey, without a deducible trace of embarrassment asking the Board for recognition of the several additions to his Police work over the past five or six years in his representing the Company on the Board of Guardians, the Assessment Committee and the Board of Works, all of which have involved many evening attendances at meetings, etc." A trifle abashed, the Board record their appreciation of Mr. Sheppey's "valuable aid in the Company's interests in certain parochial respects" and award him £50.

For some considerable time after this, the Minute Books are silent on the subject of Police. This was the period during which the new Dock was being built by the Company at Tilbury. The Board found themselves also concerned with the storage of frozen meat from the colonies on or in a hulk in the Thames. There is also passing mention of a Railway Company's Constable whose activities approach the Docks geographically. Then we turn again eastwards as the effects of the establishment at Tilbury showed themselves fiscally. The Board sought ways of cutting expenditure in all Departments. Departmental Heads were asked to submit reports, and Sheppey did so among them. His was a brief report and forthright, stating that with certain cuts and alterations which could be made, the Police Department could attain savings of £1,000 per year.

In October, 1887, there is an important Minute referring to a report by Mr. Sheppey of the grave difficulties of keeping order on and around Brunswick Pier on Sundays and holidays. It seems that this had suddenly become a place of high fashion, not to say a social nuisance, though the details are not set out in terms. Sheppey says that he had already applied to the Metropolitan Police for assistance (Rowan and then Mayne had both now retired and the Commissioner was then Sir Charles Warren who was shortly to be uncomfortably involved in the Jack The Ripper affair) receiving the reply that as the Pier in question was the Company's private property, the Met. Police would take over its policing only upon substantial payment. The Board discussed the matter at length and finally it was decided that a Notice should be put up at the Pier Entrance to the effect that, the Company having thrown open this section of their private premises on sufferance for the recreation of people in the neighbourhood, "must look to those who make use of it, to keep order in it". It was decided that if this did not work, the Pier would have to be closed to the public.

A month later, Sheppey applied to retire on pension. No reason is given. The Board discussed the point and decided that no officer could apply for a pension except at the end of that year in which he had reached the age of 65 – unless it was established that through age or ill-health he was unfit to carry on. Despite this, on January 1st, 1888, among the Company's Officers retiring on pension is included the name of "T. H. Sheppey, Principal of Police".

There is, strangely, no formal Minute appointing Sheppey's successor. However, the very next Minute, apparently of a wholly economic nature, showed the nett savings anticipated in each Department over the next twelve months – and the figure against the Police Department is no less than £1,800. It seems that the Board thought that by increasing the hours of constabulary duty from 8 to 12 per day, in return for a slight increase in pay but with a consequent reduction in the numbers employed in the Department, these savings could be made. The Minute indicates that the question had been raised whether these extra hours might not be excessive for efficiency but – "Mr. Cahill so strongly represents that his plan would be satisfactory that the Board proposes to adopt it for a month on trial." In fact, Cahill did succeed Sheppey, but whether he had already done so by this time is not clear, there being no record of his appointment.

The Board's attitude towards appeals on charitable grounds was notable for its happy inconsistency! Here, for example, was Sheppey, from retirement, politely asking whether his ten years service in the Metropolitan Police before he transferred to the Company might not be taken into consideration when his pension was calculated. The Board declined – and brusquely. And yet this attitude was seen to change dramatically over the ensuing years.

In May, 1888, Brunswick Pier was again in the news and the Minute Books. It was decided to post a Constable at the gate and to admit, through him, only orderly persons. One thinks at once of the nun, posted during 1971 at the Vatican entrance in Rome, to prevent those without sufficiently modest clothing from entering – she had a nervous breakdown which was certified as being due to the accumulating effects of mass hatred. The Minutes do not, however, record any effects upon the Constable on Brunswick Pier!

In the following month, the Board authorised an allowance of 30/– per year to any policeman holding the badge of the Order of St. John in First Aid. 26 members put in immediate claims. The figures set out, show that during the previous two years there had been 669 accidents in the Docks, Police Ambulances being used in 102 cases. Men qualified in First Aid tended 100 casualties, many of them earning praise from Hospital surgeons. In at least two instances, proper and immediate First Aid saved the lives of the injured.

Things were by now beginning to happen on the greater canvas of the Dock Companies' histories. As 1888 came to its close, it was announced that from January 1st, 1889, the East and West India Dock Company and the London and St. Katharine Docks Company would be worked as one. There was to be a special Committee set up to cover the merger called The London and India Joint Docks Committee. Meanwhile, the sequence of Minute Books continues for a time.

On March 17th, 1891, the death is recorded of Mr. T. H. Sheppey, who had been pensioned from January, 1888, at £229 per annum. And I may mention at this point that in 1893 there was an appeal from Mrs. Sheppey for help in getting her three daughters and herself to California, where they had relatives to assist them. "It has," says the Minute, "proved impossible for them to live and pay their way in England especially with the collapse of the Briton and Medical Insurance Company in which they had sunk all their savings. The three girls were all too ill to carry on their planned careers in literature and art". Immediate action was sanctioned by the Chairman and later ratified by the Board – action which is quite incredible in its passing revelation of money values in those days not, after all, so very long ago. First-Class passages from England to Baltimore were obtained for them by the Company at a cost of £4 4s. 0d. each, and Railway tickets from Baltimore to California at £10 each.

In March, 1895, we read of the death of another faithful servant of the Company's Police – Thomas Gilling, lately Inspector, who had been pensioned off in 1886 after 36 years service. The Board granted to his widow the continuance of his annual pension of £87 – for one month precisely. How they expected her to live after that one cannot imagine.

Now the Amalgamation Act was being prepared, which led to the birth of a brand new Company in its own right, on a date which could scarcely be more appropriate – January 1st, 1901. But we must here pause again and once more put the clock back as we trace this major tributary from its source to this point. That source lies a long way back – for the London Dock Company began in 1804, a mere five years after the West India Dock Company Act, and its premises were nearer the heart of the City than the Isle of Dogs.

Section 5. The London Dock Company, 1804-1864.

The London Dock, nearest to the City until the building of the St. Katharine Dock, nearly twenty years later, actually opened for business in 1805. But its Minutes show that the Company had set up several sub-Committees, one of which dealt with Appointments. And in the earliest group of Minutes, it is determined that there should be a Dock Company Police Force, along lines not dissimilar to those then operating in the West India Docks. There is from the start a clear distinction between police, who are to be sworn in at Wapping by the Magistrates, and watchmen – notably less important and of a private nature.

On November 6th, 1804, it was decided that the policing not only of the Docks but of the Warehouses including the vast blocks in Cutler Street, should be by an establishment appointed by the Company. And then the Company seem to run temporarily off the rails, as it were. For they speak of a Force of 30 Watchmen, above whom were two Head Constables and one Superintendent to command them, the title of the last being Captain of the Watch. There were directed to be constructed twenty Police Boxes and a Watch or Guard House. There were also to be created four Horse Patrols for the night watch.

In February, 1805, the error thay had made was corrected, and John Harriott at Wapping was requested to swear in all the Company's watchmen as Constables. This was soon done.

Contrary to expectations, in comparison with other Forces, there is no mention of the identity of the early Constables, save one – Archibald McDonald. In this instance, there were doubtless too many, and as to McDonald, the fact that he was appointed alone, a month before the formal opening of the Docks, indicates that he was probably the first Principal of the new Force.

On August 13th, 1805, the Board received a representation from a Captain Boulderson regarding three constables still without uniform hats or coats. It was resolved that £7 be given each of them in lieu, "it being important that Constables should be distinguished by dress".

By December, letters were flowing fast and furious with H.M. Customs service, who had refused to submit themselves to search. One from the Company is interesting – it reads in part – "I am further directed to represent to you that the Company's Gatekeepers and Watchmen as well as the Constables, are all constables in law, sworn in by the Magistrates and answerable to them for their conduct as constables, as well as to the Company as servants. As the Revenue Officers have no external sign by which they are known, it is out of the question to let them pass carrying parcels and the like – this would be to invite theft and defeat every regulation."

In January, 1806, the wages of Constables were increased to £2 per week in the light of increased responsibilities, and two more Constables were appointed, William Clark and John Watkins, sworn in on February 11th.

The following October, a letter was received from John Harriott, suggesting that as among the many Byelaw offences possible to be committed there are some which require the presence of two Magistrates to be heard (those dealing with gunpowder and the like) while others could be tried by one Magistrate alone, Capt. Boulderson, like his counterpart Capt. Strover at the West India Docks, be made a Magistrate. The Board approved the idea, though one might suppose that anyone accused of a serious offence would object to a Company Officer being on the Bench which tried him.

It is September, 1808, before we find in the Minutes a first full review of the Company's Force – there is an understandable concentration on costings until then. But this review indicates that there were five Constables at £2 per week, eight Gatekeepers (Constables in law) at 28/– per week and under them, 26 Day and 41 Night Watchmen, all further sworn in as constables and receiving 3/– per shift. Over the Force is one Superintendent – not named but probably McDonald.

As often happened, the review was followed by reductions on economic grounds. The Board decided to reduce the Watchmen gradually, especially those on duty by night. Recruitment was suspended, so that wastage would account for the reductions proposed.

Early in 1810, a letter was received from the East India Dock Company, suggesting that concerted efforts be made by the East India Docks, the West India Docks and the London Docks, together – demanding power to search Revenue men, if necessary by force! Warm agreement was transmitted.

Later that year came the serious labour troubles with riots and strikes abounding. Happily for the London Dock Company, they were literally adjacent to the Tower of London at one point, and thus more able to obtain military assistance than the other two companies on the Isle of Dogs. In August, the thanks of the Company were sent to Mr. Kinnaird, the Wapping Magistrate for exertions to protect the Docks and preserve the peace when the labourers all struck for a rise in wages. We also deduce that a Military Guard similar to that on the Isle of Dogs was provided by the Tower troops, for in the following July, a gratuity of 25 guineas was sent on those grounds to the High Constable of the Tower, as well as 5/– to each of the soldiers who had attended the Docks during the crisis. There are also references to the building of a proper guard-house for the soldiers.

Meanwhile crime, like the poor, was always with the Company. Some of the methods of dealing with it might well raise a modern eyebrow, it is true! In August, 1815, the Board received a report from Mr. Tyrrell reporting that he had attended the examination (committal preceedings) of John Lovegrove after riotous behaviour for assaulting a fellow seaman. The Magistrate had committed Lovegrove to the next Sessions at Clerkenwell. A month later came a further report from Tyrrell, which perhaps should be quoted verbatim:

"I beg to inform you that John Lovegrove was this day put to the bar at Clerkenwell and pleaded guilty to assaulting Juan Domingo, also a sailor, in consequence of an intimation which, as directed by you, I had given him that if he pleaded so, the Company would not ask for him to be punished. The Chairman of Sessions, Mr. Watson, suitably admonished Lovegrove on the consequences which his act could have held. Lovegrove said he was fully aware of these and was thereupon discharged upon his own recognisance to keep the peace for 12 months. The reason for this action being taken was, you will recall, because he had already been two weeks in confinement, during which interval, all the material witnesses, being seafarers, had left the country."

This by modern standards is no less than shocking! Apart from the absolute rule that the prosecution may not concern itself in any way with sentence, the Crown had here, by its own neglect to hold its witnesses within reach, let the case become too weak to obtain a conviction at all. Instead of listing the case and offering no evidence, the solicitor indulged in a highly reprehensible piece of plea-bargaining and frankly conned the accused to plead guilty to an offence of which he must otherwise have been acquitted!

At this period, there were repeated applications by the Police in a body, for wage increases. These were not granted, although in July, 1821, each Constable was given a £10 bonus. At the same time, the question of the constabulary amenities was raised by the Board. Their Headquarters as a Force was referred to simply as The Watch House and apart from working offices, it contained some kind of sleeping accommodation for the Day and Night Watch. In a Minute of August, there is to be found the following:

"The building was originally only temporary and occupied by the Superintendent pending completion of his permanent office. It is made of timber and weather board and is insufficiently fire-proofed, which is bad as fires are regularly lit therein. It could be made secure by stripping off the lath-and-plaster within rooms and making walls of wood, lined with bricks, and then by plastering inside from floor to ceiling, as well as removing the external boarding and carrying up the frontage with brick. This would make the building weather-proof and it should last for many years. Settlement has taken place through the weight of the chimney-shafts, but will go no further, if the shafts are taken down and then re-built. It will be necessary to relay some of the floors, to renew some ceilings, to paint internally and externally and to set up such items as flaps for Watchmen, rails for lanterns and the like. The whole of this would cost about £100." The Board directed Mr. Douthwaite to effect the above repairs and report.

Occasionally, the Minutes still descend to the personal. Take the case of William Clark, who was sworn in on March 7th, 1806. He was in March, 1826 – exactly twenty years later – recorded as being unable to perform his duties. He was to be "paid full wages during the pleasure of the Board". His service must have been remarkable, or his condition particularly tragic – perhaps the Board knew what Clark did not. Whichever it was, Clark's death is recorded on July 11th, as is the promotion of Gatekeeper Bolton to take his place.

In 1828, another review of the Police Establishment took place. It began with some indication that the whole Force came under the Dockmaster, Capt. Boulderson, but now all was to be changed. The Force was put under the personal supervision of two Senior Officers – James Slater and Archie McDonald, who were directed to take alternate nights on duty, in return for which, they each received a £25 bonus. All police activities outside the Dock Gates were to be stopped at once. (This could have been in anticipation of the following year's creation of the Metropolitan Police). The two Police Principals were to make a joint quarterly report to the Board on the personal conduct and ability of every man in the Force.

On May 4th, 1830, the reader will not be surprised to be told that the Chairman of the Board was requested to open discussions with Messrs. Rowan and Mayne with a view to the Metropolitan Police taking over all policing of the London Docks! But before these overtures could even get under way, the Docks were thrust into the chaos of the Reform Bill Riots. It was the Treasury Minute Books to which we turned for the record of events.

On November 8th, 1831, a letter was received from the Board by Capt. Boulderson, with 'details of precautionary measures which the Board desired him to undertake, in order to guard against the possible consequences of the meeting of working classes convened by public advertisement to meet at White Conduit House on November 7th'. In reply, the gallant Captain reported that he had found "all possible zeal and integrity displayed by everyone in the Docks and that though the instructions were not posted until noon, not a single man had moved from his post until five o'clock the following morning. The emergency being now over, the same measures could and should be adopted in future instances of disorder, if any". As to the content of the instructions, the Treasury Minutes happily set these out verbatim, as follows:

"It is directed that of the Officers and employees there shall be employed 110 persons exclusive of the Night Watch, the Gatemen, Firemen and Watermen. These will be divided into eleven parties, each headed by two Special Constables to whom will be added eight veterans from Greenwich. Each party will be divided into two parts, with one Special Constable over each. Each party will then take over a Gate. All are to assemble at the Superintendent's Office at 5 p.m., section relieving section at two-hourly intervals throughout the night. The Special Constables are to carry pistols and side-arms, the men to carry staves. Should any attack be made at any Gate, one man will be sent at once to the Office, upon which, everyone not at that moment on duty will proceed to the attacked Gate, bearing bludgeons and cutlasses. All Forces at other Gates will stand fast. The man on the Pier Head will patrol the Dock outside, leaving his name at each Gate." The Gates and Personnel are then listed – involving 266 men in total.

As soon as the crisis was over, the Board sent an indication of their satisfaction to all Officers and Men. It is only later that we learn that there was also a Military Force of 100 sent by the order of the Government. The Directors conveyed their thanks appropriately. A letter was received from the Thames Magistrates at Wapping saying that the Special Constables sworn in expressly for that emergency would be counted as retaining their powers for six months.

And then, the emergency over, the overtures to Rowan and Mayne could be re-opened. Following correspondence, on December 2nd, 1831, Supt. Ian Smith of K (Stepney) Division (now "H" – for "K" is Romford) and a colleague had surveyed the Dock premises and the Commissioners now gave their opinion that to police them effectively, it would need two sergeants and seventeen men – one and nine men at night and one and eight men by day – the duties being between 6 a.m. and 2 p.m., then until 9 p.m. and then the night shift. Only one Gate would remain open – Hermitage Gate – and its key given to the Met. Superintendent. The plan was subject to review when the new entrance was opened.

The Board were surprised that the Metropolitan Force proposed was not much larger, and wrote to Rowan and Mayne stressing the enormous value of the goods in the Sheds and the vast sum the Company paid by way of Police Rates. But they were a great deal moıe surprised when, a few days later, Rowan wrote again, saying that the whole idea of the Metropolitan Police policing the Docks areas had been discussed with Lord Melbourne, who had succeeded Peel as Home Secretary, and it had been decided that the arrangements under consideration were not consonant with the Police Act of 1829, that the New Police had no obligation at all to patrol private property such as land within the walls of enclosed docks, and indeed the Met. Commissioners had no authority to relieve the Company of any proportion of their rates burden. Further sporadic mention of this topic shows that it was 1840 before the Board reconciled themselves to the fact that if they wanted Met. Police they could have them only on savagely uneconomic charges per man per hour. On March 21st, 1840, indeed, a letter from the Commissioners offered to take over the policing of London Docks by night only, for a round figure of £817 per year.

But the initial refusal was followed (as such things always are) by efforts to cut down on the existing Force. Temporarily, the Night Watch was wholly abolished, and all the emergency plans were revived as far as standing by for the expected Chartist Riots, although these did not extend to Dockland at all.

In October, 1847, a report from the local Met. Superintendent asked the Board if they would receive and pay for two hand-picked men at 24/– per week, 'as certain irregularities recently discovered by my men are causing me some concern'. The Company agreed following which there is no further mention of the intriguing matter!

In April, 1848, there were more riots, and the emergency measures were revived and again worked well. The Board sent written thanks and congratulations to all concerned – all those who acted as Special Constables received a token bonus of 2/6d.

The Minutes contain little of any interest on the subject of Police until July, 1854 – when a letter was received from the Receiver of the Metropolitan Police (the officer who even today sees to all the financial affairs of that Force) saying that the existing charge for attendance at night was inadequate, and would be raised to 31/6 per week for each Inspector, 28/– for each Sergeant and 24/6 for Constables. There would also be a charge for lanterns supplied and used.

Convictions and penalties, by contrast, are referred to in much greater detail. One related to the habit not uncommon among dockers and seamen of piercing the small rum barrel which was known as a monkey and sucking out the spirit through a hollow reed or straw. This was generally referred to at the time simply as sucking the monkey – as the illegal extraction of all kinds of liquor from all kinds of cask is still known to this day. This, upon conviction, attracted a regular sentence of nine months imprisonment – as did more than one conviction for stealing a tiny quantity of tea. A case of forgery was dealt with by a sentence of 20 years penal servitude and a common assault brought a year in gaol. Strangely contrasted are isolated examples of leniency incompatible with these standards. A docker discovered to be leaving through the Gate carrying 30 cigars in his hat, was merely fined 20/–. More expected is the ten years transportation received by three men who between them almost got away with half-a-hundredweight of tobacco. And a man named Rosetta, who was convicted for stealing 75 lbs. of mercury (a most thievable commodity, even today, as it merges at once with all other mercury and cannot thus be identified as a separate unit) was sentenced, on conviction, to be publicly whipped before being imprisoned with hard labour for a month.

Procedurally, some of the difficulties encountered by the Company's solicitor are very like those which could be encountered today, given a combination of slight negligence and bad luck. In 1858, we learn that there was a frightfully bad Magistrate at Thames Police Court, now transferred from Wapping to Arbour Square in Stepney. (It really is extraordinary how rare a phenomenon this is!) This man's name was Selfe. On a rigger named Johnson being detected stealing 27 lbs. of metal, Selfe threw the case out summarily. Understandably incensed, the Board managed to secure against Johnson a Voluntary Bill of Indictment, which cuts out all committal proceedings. The man was re-arrested and given full jury trial at the Old Bailey, when he was found guilty at once and without hesitation sentenced to four months hard labour. The Judge delivered some open and highly caustic remarks about Mr. Selfe. Then a few months later, the same Magistrate did exactly the same thing. Once more a Voluntary Bill was obtained, once more the defendant was convicted at the Old Bailey without hesitation and with judicial comments. The Board now met to consider sending a strong letter about Selfe to the Home Secretary, but Tyrrell wisely counselled against any such action unless the same thing happened a third time. (Wisely because Selfe had to be lived with by Tyrrell, probably several times a week and indefinitely, and could thereafter be relied upon to lean heavily against the Company whenever it was legally possible). The Board left the matter to Tyrrell in acknowledgement that what proved able to be done, would be done. It is implied that someone of some eminence had a quiet word in Selfe's ear, for no such incidents are reported again.

On May 12th, 1863, McDonald, Police Superintendent, informed the Board that the Regulation requiring the Gate Keys to be deposited at his house at night had become virtually inoperable, as they had constantly to be released to let out dockers working overtime and letting seamen in after late-night carousals, back to their ships. The Board duly altered the Regulation, putting the Gate Keys at night in charge of the senior man on duty at each Gate, McDonald taking charge only of those Gates unmanned and thus unopenable by night.

And from this point forward the Board's Minutes cease reference to all save the coming almalgamation between it and the St. Katharine Dock Company, which had existed since 1825. It is now therefore necessary to go back to that foundation and bring it up to 1864, before we can go further forward along this tributary.

Section 6. The St. Katherine Dock Company, 1825-1864.

Although the date of the Company's foundation was 1825, it took some time, naturally, to construct the curiously-shaped – almonst butterfly-winged Dock which was opened with due ceremony on October 25th, 1828. Meanwhile, there were problems of security even during the construction work, the more so as they neared completion. And on June 5th, 1827, we find the Board of Directors soliciting the Thames Magistrates that Thomas Edwards and John Clark might be appointed and sworn in as Special Constables under the provisions of the St. Katharine Dock Act, s.136, for the protection of works and materials. One presumes that this was done, for there is no further reference to it.

It was not until a year later – July 22nd, 1828 – that we find the first survey of the Police scene in the new Dock as it nears its formal opening. Among salary statements, we find:

"Police Office—Superintendent £130 p.a. – £140 after 5 years – £150 after 10 years. Constables – 30/– per week – Gatekeepers – 25/– per week, Watchmen – 20/– per week – Seven Constables when opening and ten thereafter."

In an interesting note of comparison which is all too rare, behold a note showing that the West India Dock Company was at the same date working with 21 Constables, and the London Dock Company with 6, both with Gatekeepers added. Also for the first time there is mention of an age limit – Constables, etc., should not be under 21 nor over 35. On August 5th, 1828, Sgt. Major Baxter, aged 39, who had served 23 years in India with the 13th Light Dragoons, was appointed Superintendent of the Company's Police.

As to appointment – on August 15th, it was recorded that those of Gatekeepers and Constables should be in the patronage of the Directors of the Company, subject to the approval of the full Board. Complicated details, devoted to the division of this patronage, follow.

On September 4th comes a list of Byelaws regulating, among other matters, the closing of the Gates, allowing the Police Superintendent free ingress and egress for examination or inspection or setting or relieving the Watch.

The Grand Opening of the new Dock on October 25th, 1828, seems to have gone off very well. There were no incidents to breach the peace and happiness of the occasion. Those thanked expressly in the Minutes include the Company's Police Force under Supt. Baxter.

The new Company started on noticeably better terms with the Revenue men than its counterparts. On November 28th, it was agreed in terms that the Police would take over henceforth the examination of all luggage passing in or out of the Main Gates.

Two days later, the Thames Magistrates wrote to say that the Home Secretary had authorised them to swear in the several Constables and Gatekeepers as Constables of the Realm. That very afternoon, Mr. Baxter and his men attended at Wapping so that from that date, the St. Katharine Dock Company no longer had a private security force – it had a Police Force.

Several other details follow – some of them in the Minutes of the Dock Committee which were available to me. Uniforms were at once provided on the appointments. Greatcoats and capes, adorned with the Company badge – that was basic until, a week later, there is the record of a tall, glazed hat each. Their area of jurisdiction was, for once, wider than the Docks themselves – it covered the Tower Liberties as well. Today, the Ward of Portsoken is technically outside the ancient boundaries of the City on the east, but within those same liberties. We note that £5 15s. was paid for the Warrants of Office.

Awaiting the first full survey of the Force, we find that the Board Minutes contain this. Baxter was Superintendent and below him were Inspectors James Taylor and William Mulloy. Below them, the Force was divided into three Watches – the Morning Watch from 6 a.m., the Middle Watch from 2 p.m. to 10 p.m. – and the Night Watch from 10 p.m. to 6 a.m. (These coincide remarkably closely with Early Turn, Late Turn and Night Duty in the modern Police Force.) These squads were five to a Watch save for the Night Watch which had six in it. The lowest ranks were as before watchmen. Then there was a separate body of Firemen, under Baxter but not sworn in as constables.

During 1829, there was a senstaional civil action for damages which began with a Writ served on Baxter and one of his Shift-leaders named Coxam. One gathers that information had been given by a Customs man named Hurley (also sued) which caused the Police to arrest the Plaintiff, one J. Rainbird, alleging that he had drawn a knife and had threatened Hurley in the execution of his duty. The situation was not helped by the fact that during the action, the Company dismissed Coxam for breaking regulations and being inattentive. And then, the reader's appetite having thus been whetted, not one word can be found in any Minutes thereafter as to what happened next or at all!

On May 28th, 1829, there is a Minute of some special interest. A request had been made by this, as by the other, Company, to Peel, asking for an amendment to his Police Bill giving Dock Companies exemption from police rates. Contrary to his former stony refusal to consider this, Peel now replied that when the general rating assessment was next formulated, account should be taken of the contribution which the Company were making to the policing function at their own expense. Peel said that he had so instructed the Rating authorities.

The month of November was in a sense not the month of Constable Charlie McGuire. Poor Charlie started off by being suspended for a week on the complaint of ship-owners on whose ship in the Dock McGuire had 'made observations in the hearing of passengers calculated to cause serious discontent' – whatever that might mean! Then, on his return to duty, Charlie was at once re-suspended for having lost his Warrant – having been robbed of this and other personal papers while sloshed to the gills in a brothel, locked in the embrace of not one whore but two! (The Company were clearly shocked by this example of virility!) Then, back on duty from this suspension, Charlie was found guilty of having persuaded the wife of one of the Watchmen in his squad to bring a bottle of gin which Charles had consumed on duty, presumably without sharing it. Altogether, it was just not McGuire's month. The Board dismissed him from the Force and from their service, for ever. It must be said that he did ask for it!

So far, only one wing of the new Docks had been used, and in December, 1829, the second was opened, and one sequela was the enlargement of the Police Force by one more squad plus one Sergeant named Thomas Spender to oversee it. Early in 1830, a grace-note was provided by the receipt of a letter from the Joint Met. Commissioners informing them that one of their new Constables was a man named Davies who had earlier been in the Company's service. The Secretary wrote back at once, saying that Davies indeed had – and had been dismissed – for theft!

In 1831, as we have seen elsewhere, the Reform Bill riots brought immediate emergency action, when altogether 25 Police Officers, 247 Watchmen, Firemen, Gatekeepers and Labourers and 278 Dockers were on duty overnight, though no attacks resulted. A bonus was allowed all round and everyone was profusely thanked by the Board.

In July, 1831, came personal drama of some moment. Richard Baxter had drawn his quarterly salary of £32 10s. when an unusual Minute records: "RESOLVED – That Mr. Richard Baxter be permitted to withdraw his resignation previously submitted, this apparently having been written by Baxter in a moment of irritation, feeling that he should quit the police service." And then one wonders. Was it merely irritation – or was it more serious? Could it have been pain? A Minute on November 22nd briefly records Supt. Baxter's death. He was only 43.

The appointment of Joseph Taylor, one of the two Inspectors under him, as Baxter's successor, was followed again by a review of the Police Department, as Taylor started at £120 per year, and Henry Stevens filled the gap as a new Inspector.

On October 4th, 1832, the sudden death of William Thompson, one of the Watch Commanders, from apoplexy, is recorded. His widow asked the Company for some help with the funeral expenses, being destitute with three small daughters. In the light of what they describe as Thompson's long and exemplary service and the special circumstances an award is made – of precisely £3! Thompson was replaced by James Sully, one of his former watch. (To illustrate the minutiae disclosed, Sully was to be dismissed for repeated intoxication in 1835, and was replaced by George Goffin, who resigned in 1836 to join the Metropolitan Police – and so it goes on.)

Regarding the rates, Peel evidently meant what he said, for when the Assessment for 1834 was made, a quarter of the police rate had been deducted by reason of the Home Secretary's action.

A little later, we find a reference to arrangements having been made with the Met. Police Commissioners for mutual assistance in any emergency that might arise.

And then in August, 1843, we find a report of the Dockmaster relating to the pecuniary embarrassment of Mr. Taylor, the Police Superintendent. The circumstances, not even outlined, "were such as to render it expedient that his services be dispensed with". In the next Minutes, a statement from Taylor was read in which the former Chief of Police, "threw himself upon the Board's mercy, begging them strongly and pathetically to permit him to resign instead of being dismissed". The boon was most solemnly granted in the light of the length and quality of his previous service. Taylor's resignation was dated August 12th. Nine days later, Rowan and Mayne, upon being requested by the Company, recommended one of their former sergeants, John Passmore Mumford, who had served for 12½ years in the Met., for Taylor's successor. Mumford, though only 34, was duly appointed. The Board agreed that he should have the advantage as regards superannuation of his previous police service as if this had been with the Company.

On April 18th, 1848, occurred the Chartists' Riots. They had met on Kennington Common and had threatened violence to everyone who opposed them. No less than 567 St. Katharine Dock men from the Docks and Cutler Street Warehouse, were all made Special Constables. The more efficient were selected for immediate service and a store provided by the Company contained 249 pikes, 175 cutlasses, 75 pistols, 24 muskets and a lot of ammunition therefor. In the event, the Chartists did not advance to, or towards, the Docks. The emergency over, the customary thanks and bonuses were distributed by the Board.

But if the political front became more quiet, the natural enmity between the Docks' Police and the Revenue men increased in both volume and seriousness. Retaliating for the arrest and prosecution by the Company of two Customs Officers for theft of brandy, the Customs began a campaign of stringent searches of whatever places in the Dock the Company men would frequent. Indeed, this activity interfered with work, at one stage. The Customs laid information with the Metropolitan Police, as a result of which a warehouseman and three of his staff ,all trustworthy employees, were arrested and whipped off smartly to Newgate, pending their trial, for stealing molasses. In due course, the four victims were acquitted when it was shown in evidence that in great heat, molasses swell and some has to be drawn from each cask to prevent bursting. This was a fact well known to the Docks Police, but not to the Metropolitan – though the Customs should have known it well enough. The Company sent a petition to Parliament asking for a full enquiry into the management of the Customs service. It was not even acknowledged.

In June, 1849, the Company succeeded where all previous efforts had failed – it obtained the services of four Metropolitan Policemen to supplement its own Force, within the Dock Walls, free of charge. Mr. Mumford reported that the arrangement worked well enough, but a further application by the Company for two more Met. men at Cutler Street Warehouse was, if not rejected outright, than at least deferred.

Mumford's salary was now raised to £160 plus gratuities each year, to which a free dwelling house was added. He was also allowed easier hours of duty.

A passing reference in the 1850 Minute Book is curious, insofar as Mumford is an ancient Cornish name, rarely found in the East End of London. For among the newly recruited Constables to the Force under Mr. J. P. Mumford, appears the name of Henry Mumford. Quite possibly it was the Superintendent's son. If so – how nice!

From time to time, the Minute Books record the Board's continuing expressed appreciation of Supt. Mumford's zeal and assiduity. To his salary and privileges is added an annual allowance of £20 for the wages of a servant in his free accommodation, as well as a £7 addition to his clothing allowance.

But at this point the Minute Books start concerning themselves wholly with the amalgamation of the Company with the London Dock Company, and we can now turn the pages forward once more to follow the law-enforcement history of this thriving new Company up to its ultimate merger with the East and West India Docks Company.

Section 7. The London and St. Katharine Docks Company. (1864-1889)

With matters of far greater significance affected by the amalgamations, it is quite some time before the Minute Books of any new Company contain any direct reference to Police. In many instances, such matters as arose were dealt with wholly by Sub-committees, whose records are no longer extant – the Board of Directors often approving unrepeated Committee Minutes of which no trace remains. And as another indication of the increased sophistication of Minuting as compared to the good old days of the West India Dock Company – the same basic sized Minute Book of 500 pages which used once to cover six months work is, by 1864, found to cover five full years.

It should also be mentioned that the amalgamation noted above was one containing not two elements but three – for there had been founded in 1850 the Victoria Dock Compan,y which had been opened for business in 1855, and this, too, was amalgamated in 1864. However there are no Minute Books of that Company for those early years of its life, and it is first mentioned as 'an existing part of the formation of the London and St. Katharine Docks Company' in 1864. So the Victoria Dock was part of the assets. And indeed, we may deduce that it was looked after by some form of Police Force. For one of the earlier Minutes of the new Company refers to Thomas Grigg, Assistant Senior Constable now transferred from the Victoria Dock Police Establishment to the Upper Division of the new Company.

On April 9th, 1867, is mentioned a list of Constables submitted by the Company Secretary for annual swearing-in before the Magistrates at Shadwell (presumably there since Wapping transferred to Stepney, as being materially nearer the St. Katharine Dock, if not the Isle of Dogs).

In 1868 there was more public strife in Dockland, and on January 1st of that year a Magistrate actually attended each of the Docks in turn in order to swear-in as many of the Company's employees as were willing, to be Special Constables. And at the same time as arranging this, the Board formally delegated to the Company Secretary the authority to see to the provision of constabulary warrants whenever the need arose.

And still, for all the sophistication in Minuting affairs, there is the occasional personal tragi-comedy to enliven the interest. For example, the Board solemnly discussed an application for re-employment made by William Anderson, formerly Gatekeeper and recently dismissed for being found on duty with a bottle containing a mixture of wine and water. The application is not merely rejected – "it cannot be entertained at all" says the Minute. (As a devotee of wine, the author applauds the decision. No man who could mix wine with re-cycled sewage could be reliable enough to be part of any police service!)

On May 18th, 1873, Supt. Mumford was placed on the Superannuation list, because of age. He was replaced by Head Constable T. Grigg, who had some years earlier been transferred to Victoria Dock and who had since become Acting-Superintendent of that Dock. Grigg's salary was stated to be £140 going up annually to £200, plus £10 uniform allowance and free quarters. At the same time, the consolidation of the three Docks – London, St. Katharine and Victoria – was related to the Police Department and treated as three Divisions, enabling men to be posted from one to the other and being considered as a whole in matters of pay, promotion and suchlike. The Board delegated the authority to handle all Police questions to the General Manager – the first reference to the Chief Executive under that title. In early course, he directed that each of the three Docks should have a Superintendent to command its police establishment – one of the three being the most senior and denoted Chief Superintendent – the first of this new line was Supt. Hearn of the St. Katharine Dock Division.

Some of the painstaking care with which the Directors treated Police matters may be found in September, 1873, when an unemployed man named John Sullivan was stopped at No. 3 Gate, St. Katharine Dock with 15 lbs. of coffee concealed about him, which he had stolen from "B" Warehouse. He was arrested and charged, tried and given two months hard labour on conviction. The Board directed enquiries to be made as to how Sullivan had escaped detection before reaching the Gate. Why was the plunder not originally prevented? Apart from police – what were the Warehouse staff doing? Supt. Hearn reported fully within seven days, and the Board commended his vigilance and zeal.

A large and recurring number of Minutes concern general security. For example, Mr. S. Day, Foreman of No. 11 Warehouse, London Dock, was fined 5/– and severely admonished for leaving the sliding doors of a Jute cargo warehouse unfastened. Also discussed at the same meeting was the action of P.C. Browning. It seems he stopped two men at a Gate, suspecting they had stolen goods on them. Search revealed four bottles of stolen brandy. As he gathered these into his arms, the men dashed past him and away. Browning had chased them, but never stood a chance, his running being impeded by the four bottles which he had not dared let go. Browning was reprimanded.

Another interesting entry is on March 5th, 1874, when the Board directed the payment of 5/- reward to a Cutler St. Warehouse labourer named Lewis Jordan for "his praiseworthy conduct in giving the Police such information as had led to the conviction of E. Lewis, Customs Officer, for stealing a quantity of tea".

The Meeting of February 11th, 1875, brings a note of drama into our story with a reference to the disappearance from his beat of P.C. Edward Snashall, stationed at Victoria Dock. He was believed drowned - indeed at their next meeting, the Board heard that his body had been found on the other side of the Dock from his beat. His death was formally attributed to 'foul play by the Fenians', though the evidence is not disclosed. A gratuity of 3 months full pay was given by the Board's direction to his widow.

Even more mysterious is the Minute of March 16th, 1876, which records the Inquest on a London Dock P.C. Jacob Tolhurst. He had been found on his beat on the south side of the eastern dock, suffering from the effects of poison which he managed to state had been given him by an unidentified man on the quayside. The Inquest found 'death due to strychnine poisoning being murder by person unknown'.

At this point, as with earlier instances, the attention of the Board, and the only Minutes recorded, are on the subject of a coming amalgamation with the East and West India Docks Company. This was in the event concluded in 1900, but for twelve years before that the two companies ran in harness, being administered by a Committee whose activities did include the Police Department. This Joint Committee has left its own set of Minute Books containing the occasional reference to police matters. Thus, and although this is not a company in the true sense, it deserves to be regarded as at least a transitional source and it will be dealt with accordingly here.

Section 8. The London and India Docks Joint Committee. (1889-1901)

One of the cardinal points to receive attention at this period was Labour Relations and how they related to security. The reader must not however compare this with the position today, for in the closing years of last century anarchism and violence prevailed. (We are better off today than we realise!) On September 10th, 1889, the Committee had to arrange and send a deputation to the Home Secretary with evidence that men currently on strike were using physical intimidation to prevent others working. The Chairman of the Joint Committee, indeed, reported more than once in the Minutes on letters and meetings he had engaged in with the Commissioner of the Metropolitan Police (at this time Sir Edward Bradford) on the topic of strikers' conduct and the way the Committee's difficulties had been increased by the neglect of the Met. Police to take prompt action when requested, outside the Docks where the Company's police could not act. Eventually, Counsel's Opinion was sought on the question of what, if any, sanctions could be brought to bear upon the Metropolitan Police. The resulting Opinion, later received through the Company's Solicitor, was 'laid on the table' and not referred to in detail, but since there is no later reference to it at all, one may conclude that no remedies were suggested.

Interestingly enough – at this time the Chairman of the Establishment Committee put to the main Committee his Book of Instructions to Docks Police, which the main Committee warmly approved. Alas, no details are given, nor have our efforts revealed any sign of an extant copy – though of course one just might exist today, lying at the back of some old drawer or cupboard.

And then the question of sanctions against the Metropolitan Police rears up again. This time, the Solicitor was told to secure the Opinion of the great Harry Poland, Q.C., but Mr. Poland returned the papers without an Opinion for personal reasons and the Instructions were sent to another Counsel whose report was in due course 'laid on the table'.

It must now be remembered that with the India Docks Company's assets now held by the Committee came Tilbury – which was the centre of a particularly violent strike in 1889. Just before Christmas there was a letter from the Essex County Council asking the Docks Joint Committee for £190 towards the extra expenses incurred by the Essex Police during the late dreadful strike at Tilbury. The Committee replied stating that as ratepayers they were entitled to full police protection, but as a tribute to the efficiency of the Essex Police in giving the Committee's Police assistance as requested, they would gladly pay the sum requested.

In May, 1890, one member of the Committee, Mr. Morris, M.P., reported the substance of a rapprochement he had effected with Sir Edward Bradford, from which derived promises of immediate and full support for the Docks Police, whenever necessary.

November of that year saw yet another savage strike at Tilbury, and messages of thanks rolled around between the Forces involved. The date of November 3rd is mentioned as that on which the altered Regulations for the employment of labourers came into force. It would seem that recent strikes against the Conservatives' Industrial Relations Bill were not exactly without precedent!

There follows an intriguing mystery, unsolved by me. Early in 1891, the Shipping Federation wrote to the Committee asking for more police protection within the Docks. In reply, the Committe stated that it had been decided to disband and withdraw the Docks Police altogether! This pronouncement came as scarcely less of a shock to the author than it must have done to the Federation! Since no trace of any such idea was minuted, and since no moves to implement it ever took place, it must have been sheer bluff – though one would have expected something to be minuted on the subject of so basic and substantial a bluff being undertaken. As it is, there is no further mention of the matter and the Committee turned to the topic of the installation of a telegraph wire to connect the Divisional Police offices at London Docks and West India Docks.

And then comes high drama, which began in May, 1892, with a report to the Joint Committee from their own Establishment Committee on the recent communication with Sir Edward Bradford regarding the possibility of the Docks being patrolled by the Metropolitan Police. This turns out to have been merely another of the umpteen approaches by the Docks Companies on this topic generally, stemming from the view of a small ginger-group of members that if the Docks Police were to disband, the Metropolitan Police would just have to take over, anyway. The effects of this particular volcanic eruption could still be seen in January, 1893, when the Joint Committee Chairman reported on his talks with Sir Godfrey Lushington of the Home Office, who had said that the Metropolitan Police simply would not police the Docks whatever the Committee did, and that was that. There was no obligation on them to patrol private property. Not only were the interpretations placed by some few persons on the Metropolitan Police Act, 1829, unacceptable nonsense, but if the Committee were so rash as to take this to Court, and if the Courts were to decide against the Home Office, then the Government would at once rush through Parliament a short formal Bill to relieve themselves of an obligation which had never been contemplated. The Joint Committee regretfully decided to forget all about the matter, especially as Sir Godfrey had promised Met. Police assistance in the event of further industrial unrest.

The next Minute serves as a happy and interesting comparison with today. There was a very active Docks Police Life Saving Society which had won a vast shield in national competition. The team were received and presented to the Committee, much congratulatory oratory is recorded – in particular for P.C. Russell, the Secretary/Instructor – and the shield was hung in the Board Room. As will be known to readers, the P.L.A. Police Team have won prizes national and international, again and again, proving themselves unbeatable for long periods. It is pleasing to see the start of so excellent a tradition.

The topic is taken to a personal level in November, 1898, in a Minute recording the presentation by the Chairman of a bronze medal and a Royal Humane Society Certificate to P.C. Bennett for a brave rescue of a drowning man in Tilbury Dock. The author has seen a number of similar well deserved awards made to P.L.A. Police Officers during the 1960s and they never fail to inspire.

As if by way of a parting gesture to the Company, the port's lightermen threw a major strike, but happily it was settled before the Committee formally handed over all administration to the successors for whom they had been holding on – the new London and India Docks Company – to whose Minutes we now turn.

Section 9. The London and India Docks Company. (1901-1908)

It must be recognised that at this stage of commercial development almost all the day-to-day routine concerned with the Docks Police was recorded, if anywhere, in the Minutes, not of vast Dock Companies, but of the Sub-committees set up by them. The size and importance of the Force is in almost exact inverse proportion to the recorded details of its administration. And even apart from the flow from other tributaries yet to be examined, the London and India Docks Company (which embraced the Royal Docks at Tilbury – indeed every group except Surrey and Millwall) were the administrators of a very large and important Police Force.

The first reference in the new Company's Minute Books to Police concerns that missing but valuable Instruction Book referred to a few pages ago. It is listed with other items taken over and adapted for the use of the new Company's Force.

The next is a reference back to the Lightermen's strike so lately settled. The Company settled a bill from the Metropolitan Police for assistance given, most amenably even though the amount was £750. Their gladness is explained by mention of an agreement that the Lightermen's Company would pay £500 of this. Now that's the way to settle strikes!

The Chief Superintendent of the Company's Force was Mr. Cahill, who had been top man of the West India Docks Division. He reported in September, 1901, on a major fire at the West India Meat Depot. Investigations had revealed spent matches, cigarette stubs and clay pipes in the area of the fire's starting point. The Board exhort the Police to increase the energies then devoted to stopping smoking in the Docks, the fire risk being enormous.

There was continuing trouble with the Customs, of course. A letter from the Secretary to the Commissioners for Customs and Excise set out the conditions upon which their men would continue to suffer the occasional entry and search of Bonded Warehouses by night – conditions which included payments to Revenue men at overtime rates. The matter was dropped, but a little later there is a reference to the Establishment Officer having been involved with Customs on the occasion of an official enquiry into Police allegations that a particular Customs man had been sucking the monkey at London Dock. Surprisingly enough, Customs were co-operating fully and the Board record their pleasure – at which point, alas, nothing more is heard of a promising brou-ha-ha.

In June, 1902, the Minutes revert to fire-fighting. It seems that the London Fire Brigade had just been founded and looked down on all other fighters of fires. The Chief Officer, indeed, had sent a letter requiring the Board to order that in the event of a fire being discovered within the Docks, the Police, whose primary duties lay in fighting it, should do nothing save to send for the L.F.B. The Board recorded their displeasure at what they considered to be a serious insult and directed no such change in arrangements!

The only other reference to Police in the Company's Minute Books is a happy one. It seems that for Thomas Whelon, a docker, life had gone past all bearing. He had reached breaking point one cold morning when he had mounted the footbridge over a neck of London Dock, and had hurled himself into the water. Scarcely had the splash subsided when there was another nearby, as P.C. Layton hit the surface. Layton dragged the protesting Whelon to the quayside and willing hands. The young P.C. was awarded the Royal Humane Society's Testimonial on Vellum, and the story ends with the presentation of this by the Chairman of the Company on April 30th, 1907.

And that is the last reference in their Minute Books to the Company's Force, which the reader has seen grow from its historic start to this point when, as also happened with the other and much smaller Group whose origins we now turn to trace, they were about to become the elements making up the Port of London Authority – with its surviving and much respected Police Force.

First, though, we turn to the Company which was founded to build and administer Docks on the southern part of the Isle of Dogs – the Millwall Docks Company.

Section 10. The Millwall Freehold Land and Docks Company. (1864-1870)

There is in fact so little reference in this Company's Minute Books to any Police Force that one might be forgiven for thinking that it never had one at all. But three entries make it certain that they had.

The Company was formed in 1864. In February, 1866, its Consulting Engineers report that the excavations which were to lead to its western entrance had been completed and that the excavation of the new main dock was proceeding apace. There follow references to the dock construction being well advanced and to a second and north/south dock then being excavated. (This second dock was in time joined to the South West India Dock by a cutting.)

And then – on January 14th, 1868, we find "RESOLVED: That A. Palmer be appointed Head Constable at a salary of £2 10s. per week and that he be sworn in accordingly by the Magistrates."

At the next Board Meeting after that, in the course of a long report by the General Manager to the Board, a section is referred to as dealing with the policing by the Company of the Docks, together with the duties of gatekeepers and firemen.

The Dock opened for business in March, 1868, and in the month following appears the only remaining reference to police. It is a sombre one. "A Police Constable of the Company's Police Force has been found drowned in the Dock." That is all. The poor fellow is not even given a name. Sic transit gloria mundi!

Section 11. The Millwall Dock Company. (1870-1908)

It is interesting that the first reference to police in the Minute Books of the Millwall Dock Company should concern the same man, A. Palmer, as was first mentioned in the books of its predecessors in title. In two years and a few months, Palmer had done well for himself. For here – "The General Manager reported that Capt. A. Palmer, the Company's Chief Constable, who was originally with the Millwall Land Company before the creation of the Docks, is now suffering from heart disease and unable to carry on his duties." Regrets were duly recorded, and a pension of £70 per year was awarded Palmer, who passes from our story.

In 1876, the Board received a Petition from the Police Force generally, asking for some payment to be made to policemen on sick leave when their sickness was plainly due to their duties, particularly night duties. Up to half pay upon strict proof was permitted. A letter of thanks from the Force was read to the next meeting.

But such details apart, the over-riding interest of the Millwall Dock Company to any historian centres around the sensational scandal which did not break until February, 1899. Then is recorded in the Minutes the shattering fact that Mr. Birt, the Company Chairman and formerly its General Manager – the man responsible above all others for the build-up of the Company's business – had absconded on the eve of the publication of the Annual Accounts, having been found to have been falsifying the Balance Sheets for a number of years. To follow this path ahead for a moment – in May, 1899, he was found, tried and convicted. Whether it was shame or kindness or both, the sentence he received was not recorded in the Minute Books.

The remaining references to Police in the Minute Books are all surprisingly personal. The first calls for congratulation. There had been a serious outbreak of fire at "P" Shed, when a case of straw-packed glass had been found alight. The fire was extinguished with such speed by P.C. Orr and Fireman Pike that little damage was done and a major fire was prevented.

On April 21st, 1900, it is sadly reported that P.C. Head, who had met with a nasty accident at Glengall Gate the previous February, had died on April 20th in Poplar Hospital. The case is mentioned as coming within the scope of the Workmen's Compensation Act, 1897, and Head's dependants were entitled to a little over £222. Deducting payments already made, £202 remained outstanding and the widow was drawing precisely £2 per week.

An interesting letter from the Company's solicitors early in 1901 reported that a docker employed by the Company had been given six months imprisonment for stealing skins from the Dock, for it prompted a decision by the Board that in all future cases of theft, the decision to prosecute or not should be left to the Chairman of the Company on information given him by the Police. This obviously relates only to cases where the Company is the only loser and is in a position to discipline the offender, and not to what might be called public crime which the police, under their oath to the Magistrates, were in any event obliged to prosecute whenever the evidence justified it.

The Boer War was of course in progress at this time, and the last reference to the Millwall Dock Co. Police records the receipt of a letter from the Soldiers and Sailors Families' Association regarding two soldiers who had been in the Company's Force. They had been killed in action. The Board sent messages of sympathy to the widows and put through an allowance of seven shillings per week to each of them.

And having noted this, we must turn to the story of the only Docks Group on the south bank of the Thames. And, though it is of less significance than that of the major companies, its source as a tributary entails a final journey by the reader back to 1800 – in which year was created the Grand Surrey Canal Company.

Section 12. The Grand Surrey Canal Company. (1800-1855)

Happily, the first item in the first Minute Book of this Company puts the reader right in the picture on the ground floor, if such a mixture of metaphors is not unforgiveable!

For it takes us back instantly and vividly to the afternoon of Tuesday, November 14th, 1800, at the first General Meeting of Shareholders in the Intended Company held at the London Tavern – Admiral Edwards in the Chair. A report from the Engineers having been read, it was unanimously resolved that: "the execution of a navigable canal as surveyed and planned, passing from the Thames at Rotherhithe to Deptford, Peckham, Camberwell, Walworth, Newington, Kennington, Vauxhall, Stockwell, Clapham, Streatham, Balham, Upper and Lower Tooting, Mitcham, Croydon, Merton, Morden, Kingston, Malden, Ewell and Epsom, with collateral cuts to other places in its vicinity – which canal may in time be extended by way of Southampton to Portsmouth – WILL, by forming a cheap, easy and certain water-conveyance for all kinds of articles, be productive of the most important advantages to those parts through which it passes, as well as to the Metropolis and to the Nation in general."

Thinking as one reads this of the shabby, stagnant, sleazy stretch of insect-infested, olfactory-offensive ooze, a death-trap for odoriferous urchins, into which this pristine project has finally devolved, it is hard to imagine its grand original conception as it took shape in the minds of the Shareholders in the new Company. But it must be remembered that the development of the canal, as with so much else, changed radically – first with the Industrial Revolution and later with the invention of the internal combustion engines, so that comparison is difficult, if not impossible. But it is salutary to reflect on what the canal might have been, had it not been for those two developments.

Next into that Minute Book is copied the text of a letter requesting that the Engineer to the Company should attend the offices of the Navy Board. The letter concludes with a copy of its signator – Nelson.

But all this is but background, and the researcher must plod slowly on, alert for the first mention of Police or, in this instance, Rangers. And the first mention comes in a report of a meeting on November 1st, 1802 – a mere five days after Captain Bartlett was sworn before Colquhoun and Harriott at Wapping. The reference is to the appointment of one, Thomas Warden, as Overseer of the Canal at a wage of £2 per week.

At this point, the pitfalls of concentrated research commanded our attention. In every Company other than this one, the history of which we have covered through its Minute Books, the first steps have always concerned the excavation of a Dock, with enclosed walls and often a ditch. Only then does security receive attention. But here, the trees on which one is concentrating hide sight of the wood. No Dock was built as a first step. And yet from early on there are direct references to the Dock.

The answer lies further back in history than any of our story, save for the first part of this volume. It dates from 1677 and the creation by a remarkable woman named Mrs. Howland of what was by a long chalk the first enclosed Dock in Britain, possibly in the world. Perhaps one is inclined to credit her with more romantic interest than she deserves. Perhaps she was merely an absentee land-owner. But a vast area of land was dug out and filled with water from the River on the south bank, a lock making the entrance manageable. This, in essence, was the Howland Dock.

Like all great ideas, it was mocked much as an eccentricity. And this served but to emphasise the dramatic change of popular view in 1703. One must remember that the Thames from the Pool to Greenwich was often packed so full of ships that one could cross the River on foot by stepping from one ship to another. This is confirmed by prints of the time as well as contemporary records.

Now there hit London in 1703 a freak storm – a gale – little short of a hurricane. It wrought great havoc among the hundreds of ships jamming the commercial river. And the only ones to escape any damage at all were those safely lying in Mrs. Howland's Dock which was enclosed not only geographically but arborically, being surrounded by tall poplar trees, as engravings show.

It was this storm, and its effects, that turned the minds of the Honourable Companies across the Thames towards the merits of enclosed Docks. It took nearly a century to start them. But when the West India Dock first opened, the Howland Dock, its poplars proudly waving in the wind, stood on the Surrey bank. It was only later that the Howland became, because of the trade that dominated it, re-named the Greenland Dock.

Reverting against this background to the Canal, the building of its early part went slowly on and in March, 1808, the Company appointed several day and night watchmen for the security of the Company's property. This is still far short of a police force sworn in before Magistrates, of course. The two first watchmen were named Thurnall and Price – one for day duty and ther other for nights. And later we may read how the Company adapted a craft of some kind (almost instinctively such a wording makes one think of Peggoty's upturned boat!) for the shelter of these two men. Construction of the canal was now being done by night as well as by day, behind protective fencing.

And in December, 1809 – at last! – "It is resolved that some of the Company's employees shall be sworn-in as constables, to prevent sundry depradations."

The Canal water at this stage was clean enough to hold fish, for the constables are told to warn-off anyone fishing there without a Company's permit. (Comparative rules are laid down in the Port of London Act, 1968). But – quis custodiet ipsos custodes? In August, 1810, Thurnall and Price, sworn constables, were discovered to be running a small but juicy little business in ships' stores on the side! Captain Smith, the Company's Head of Operations, was told to discharge them immediately and to appoint two others to replace them.

Then on October 18th, 1811, there is the first reference to a Canal Ranger. He is to come within the Committee of Works 'and shall be provided through them with a greatcoat and a gold-laced hat'. And shortly afterwards, he is identified for us as James Croxton. His first reported action concerned a man named Griffiths, who had started to take water from the Canal for his own private use. Discussions resulted in this being permissible by licence to be obtained for £2 per year.

In September, 1813, the Company moved its base to Rotherhithe, and began to retrench in personnel as well as operations. Among those made redundant were the two policemen. (The Ranger was retained).

Then, on December 23rd, 1813, a Special General Meeting of Shareholders was held. They were given a written report on all work to date. And under the heading of Security, there was to be erected a small Lodge at each end of the Canal to serve as a station for the two watchmen – one in each – they being required to double the duties of watchmen with those of 'half-penny hatch-keepers', for which purpose they worked in conjunction with a lock-keeper. (Hatch and Lock are used interchangeably here). Also mentioned at this meeting is a reference to a high and closed fencing near the southern boundary of the Canal. This is odd, in that the Canal runs basically east/west, here, although there was the Peckham Arm which did run south and may have needed protection.

A Minute in the following February reveals that the Company were not above accepting auxiliary help from the parishes through which the Canal ran, as "Mr. Penny, the Rotherhithe Parish Constable requests a small donation for his services during the past year – keeping an eye on the canal banks, etc." The Board deflect the Bill through to the Dockmaster to see to!

The Minute Books now reveal, once the thread has been sorted out and fitted together in sequence, a personal drama, of which the hero – or at least the chief character – is one, Thomas Clay. Clay was one of the two Hatchkeepers. He was asked in the summer of 1816 if he would do extra duty as a Canal Ranger. He agreed, and his wages were to be decided upon. In August, he put in his weekly report on the Canal, and added a plea for attention to his numerous polite requests for his extra wages. The Board instructed the Dockmaster to send him £1 on account. In October, Clay raised the matter again. He asked with his weekly report not only for the wages due but for a greatcoat as well. The Board again granted £1 on account and directed the purchase of a greatcoat second-hand and not costing more than 20/–. In December, reporting that the towpath needed repair in several places, the Board directed the Dockmaster to report generally on the wages position. In January, Clay put his request into a new form – 1/– per day on top of the Hatchkeeper's salary. £2 on account was authorised by the Board. Two weeks later, the Board seemed to be wondering whether there might not be right on Clay's side. Finding that the last payment on account had not been made, they sent for the Dockmaster. Matters were still unresolved by August, 1817, when the Dockmaster reported that Clay had been arrested and imprisoned for a £3 debt. The Board directed his immediate release on payment of the sum due, and the Secretary was charged with a full investigation. After several months of silence, the December Board Meeting included a report by the Secretary that Clay had been rude and offensive to him personally. The Board discharged him forthwith. A man named Carr was then appointed in Clay's place. He was sworn in as a Constable. But the Board had not seen the last of Thomas Clay. On January 14th, 1818, he appeared in person before the Board, delivered up his staff of office – hollow, and containing his warrant – and demanded that his past wages be paid. An immediate donation of £6 on account and without prejudice satisfied him, and Clay left the Board Room – and indeed our story, for there is no further mention of him at all.

The next event of any importance in the Minute Books takes us to the summer of 1821. On August 2nd, the Secretary reported that nuisance and damage had been caused on the Canal banks and bridges by men and boys of the lower orders. A number of the Company's Police Officers (the first mention of such a body) volunteered to do extra duty on the following Saturday for 10/6 per head. The Board considered the suggestion exorbitant and asked the Secretary to sort matters out with the local Magistrates. The Secretary tried, but was unable to obtain satisfaction and the 10/6 per man was agreed to. The course was, it seems, justified, as the Police, not without great trouble to themselves, cleared the Canal banks and prevented the roisterers from doing much dilapidation. One man was arrested and later sentenced to 3 months imprisonment.

Over the next two or three years there are passing references to the nation's (or London's) difficulties in the field of law and order, as the old Parish Constable system finally failed. Mobs, for some reason, regularly assembled on the banks of the Canal at week-ends, countered by squads of the Company's Police.

In July, 1825, Thomas Clay's replacement, Carr, died and Gordon Lewis of Peckham was appointed to the post. Sums between £6 and £9 were paid out weekly to Special Constables for Sunday duties along the Canal, principally to stop bathing, which was continually attempted despite warning notices posted all along it.

References over this period suggest obliquely that the Canal Company had carried their Canal across the width of the Howland Dock, with a lock installed on either side, north and south. On the north, the Canal ran on to join the Thames at Rotherhithe. Out of this, in due course, came the existence of the basin which lay between Albion and Island Docks in the Surrey Group as it was all to become. There was a land access to the Canal, as we know from reports in 1827 that it was out of repair. The Company's reaction was to erect large gates wide enough for wagons with a brick pillar on either side. On one side within these pillars was the lodge which accommodated the constables on duty thereat. But still there is no mention of the formal foundation of such a Force as plainly existed.

And then in October, 1828, the Minutes refer to a return, listing the ranks and names of the Company's Constables, Gatekeepers and Watchmen that had been sent as requested to H.M. Customs and this in turn was followed by a direction that the Secretary arrange with the local Magistrates for all Hatchkeepers to be sworn in as constables. In consequence, five more constables are created – and the local Magistrates for this purpose were revealed as those at Wapping. In January, 1829, five more Constables were sworn in directly – named on this occasion as Taggart, Sawyer, Pike, Sam Smith and Matthew Buck, and presented with their warrants of office.

That November, P.C. Pike had occasion to arrest one, Joseph Adams, a master baker of Rotherhithe, whom he had caught red-handed netting fish from the Canal. The next week, the Secretary was sent to the Magistrates to receive on the Company's behalf the fine imposed under the Company's Byelaws. In February, 1832, by the way, Pike, referred to as Constable and Canal Ranger reported the need for some assistance along the towpath. And this is followed by the first reference to the Metropolitan New Police, to whom the Company had sent an unavailing plea for help. A week later, on July 26th, the Secretary read the reply received from Rowan and Mayne, who had ordered all Metropolitan Police in the area to remedy the evil complained of. They asked also for the Company's reports of any instances of unwillingness by their men in performing this public duty.

The total labour force of the Company cannot have been large, for a Minute of November 15th, 1832, required the Day Constable at the main gate to record the names of the Company's officers and servants and their times of entrances and exits, so that fines could be levied on those arriving late. (One can imagine the reactions of today's Union members!)

For a time, there are no further references to Police. And then in February, 1835, Pike reported that he had been assaulted for refusing a local estate-owner named Hudson to pass the Toll-Gate on horseback without paying toll. The locals were talking about burning the Gate down. But others found it of advantage to them – men such as the Post Horse Duty Officer (a species of Revenue man) who now asked that Pike should make all horse-duty collection as well as his own tolls. The Board declined the suggestion.

In July, 1837, a letter was received by the Board from a local doctor referring to several recent instances of drowning in the Canal. The Board shilly-shallied, but the facts were repeated and eventually, the assistance of the Metropolitan Police was obtained.

Meanwhile, old habits die hard, and with an amused sigh we find in the following October that a watchman was dismissed for intoxication. Other habits, too. "The Secretary is desired to ascertain whether arrangements might not be possible for the policing of the Canal and locks, to be effected entirely by the Metropolitan Police." As in all other instances, nothing proved possible, though Mr. Mayne observed in a letter that 'the Bill now before Parliament' (this would be the Metropolitan Police Act of 1839) 'has a clause enabling public bodies to hire a few Metropolitan Police at a time for fixed rates'.

In the following June, the Thames Magistrate, Mr. Ballantyne, swore-in six additional Constables for the Company's Force – named as John Taggart, Jim Johnson, Stephen Carson, Robert Kidd, Billy Buck and William Pike – this makes two William Pikes in the same Force. To them, William Adams was added in his new capacity of Constable, Head Messenger and Superintendent of Fishing. Meanwhile, the Metropolitan Police hiring clause duly became law but the rates permitted were greater than was financially viable.

Constable Cooke, the Secretary of the Company's Angling Club, zealously apprehended two members of the public for fishing and, in June, 1843, took them before the local court where they were fined. But another reference to judicial affairs at this time is less clear. The Board was asked by the Company Solicitor whether they intended to employ Counsel at the forthcoming trial at the Old Bailey of one, Parsons. The Board replied to the effect that they would not do so but would leave the prosecution to the Court. The arresting constable, one of the Company's men named Wylie, was advised of this decision. There is patently an error in recording the fact, here. No court can prosecute, and at the Central Criminal Court no-one save a legally qualified barrister has any right of advocacy for the Crown.

Throughout the Minutes, references abound, of no special relevance in themselves, but from which relevant and interesting facts may be deduced. An example is a Minute of August 15th, 1850, which sets out the terms of employment of a Night-Watchman, which makes clear that these were largely recruited from pensioned policemen of very good character to supplement existing pensions. A certificate of police service was requisite, and the wages were 9/– for each duty of midnight to 6 a.m. Similarly, we know that the Canal Ranger had among his many duties, one of recording the hour of his passing each Hatch in the appropriate book kept there.

In July, 1857, occurred an incident not without legal, as well as dramatic, significance. One of the Company's Hatchmen was accused at Lambeth Magistrates' Court with assault on a Mr. Goring. The defence of the accused, James Varnham, was that he was a sworn Special appointed to protect the Company's property. He had observed Goring on the Canal bank, urging on his dog, which was swimming about in the water. Goring alleged that the dog had escaped from his control and he had trespassed technically in order to retrieve his pet. Varnham arrested Goring, not without a struggle. Goring refused to give his name and address and claimed to have been hit several times by Varnham. Mr. Elliott, the Magistrate at Lambeth, considered the Byelaws, heard the facts and decided that the fight had taken place on public – not Company – land. This entitled Goring to resist arrest and made Varnham guilty of assault. He then fined Varnham 20/– together with 2/– costs and 10/– damages to repair Goring's torn coat. Mr. Elliott then went on to inform everyone that the Company's police officers had no right to detain anyone not on Company property, and in any event, arrest for trespass – then, as now, a purely civil matter – was illegal. The Board directed that written instructions to this effect should be circulated to all members of the Company's Police.

In June, 1861, 25 more Constables were sworn in, only one being named and he, for some reason, bearing the traditional fictional name of John Doe. Shortly after this, a Minute refers to the duties of the Canal Rangers – they had to be sworn-in as Constables, and were charged to prevent all trespasses, nuisances, disorderly conduct, to stop all bathing whether indecent or not and prevent all damage to the bridges, works or property of the Company. This schedule related to the retirement of Ranger Pike and his replacement by one Peter Miller.

The Minutes then become concerned with the coming merger (in 1865) of the Company with the Commercial Dock Company, save for recording the strike of 1864 and thanks to the Grand Surrey Canal Company Police for assistance during it. Thus, at last the formal title of this unusual and brave little Force is recorded, even if only on the very last page of its Minute Books.

Section 13. The Commercial Dock Company. (1810-1865)

The first of this Company's Minute Books is dated 1807 – some time before the passing of the Act of Parliament which was to give it its legal existence! But among the detailed instructions there given to the Dockmaster is the following:

> "He will attend to the Watchmen and the Porters, ensuring that both are vigilant and active. At 8 p.m., he shall toll the bell at the Guard Room, whereupon the Gate shall be locked and the keys given to the Captain of the Watch, after which nobody may pass in either direction without giving the countersign, unless he is accompanied by the Dockmaster personally. There being but three entrances, one by the Guard Room, one by the northwest corner and the third by the Counting House, he shall see that all three are manned all day each by a Constable, who shall ensure that nothing leaves or enters the Dock save that it is subjected to examination."

On July 2nd, 1808, the Officer of the Military Guard (the war with France being then existent) wrote to suggest that the Guard might be reduced to a nominal one, under the Sergeant, adding that 'if the Company do not agree, then the Guard will be withdrawn altogether!' In fact the Guard was removed altogether during 1809. The Board of the Company thereupon resolved to establish a Force of Constables.

Details of this being done were doubtless recorded in a Committee Minute Book not now extant, and the next reference to Police in the Board's Minutes is on January 12th, 1812, when a request was sent to Mr. Colquhoun at Wapping that he should please swear in Joseph Ails 'as an added Constable is badly needed, currently'. (Ails was dismissed the following year for improper conduct of some kind.)

The next reference in the Board's Minutes of any consequence is in January, 1825, the details of the Company's return to the Magistrates of all those holding police warrants being set out in full. They were:

Const. R. Myers	—	At Main Gate.
Const. Wm. Tibbals	—	At Timber Ponds.
Const. Jas. Chiverton	—	At the Bridge.
Const. Wm. Smith	—	Among the Watermen.
Const. John Day	—	At Main Gate.
Const. Wm. Warren	—	Night Duty Officer.
Const. Jon. Cowland	—	At Gate Near Offices.
Const. Stephen Mears	—	At South Entrance Gate.
Const. Wm. Little	—	At Waterside Gate.
Const. James Hayes	—	At Lockside Gate.
Const. Jn. Walker	—	At York Street Gate.
Const. Wm. Matthews	—	At Horseferry Gate of No. 6 Dock.

A Minute of February 25th, 1831, is unintentionally hilarious – "Resolved that a new suit of clothing be allowed to Constable Smith, he not having had any for two years". This is, in passing, the sole reference to uniforms in the Board Minutes.

In May, 1835, P.C. Burridge was granted reimbursement of expenses incurred by him in pursuing the receiver of four casks of stolen tallow. No amount is specified.

Deaths of serving policemen are recorded from time to time, usually with the name of the replacement for them. Among these, Constable Chiverton, the Bridge Constable, was replaced by his son, who later, with P.C. Tibbals at the Timber Ponds, received a wage increase of 5/– per week.

The Company eventually acquired a veritable maze of eleven Docks all interlinked and this doubtless explains new constables being sworn in often in batches of six or eight. The size of the Force, though not directly stated, was certainly not small in 1850 when the reader will not be surprised to see an application to the Metropolitan Police to take over the policing of the Docks area. The matter was considered and a fee demanded which was far above the existing cost to the Company. Plus ca change, plus c'est la meme chose!

The next small increase in the Company's Force is of interest in that it mentions the ages of the new members – respectively 32 and 28. So the familiar figure of fiction, the fat, middle-aged, solid copper, is by no means accurate, at least in 1851!

A new Police Lobby was erected shortly afterwards, at Iron Bridge Gate, and a few lines later is recorded the swallowing by the Company of a little old Company calling itself the East Country Dock Company, which had existed in fact since 1811, but which had no semblance of a Police Force.

In August, 1852, the Company Minutes record the issue to all the Company's Police and Watchmen with rattles, so as to attract the attention of a colleague within earshot. This was consequent upon the escape from custody of a thief.

For almost a decade the Board Minutes are bare of all mention of Police, but on January 4th, 1861, the Police Superintendent reported that his Force was insufficient to fulfil its task. More Constables were at once authorised, and at the same time, a change of title was promulgated – Patrol Rounders were to be known as Constables. A week later, a new Constable is mentioned by name – J. Steer – and his wage – 20/- per week. The title of Head Constable clings to that position which we know as Sergeant, and Inspectors are still Surveyors. In fact, Steer's progress reveals another fact, not without interest. It seems there was a period of Probationary Service to be got through, and it lasted two years. In February, 1863, Steer, having served this period went up from 20/- to 23/- per week.

And now, as usual, the Minutes become gradually limited solely to the negotiations which precede in this case the coming amalgamation of the Company with the Grand Surrey Canal Company and there is no further mention of Police.

Section 14. The Surrey Commercial Dock Company. (1865-1908)

The formal merger having taken place, the new Company came into legal existence in January, 1865. And on the following February 2nd, the Minutes record the receipt and perusal by the Board of a Joint Report by the two Police Superintendents, which recommends, among other things, that the Force may be supplemented when necessary by Metropolitan Policemen at standard rates, up to three by day and one by night, at the discretion of either Superintendent. An appointment of a Canal Ranger shows that this Office continued, and at a wage of 40/- per week.

The new Force was divided into two Divisions, each representing the manor of its predecessor. Both, from time to time, used their powers to hire Metropolitan officers, but not often – the figures cited reveal that the Constable's wage was never above 25/- per week, while the hiring cost per man was never less than 30/- per week.

There was an informative discussion in 1866 about Special Constables. The Surrey Division secured the Board's permission to have fifteen of its dockers so sworn-in. But not only had the Special Constables Act been passed by Parliament in 1861 – there was power to create Specials in this, and indeed in each of the Dock Companies' Acts. Therefore, the Board asked its Solicitor, Mr. Druce, whether one course might be more expedient than the other. Mr. Druce replied unhesitatingly that the 1861 Act should be used. The Board promptly directed that not only the new fifteen men but every man in the Division should be re-sworn under the 1861 Act. On September 4th, 1865, a further group were sworn-in, the place being Surrey Sessions House, Newington Causeway – the building later housing London Sessions.

In November, the Surrey Division Superintendent proposed to the Board that their area be placed in charge of the Metropolitan Police each night. The Commercial Division merely asked for eight more night duty Constables, but the discussions that followed led to their proposing that they, and not the Met., should police both Divisions by night. A full discussion was mooted, and subsequently deferred more than once. It eventually took place on June 29th, 1866.

At it, and pursuant to it, there was agreed a reconstruction of the whole Force, under the single Superintendency of Mr. James Ross. All Constables and Gatekeepers of both Divisions were amalgamated and placed under one Inspector and two Sub-Inspectors. The Inspector's name was Rimmer, and one of the two Sub-Inspectors was John Steer whose recruitment in 1861 will be remembered. All three received the same basic wage – £65 per year.

The new unified Force seemed to settle down well. In 1868, the differential expected between Inspector and Sub-Inspector was restored, Rimmer getting £75 p.a. to Steer and his colleague Bradbere's £71 p.a. Also, the ad hoc use of the Metropolitan Police became noticeably less per quarter, as the figures show.

For some reason we have not been able to discover, Trinity Monday was a full day's holiday for every man in the Force. Agreement with the Commissioner, Sir Richard Mayne (Col. Rowan having retired) set a charge for his men doing this duty annually for a fee of £10. Another mystery, allowing £25 for books for Constables may possibly be no more than a misprint for boots, which seems more likely!

In April, 1876, Rimmer was made up to Chief Inspector and his salary raised to £100 p.a. And in 1878 there was a discussion at Board level, details of which are not given, beyond stating that it concerned the policing of the Docks, and, exceptionally, in an atmosphere which the Minutes describe in terms as acrimonious. The ending was an exactly equal vote for and against whatever proposal was ultimately put, and the matter is left there, no mention being made of any casting vote.

In 1882, Chief-Inspector Rimmer reached retirement age, and his post was advertised. No less than 133 serious applications were received! A short-list of seven was eventually made out, the final selection being left to the Chairman and Vice-Chairman. Frustratingly, the name of the winner is not given – though one would imagine that Steer and Bradbere would have been favourites. After a further discussion – less acrimonious than before, one hopes! – in April, 1883, the power to appoint new Constables was delegated to the Docks Committee – whose Minute Books do not, alas, exist today.

In the following July, there was a Board discussion on the duties and hours of Constables generally. Old problems are still with us, too. In the same month, the Secretary told the Board that he had received numerous complaints from residents in the Canal area of disorderly conduct by boys who crowded the bank every Sunday to bathe. The solution decided upon was for ad hoc supplementation of the Force by Metropolitan officers.

In December, 1887, the Secretary reported the receipt by him of a request by H.M. Customs service for a number of the Company's Police to obtain Customs Powers so that they might seize contraband goods in their own right. The Secretary thoughtfully added that he had contacted all the other Docks Companies, every one of which had already declined the same proposal when it was made to them – it being no more than a device to lighten the Customs' load and increase that of Police. The Secretary was told firmly to decline the suggestion accordingly.

In October, 1888, the position of Chief Inspector again fell vacant, and from numerous applications, a short list of four was made out. The Chairman and Vice Chairman selected Mr. John Abraham Lecoq, formerly a Met. Police Inspector, which the Board ratified. His wage was to be £110 per annum, rising to £150 p.a. plus free coal, gas, uniform and accommodation. After a probationary period of three months, Mr. Lecoq's appointment was confirmed by the Board.

In October, 1890, the Board considered the position regarding Fire Precautions. They suggested increasing a section of the Police Establishment for this purpose, and also went into the details of available insurance. Eventually, two sergeants and four constables were thought to be enough, with the Docks Committee having power further to increase this if they considered it necessary. Additional Insurance was rejected as an alternative.

The puzzle about Trinity Monday still continues. Each year, a Minute gives the cost of arranging full cover of the Canal by the Metropolitan Police for 24 hours. The reason is never even hinted at. The Minute ends with a slight non sequitur – "Hudson and Co. to be paid £6 4s. 6d. for Police Whistles". Better than rattles, any day! Though rattles are even today used to keep contact in thick fogs.

The problems of manpower generally had clearly resolved themselves satisfactorily. There are no references to the Metropolitan Police being paid anything at all for many years over this period – except for the Trinity Monday charges, of course.

Constables were included in the Company's Superannuation Scheme, four of them being named as reaching the qualifying age in September, 1897.

Industrial disputes seemed also to be less frequent, and the entry of March 7th, 1901, stands out by its rarity – "£5 is payable to the Metropolitan Police for their assistance at Lavender Dock Entrance during the Lightermen's strike."

On March 28th, 1902, the Superintendent of the Force reported that he had received a petition signed by every man in the Force, regarding hours of duty. The Superintendent followed this with a solution which, maddeningly, is not detailed! But the Board confirmed it, whatever it was.

In 1907, even the problem of Trinity Monday on the Canal was solved without Metropolitan Police aid – "The Company's Police having taken steps effectively to close the Canal altogether, that day" being the wording used. It is satisfying that for at least two years before the Company dissolved into being one constituent part of the Port of London Authority, their Police Force was handling every one of its problems unassisted by the Metropolitan Police.

Section 15. Conclusion.

And here the vital part of our story which concerns the establishment of a Police Force by each of the Dock Companies, closes. Looking back over it, one wishes only that more of the Committee Minute Books had survived, despite the extra work that this would have entailed by way of research – for the picture would then have been that much more complete. However, the main objective has been achieved by this infinitely painstaking research and we have seen at least in clear outline the course of each of the tributaries which have between them contributed materially to the ever-widening stream of our history.

The commercial and political creation of the Port of London Authority by the joint and several efforts of Winston Churchill, who conceived and planned it, and Lloyd George, who put it into effect, is a story too well known and too widely documented to need re-stating here, and all that is necessary for us to say is that the river to which we have likened this study of law enforcement in the Port of London, is now in full flood.

PART FOUR—FULL FLOOD

The formation of the Port of London Authority — Its strides towards law enforcement — The development of the new Force and its continuance.

PART FOUR—FULL FLOOD

On March 3rd, 1909, a meeting was held in Whitehall under the chairmanship of Rt. Hon. Winston S. Churchill, M.P., President of the Board of Trade. Having recited the terms of s.1 of the Port of London Act, 1908, in full, the record continues:

> "Now therefore, the Board of Trade having thought fit to appoint the first Chairman, do so in pursuance of the powers conferred upon it appoint Sir Hudson Ewbanks Kearley to be Chairman of the Port of London Authority."

Thirteen days later, on March 16th, at 109 Leadenhall Street, City of London, Sir Hudson duly presided over the first Board Meeting of the new Authority. The occasion certainly called for oratory – a talent with which Sir Hudson was richly endowed. Extracts from his inaugural speech must be quoted.

"On the appointed day, March 31st next, we shall have transferred to us the three Docks Undertakings hitherto conducted respectively by the London and India, the Surrey Commercial and the Millwall Docks Companies. In addition to their properties we shall take over all their staffs, their workmen and their trade. Our grand initial responsibilities will be to weld these into one control and management.

"The Port of London has a great history. Recently in the British Museum I found the Seal of the Port of London used by Edward II consisting of the royal arms as they then were – three leopards, surrounded by four swords – which is an allusion to St. Paul, the patron saint of London. . . . The legend inscribed on that Seal is that of Edward II when in the Port of London. It is a happy coincidence that the reconstitution of the Port should be by an Act of Parliament passed under another King Edward – the Seventh.

"Twenty years ago, the largest ship afloat was 550 feet long. In 1902, the Oceanic, the largest then afloat, and 686 feet long, was capable of entering Tilbury Dock. And today? The leviathan of the moment, the Mauretania, 760 feet long, could not squeeze into Tilbury. Let that astonishing growth in seven short years remind us that the dominant factor in the prosperity of any port is the accommodation and facilities that it affords."

And with these and more rolling platitudes entirely appropriate to the great occasion, the first meeting of the Authority passed into history. In a short time the Minute Books (which are from the first printed in bound volumes, to the intense relief of the author!) come down to the minutiae which make them so fascinating. The first direct reference to police lies in a Minute of May 6th, 1909, which concerned J. Daly, a Constable at Surrey Docks who had been certified as medically unfit through consumption for all further duty. He had served 7½ years and did not qualify for any allowance. The Board have him one month's notice and directed that sick pay continue till this expired, whereupon he should have his pension contributions, amounting to £5 0s. 10d. sent to him. Perhaps the Board felt it was too soon to set a precedent of humanity!

Another Minute enables us to deduce the salary of the police then current – a Second-Class Constable, on promotion to First-Class Constable, went up from 25/– to 26/– per week, which sum could rise gradually to 32/– per week.

A Minute from the next Board Meeting reports several convictions obtained by the Authority's solicitor. One is for throwing rubbish into the Thames from a ship, which attracted a fine of £5 with costs of £2. Another is for advertising on the Thames from a ship – fined £3. The former offence, although it is rarely that the offence is witnessed and the culprit identified, brings several convictions still, each year.

Ignoring early inevitable references to Constables being summarily dismissed for being drunk on duty, the reader may sigh to learn that on May 20th, 1909, 'it was moved by Mr. Duthie, seconded by Mr. Broodbank and agreed that it be referred to the Organisation Committee to consider the advisability of approaching the Home Office with a view to possibly transferring the policing of the Docks to the Metropolitan Police'. (One pictures a pantomime and a drop-sheet coming down from the flies to where an ebullient comic cries, "Now, you all know the words – everybody join in!") But perhaps we do Mr. Duthie less than justice, for at the very next meeting he insisted that he add to his proposition the words "or in the alternative that steps be taken to reorganise the existing police service of the Authority". The words, whether previously mentioned or not, were inserted.

In fact the Minutes are silent as to the development of these negotiations but fortunately we have been able to refer to a collection of other papers related to the P.L.A. Police, which enable what happened to be followed in detail. On June 30th, 1909, the Authority's Secretary, Mr. Philipson, reported to the Committee on the existing details of the as yet unaltered Force – or Forces. Supt. Cahill led, with a personal clerk, there were 10 Inspectors, 25 Sergeants, 386 Constables, 13 Barge-Searchers, 18 Firemen and a Messenger. The cost of their Wages, Uniforms, etc., came to £26,000 for the London and India Force, £7,000 for the Surrey Force and £3,500 for the Millwall Docks Force. To the total of £36,500 the sum of £3,000 had to be added as being paid annually to Police Pensioners. The Authority were further liable in total for £9,000 per year for Police Rates though no service resulted. Thus a grand total of roughly £50,000 was incurred.

Having thus costed the Force, Mr. Philipson set out briefly the history of the many applications made previously by the several Companies and laying particular stress on the 1891 application by the London and India Joint Docks Committee, as this contained a vital point of law. The Metropolitan Police had previously always contended that they had no rights or duties on private property and the Committee claimed that as the public had in certain instances a right of access to the quays, they were public property and thus within that which fell as a duty to be publicly policed. Dissatisfied with the refusal they met, the Committee had taken Counsel's opinion, which had given them no more than a slim sporting chance. The point most in their favour, said Counsel, was s.5 of the Metropolitan Police Act, 1839, running in part that the Met. should have powers and privileges of constables also in Berks. and Bucks. and "upon the River Thames within or adjoining the City of London and the Liberties thereof, as well as in the several creeks inlets and waters, *docks*, wharves *quays* and *landing places* thereto adjacent . . ." (Author's italics). The Chairman of the Committee, spurning diplomacy and protocol, had gone straight to Sir Godfrey Lushington, the top Civil Servant. He met as great a tartar as himself! Sir Godfrey said that if the Chairman's view was upheld by the courts, the Government would pass a brief Bill in two days to relieve themselves of an obligation with which it was never intended that they should be encumbered. "The question" now reported Mr. Philipson, "was not further pressed". Game, set and match to Sir Godfrey!

But now Mr. Philipson's informative report was accepted, and the P.L.A. succeeded in obtaining a meeting at the House of Commons on 24th November, 1909, with the

Home Secretary and the Met. Police Commissioner. Sir Hudson Kearley (who was accompanied by Messrs. Philipson, Duthie and Torrey) cited the £50,000 annual cost of their Force and stated that public policy demanded a radical change. Sir Edward Henry, the new Commissioner, in reply, said that their investigation revealed that the Docks Police Forces were badly organised – there was one supervisor in rank to eight constables, compared with one to five in his Force – and while each constable cost P.L.A.£90 per year, each Metropolitan man cost £130. He thought the pilferage percentage was probably even greater than Sir Hudson feared. The Home Secretary decided that a group of experts should evaluate and cost the whole docks policing enterprise.

June saw a touch of welcome humanity in the Authority's treatment of one, P.C. Light, who had developed heart trouble and who was now given a small pension on his retirement, for his life. Later in the same month the Board, upon being informed that the London and India Division of the Force worked longer hours for better terms than the rest, lined up the Surrey and Millwall Forces with it. Cahill was now appointed P.L.A. Chief Police Officer, at £500 p.a. plus £40 accommodation allowance, plus £27 travelling expenses on ordinary duty. As a matter of interest, the same meeting saw the re-appointment of Deloitte, Plender and Griffiths as Authority's Auditors at £600 p.a. and of Rees and Frere as their Parliamentary Agents at a £105 retainer. Both these distinguished firms serve the Authority still in thes ame capacities, though at materially larger fees!

It seems the fate of the Police Department that many small and unimportant incidents fall to be dealt with by the Board and appear in all their embarrassing glory in the printed Board Minutes. Thus does a lowly junior constable, dismissed for taking articles out of the dock without a proper pass, get a Minute all to himself, as do two others, caught smoking on duty and likewise summarily dismissed. And so the story continues. Police officers retire on pension, are dismissed, are taken on, become ill and sometimes die. Occasionally there are points recognisably parallel with the Force today. It surely does not take a policeman to feel, if not actually disgruntled, then at least not particularly gruntled on reading that two dockers were convicted for offences in the same dock (Royal Victoria) on the same morning. One, convicted for loitering with intent, received twelve months hard labour. The other, for assaulting a policeman, got two months.

In January, 1910, Mr. Philipson was formally made General Manager of the Authority at an inclusive salary of £4,000 per year.

The Minutes refer to regular monthly reports from Cahill, though no details are normally given. Details of convictions and sentences, by contrast, are usually set out – as a rule and by today's standards, the sentences were rarely lenient, usually hard and sometimes positively callous.

At last, in August, 1910, Sir Edward's report, bespoken by the Home Secretary, was received. Although this is not even mentioned in the Minutes, it was elsewhere obtained in full. It excludes Tilbury, of course, this being way beyond the Metropolitan Police District. Then it begins by stating a position which was to be re-stated almost exactly in 1971, as we shall see. "A considerable proportion of the total strength is required for Gate duty – if the Authority reduces the number of Gates kept open at night, or the hours during which they are opened at all, there will be a material reduction in the number required." He insisted that a Criminal Investigation Department was essential. If the docks were to be taken over by the Metropolitan Police, he observed, there might have to be a Docks Division or possibly even a Force within a Force, for the work was extremely specialised. Proper Police Stations would have to be built, as well as Section Houses for unwed constables. As to numbers which the Metropolitan Police would need if they took over, they would have to be dramatically increased. Taking the Royal Group as an example, it was 722 acres in area, and was then policed by 108 men of all ranks, doing three shifts between them, and it contained 573 warehouses holding goods of immense value, and had 17 Gates, nine of which were 24-hour ones. This can be stated as one man to 6½ acres, whereas in Liverpool, for example, where there were only 25 warehouses and far less of a policing problem, there was one man to 3½ acres.

Sir Edward next set out the numbers and ranks he considered to be essential, and their equipment, which included an electric launch to patrol by water, and a row-boat for detectives (Who says C.I.D. have always been regarded as an élite?) summarised in a long schedule. His final assessment of needs, amounted to 19 Inspectors, 86 Sergeants and 506 Constables, plus 25% again, to cover leave, sickness and crises – 764 uniformed men alone, plus the C.I.D.

Perhaps the impact of this shattering report stunned the Board. At all events, no reaction at all is recorded. But there were other matters less serious. While Sir Edward Henry had been doing his sums, Sir Hudson Kearley had been busy being ennobled. And when the Chairman of P.L.A. went to New Scotland Yard on November 10th, 1910, he went under the title by which all those associated with P.L.A. and its past will know him best – Lord Devonport.

At the meeting referred to, points of detail were settled and financial calculations made. The conclusions were indeed stunning. If the P.L.A. Force continued but enlarged to a sufficient strength to do their job adequately, its cost would be £80,000 per year. If the Met. took over at lowest possible fees, it would cost the Authority no less than £120,000 per year.

On January 11th, 1911, Mr. Philipson sent all his Board Members a private letter, reviewing all the events leading up to the current question of whether the Met. should take over policing the Docks. Then he cited the main totals such as those mentioned above. More valuably, perhaps, he set out the comparative advantages and disadvantages of having a private or a public Force. These are so germane to the issue and to our story that they must be quoted in full.

"The advantages of using a public Force are:

1. That, being the official representatives of law and order, the police have greater prestige and authority in the eyes of the public.

2. The standards of discipline and efficiency would be greater.

3. There would exist a closer co-operation between the police in the Docks and those outside.

4. Newly-qualified constables would have facilities to exchange surroundings with other Divisions – even other Forces.

5. That since the Metropolitan Police Commissioner was a servant of the Crown, the Docks police would be, as it were, at one end of a chain, and the other end of which would be held by the State, to which the Authority could turn in difficulty or emergency.

"The advantages of using a private (P.L.A.) Force are:

1. The retention of control in the Authority's hands.

2. Closer co-operation between Police and Dock Officers than was likely if a public Force kept order. Also, owing to the rigid regulations of the Met. Police, trouble might arise between them and merchants or ship-owners, to the detriment of business.

3. The lower cost of having a private Force.

4. The fact that the introduction of the Met. Police could not be wholly effected for three years."

The General Manager's letter ended with the interesting fact that a petition had been received from 173 ship-owners and merchants of the Port of London urging that the policing of the Docks should be taken over by the Metropolitan Police, and the London Chamber of Commerce had said that if the P.L.A. Police was to continue, a more effective means of stopping pilfering would have to be devised. Clearly the reputation – and the morale – of the Docks Police could scarcely have been lower in all their compound history. Some illustration of the state of affairs prevailing may be provided by the report of a Sub-Committee set up to investigate disciplinary offences in 1911. This body ended by recommending "(1) That the Discipline Books be arranged and recorded in a manner similar to the Defaulters Sheets in the Metropolitan Police. (2) That they be fully and properly and diligently kept. (3) The punishments imposed should not be so noticeably more lenient than those which were standard in the Met. Police."

Even so – Supt. Cahill's task connot have been at all easy. One wonders whether he dreamed of being given the authority necessary to do the job properly. If so, he was doomed to disappointment. The ball which was to prove decisive was started rolling in March, 1911, with the engagement of Mr. R. F. Godfrey-Fausset, late of the Indian Police, to investigate the Dock police system and advise on its reorganisation. There is no hint of how the Authority came to know of this gentleman, nor how he came to be selected, though it may be that the Home Office had more than a little to do with both.

The Fausset Report was very long and very comprehensive. He began by saying that while the total manpower in use was 468, he was going to need no less than 808. He wanted 26 Inspectors, 55 Sergeants and 639 Constables, plus a C.I.D. of 36. These numbers would allow each man to have one day off in every seven. Gate Duty – the most arduous and important of all those preformed – should be an eight-hour one, not the present twelve-hour stretch. Regarding the beats covering the total of 2,186 acres containing 1,200 warehouses and hundreds of other buildings, he wanted them enlarged. He described the wooden fencing round the Docks in most areas as useless as a protection against thieves. He added with sagacity, "Save in grave emergency, beats should never be denuded of constables". He proposed patrolling by 36 Constables over the 24 hours, as 'constables on the beat can easily be located by thieves'. He planned water patrols by electric launches. Outlining his plans for a C.I.D., he said, "it is thought that only a small proportion of dock thefts can be detected by the present under-manned and over-worked Force, whereas apart from detecting, the mere existence of a C.I.D. will be a strong deterrent to evilly disposed persons." Under the Chief Inspector whom he would place at Headquarters, he proposed five Sub-Divisional Inspectors one in charge of each of the dock groups, living on the ground. As in his view one of the chief present drawbacks was lack of supervision, he required many more Sergeants to save "too much discretion of constables". He wanted the searching of barges increased, though recognising that no fully effective searches of every barge was possible, but suggested occasional surprise visits to barges by the C.I.D. He demanded a Training Inspector and an Instructional Centre, saying, "At present, men are being sent out to duty to some extent unaware of their work. This must be remedied." Recruits, should become useful after three months intensive training and would then be on probation for a year, subject to instant dismissal and moving only in company with experienced officers. Promotion should require a certificate showing special training duly completed, good character and competence. His salaries proposed included a Chief Inspector's £200 - £250 down to the 14/– per week at which a trainee constable would start working up to 33/–. Detectives would earn 7/– per week extra, for their long hours and plain clothes. Entry should be between 21 and 27 years of age. Retirement should be 57 for Constables, 60 for Inspectors, men with 33 years service being able to retire at two-thirds full pay. The contribution should be 2½%. He supported rent assistance for those living other than in the Section Houses, citing Liverpool as doing this. He ended with a section generally entitled General Management and Discipline. This should rest wholly in the hands of the Chief Police Officer subject to overriding control by the Authority's General Manager. He recognised that there were a number of dead heads whom it would be necessary to pension off, and others who might be persuaded to transfer. The minimum height should be 5 ft. 9 in. A medical test must precede acceptance. A "Conditions Of Service" book must be drawn up and issued. He ended by estimating the annual cost of the whole Force as £67,000 plus £2,500 for uniforms.

It was a splendid start. The Board considered it and reserved their decision pending the General Manager's costing check. Mr. Philipson's confidential report is (again in authenticated documents but not in the Minutes) extant. He went into the costs of the proposed pension scheme in detail and estimated this as £20,000 per year nett. Then he went further, sowing a seed which was later to germinate fully in practice. A passage of his report must be quoted direct.

"The primary object of the proposed improvement in the Police service is the efficient protection of property in the keeping of the Authority. Advantage would also be derived by those who have business in the Docks, even though they have no goods lying here. It would, I think, not be politic to levy additional charges directly. A special police rate would be but one addition to London's heavy charges and our own dock rates and charges must cover the cost of effective police supervision. It would be hard to apportion in detail that part morally due from Dock users and that which primarily suits the Authority's needs. Police supervision, however, if proper, is one of those factors which render a port attractive and therefore one which promotes trade. Thus – when the next general revision of dock charges is considered, I think the costs of the new police service must be borne in mind."

On August 3rd, the Board formally approved the decision of the General Purposes Committee agreeing to the principles outlined in Mr. Godfrey-Fausset's report, and suggesting that the post of Chief Police Officer of the Docks Police should be advertised forthwith.

Eighty-seven applications were received in response to the advertisement. A number were selected for interview, and two names were finally submitted. If Cahill was among the applicants, he was not on the short-list. The two names are Mr. R. F.

Godfrey-Fausset and one E. C. Stuart Baker, J.P., F.L.S., Senior Dep. Inspector-General of Police for Bengal and Assam*. On November 16th, the Board met to meet and interview the two candidates. The strong favourite was clearly Godfrey-Fausset – whom the Committee had appointed to investigate and whose long and detailed report had been accepted in terms by the Board. Granted that some men never do themselves justice at any interview – the reader would be no doubt surprised to be told that the post was given other than to Mr. Godfrey-Fausset. In which case, the reader is in for a major shock! Of the 21 votes available, Mr. Godfrey-Fausset received a measly six, while Mr. Baker swept the board with the other 15. The Board thereupon made the appointment, and Mr. Baker was called back into the Boardroom and told the decision. At which point, Godfrey-Fausset passes for ever from our story.

Baker was asked to do his own report on the Force and the plans for reorganisation. His report was even longer than the last, and it was printed so that copies remain for detailed study. It is dated October 2nd, 1912. A summary of those points where he differed from his predecessor is necessary, though they are not of any great significance. On uniforms, he stressed that the work from its nature taxed the durability of these – more so than those of the City or Metropolitan Police. He insisted that summer and winter issues, of different weight, should be supplied. He detailed a system for indenting for these and other replacements. For the first time, he adopted a badge system which corresponds greatly to that which we know today, – a crown for the Superintendent, three stars for the Chief Inspector and two for the Inspector. The General Purposes Committee thrashed out the details with Baker in person. Finally, they resolved: "The Committee decline from expressing a final decision on Mr. Baker's report, but they are impressed with the necessity to start a C.I.D. immediately and recommend that Mr. Baker's proposals in this field should be accepted at once. The C.I.D. should have one Det. Chief Inspector, 6 Det. Inspectors, 12 Det. Sgts. and 20 Det. Constables, all having at least 3 years service. The appointments should be made over the next three years. This Department alone would cost the Authority nearly £3,000." The Board approved the Committee's recommendations, and appointed Mr. Bower, a Det. Chief Inspector in the Met. Police, to be in charge of the new Department. His first Inspector was to be Sgt. Tom Foster, and nine First-Class Constables became the Force's new Detective Constables.

On June 19th, 1913, the Board noted that the G.P. Committee had considered two supplementary reports from Baker, one recommending a reduction in hours, a number of promotions and correlated matters, involving in total additional cost of £13,600 to the Authority. The Board agreed, but stressed that this should be the limit until further notice.

Two short weeks later, Baker was at it again – this time, his theme was offices. The existing ones consisted of four rooms at West India Dock and a small house at Limehouse adapted for the C.I.D. He required nine rooms, a telephone switchboard and toilets – he would hand over his existing accommodation to the Division as soon as his needs were satisfied. There was, he said, a suitable building site near the North Roundhouse, to the West of the Main West India Dock Gate – it would cost £2,750 for one storey, but if carefully planned, further floors could be added later. The clarity of this statement, and his persistence, won first the Committee, and then the Board.

*Some sources hyphenate him to Stuart-Baker, but the Board Minutes, and later his own Annual Reports do not. I follow them, acknowledging the possible alternative.

Plans were made in December and a tender accepted from Whitehead Ltd., ratified in February.

Our sources of information have by this time notably increased – on top of the Board Minutes now come the Annual Chief Police Officer's reports, and sundry other documents – the author's problem becomes one of selection. The Annual Police Report, for example, has a section with the outline of Some Interesting Cases, all of which have to be most reluctantly ignored, though they could make a large book of their own. Moreover, to dip more than occasionally into the accumulation of running minutiae would mean losing sight of the wood by concentrating on the details of the trees. On the other hand, an item apparently insignificant may bear upon a later development of great importance. For example, in 1913, Baker records a decrease in crime due to the application of a new system of checking rail trucks as they arrive at Tilbury, which will be found to have its counterpart in 1977.

Baker was not merely energetic – in the service of his men, he was indefatigable. In March, 1914, he submitted plans for the conversion of an old Shed into a Gymnasium for police recreation, at a cost of £230. For the C.I.D., he acquired 12 bicycles – at £4 each! Then, 'forgetting' that recruitment had been suspended, he won authority to increase the Force by 3 Inspectors, 11 Sergeants and 16 Constables, thus enabling all save Gate Constables to serve only 8 hours in each 24. The total establishment was now 638 – the total annual cost, £61,000.

In July, extensions at Tilbury involved the enclosure of a further 135 acres by a Customs Fence. Baker used this to secure 10 more Constables, at an annual cost of £850. His conviction rate was rising rapidly, but the coming War was casting its shadow before it – "We are having to charge many men with refusing to obey their officers on ships – they claim to be afraid of the coming hostilities, but I suspect that pay rises are really at the back of it." Of those arrested during the year, only 7.1% were P.L.A. men, the Board noted with satisfaction.

But now the sands were really running out, and before September the country was at war. In the first month, out of a total of 689 policemen, no less than 313 had enlisted. Baker noted that the Met. Force, undergoing a similar crisis, were advertising for men at 50/– per week. The Authority raised their basic to 43/– with fringe benefits better than the larger Force. This was so effectively timed and placed that Baker contrived the recruitment of 98 Metropolitan Police Pensioners. As the year ended, his new Headquarters were ready for occupation.

Baker now discussed with the Board the changes which the War was making necessary. Pay bonuses, in return for longer working hours, were offered. And he personally was given some useful delegated authority to act without first seeking permission. The public were now, of course, forbidden even to approach the Docks, let alone cross Lock Gates, without a certificate signed by Baker. Cameras and sketch-books suddenly became symptoms of potential espionage. And, as Dockland began to adopt a new way of life, Baker devoted his energies primarily, and with immense success, to the true unification of five separate Forces, each with its own valued and valuable traditions, into one Force – by no means an easy task.

Christmas, 1915, was enlivened at the Royal Docks when on December 23rd a naval vessel, the *Arrina*, was in the act of departure to the River when a gunner aptly named Stout, who had imbibed seasonally but too well, fired a live shell from the after-deck! It scored a direct hit on the sluice-pit cover at the corner of the lock, doing £15 damage. The Police arrested Stout, and then handed him back to the Navy for appropriate action.

And now casualties in large numbers begin to take up increasing space in the Board Minutes – as do awards, sometimes with citations. In both, the Police figure prominently. So many do these items become that they are shown hereafter in an *Appendix* (p. 151)*.

In January, 1916, Baker reported that owing to recent increases in other Forces, the pay of his men was lagging behind. He asked for parity, which the Board granted, at an additional annual cost of £5,300. His own salary was increased by 25%, to £1,000.

With the publication of his Annual Report for 1915, Baker gives some statistics which, even taking into consideration the truism that there are "lies, damned lies and statistics"† do nevertheless throw a bright and useful light on successes in the courts. Over the previous five years, and duly broken down into groups, we find:

Year	Theft and Unl. P'n.	Assaults	Others	Total Charged	Convicted
1911	217	45	71	333	286
1912	243	91	118	452	381
1913	329	44	110	483	404
1914	353	57	260	670	561
1915	578	71	283	932	806

Commenting on these figures, Baker noted that the 1915 jump in the total was due to the Force's greater vigilance combined with greater congestion in the Docks, the abnormal employment of casual labour, and an increase in the amount of pilferable cargo, particularly in the Surrey Docks which had previously dealt mainly with stacks of unpilferable timber. One can see the Chief Police Officer endearingly backing all his horses each way – and getting away with it!

Accidents also shot up during 1915, explicably by compulsory diminished lighting and inexperienced employees, together with wartime congestion of people as well as goods.

Baker also bitterly complained that the fines for thieving were miserably small. This is less surprising than the appearance of a Minute that Lord Devonport brought the fact to the attention of Sir Edward Henry, hoping that he would use his influence with the Home Office to advise London Magistrates to use their powers more salutarily.

Even more interesting is a Minute from August, 1916, which runs: "The list of convictions and sentences indicate that the sentences imposed by the Lay Justices at Grays Court in Essex (which covered Tilbury as it still does) were inadequate to provide the least deterrent, and the Chairman will consult with the Home Office as to whether a Stipendiary might not be appointed." Such a proposition could scarcely be more than a gesture, for the Stipendiary's stipend would fall on the ratepayers. But while it is

*The opportunity may be taken to observe sadly that a similar collation cannot be made covering World War II. For some reason which is not clear, a whole collection of documents was burned, by accident or design, in about 1950. Doubtless, just such an item would have been in it.

†The author's lasting favourite example is that included in a serious American study of wife-murderers which brought forth the shattering conclusion that there was among them an abnormal percentage of widowers!

easy to accuse Lay Justices of being more likely to be persuaded by skilful defence advocates doing their professional duty (which is to win an acquittal, not to see justice done), it must be said that two of the several Benches sitting at Grays in the 1960s and early 1970s certainly attained a standard of perspicacity which no Stipendiary could ever have bettered.* In the case in point, the Home Office replied, agreeing that the fines were too low by far, but suggesting that the Authority should contrive to have its cases presented by a London advocate who would carry more weight than local solicitor-agents. (Comment, however tempting, will not be made!)

That year, Baker fired the opening shots in what was to be a long and eventually successful campaign. "The P.L.A. Police lack sufficient direct authority over shipboard labour."

On a personal level, the year was further marked by a real V.I.P. named Mrs. Hall managing to topple from the quay into the Dock water, to be heroically rescued by one, P.C. Palmer, but unfortunately further details of this intriguing incident are nowhere vouchsafed.

Admirably, the Board gave £250, as Christmas approached, to the official funds to provide Food Parcels for British prisoners in Germany. And there were to be no less than fourteen air raids in which Dockland was the target. One killed eight dockers – but on the whole, the damage was not as severe as might have been expected.†

There was an accidental tragedy when one of our own shells burst on the deck of a naval vessel in the Royals, killing three. A thoughtful appointment urged by Baker was of a Major Henderson as Supervising and Inspecting Officer to be at the Police elbow in the guarding of vulnerable points in Dockland formerly performed by the Services but now thrown upon the P.L.A. Police.

The summer of 1917 brought a concern for 56 men who, on the outbreak of war, had been probationary constables, and who had enlisted during their probation. It was first announced that they would be given permanent status as from one year after swearing-in, provided they came back to the Force after the war. A month later, it was realised that this would give them priority over Constables who had enlisted only when their probationary period ended, and a proviso had to be added, to cover.

That August, two Inspectors originally with the London and India Docks Police applied through Baker that the value of the houses they occupied rent free might be counted towards their pensions. The Board consulted their Solicitor, Mr. Turner, who with true legal cunning suggested an arrangement whereby the annual value – £30 – would be added to the Inspectors' annual salaries, and that they should be required to pay the rent. Thus the officers got what they sought without financial disadvantage to the Authority!

Throughout the war, the Authority greatly maintained morale by giving the Police constant awards, on Baker's recommendation, for meritorious service, or

*A similar brace of Benches worked at Newham, which covered the Royals, during the same period. The Indias and London/St. Katharine Divisions were covered by Thames Court (the descendants, judicially, of Harriott and Colquhoun) which had a Stipendiary for most cases. How fortunate was the P.L.A. Prosecuting Solicitor!

†The Police Federation Newsletter of March, 1968, quotes the following excerpt from an ancient West India Dock Divisional Order Book: "The Officer on duty at the Main Gate will, if he sees a Zeppelin approaching, blow his whistle and proceed immediately to the Police Office and warn the Officer on duty".

duties long over normal, the amounts varying between 5/- and £1 for Sergeants and Constables, with larger awards for more senior officers.

On May 16th, 1918, the Board considered a report which might be said to bear immense interest in retrospect. This related to agreements between the Authority and P. & O. Ltd., for consignments of silk to be received direct from ships, in sealed wagons, and taken direct by rail to Commercial Road Warehouse, already linked to Tilbury railwise – all under police supervision. No thefts were recorded. One wonders whether this might not have been the first instance of what was to develop, decades later, into the container revolution.

For two years, the volume of crime had been increasing steadily. June, 1918, saw the trial of two men whom the Metropolitan Police had found and arrested hiding in a West Ham stable, having previously stolen four casks of palm oil from the Royal Docks. The episode marked an example of happy co-operation between the two Forces, and the Authority gave £10 for distribution among those whose vigilance had brought, in the end, the recovery of all the stolen goods. By way of reciprocation, during the very next month, the Met. obtained the conviction of a West Ham lodging-house keeper for failing to keep a proper register of aliens – a sequel to an earlier arrest by P.L.A. men in the Royals of a German who had earlier escaped from an Internment Camp in Lincolnshire.

By contrast, it is interesting to note that Baker submitted a special report on the attitude of the Authority's Force during that unhappy strike with which the Metropolitan Police was afflicted during 1919. "Our Force," said Baker, "maintained an attitude during these troubles of which the Authority may well be proud. With the exception of a few days in May when a serious attempt was made by the Metropolitan men to drag our men into their dissensions and troubles, the whole Force held strictly aloof and refused to have anything to do with Unions and strife. After a slightly 'wobbly' three days, every man-jack finally recorded his word of honour to have nothing to do with either." Of course, the Corps of Specialists which the P.L.A. Police had already become, was not subject to the conditions and aggravations which had brought the men of some Crown Forces to undertake one of the most tragic and hopeless strikes ever to take place. But Baker ended by noting that of all the Force, one solitary Sergeant, with what would have been a fine iconoclasm in any other context, declined to state whether he had belonged to the Police Union or not – and was placed on the Retired List, at the age of 47. By the following November, the Police Bill received the Royal Assent and established the existence of the Police Federation, forbidding any policeman to belong to any other such organisation. And in due course a Federation on exactly similar lines was created to cover the P.L.A., and to affiliate with it.

But Baker had by no means dropped his greatest cause. His 1918 Report had stressed that the Force must be enabled to control not just the Docks but the shipping within them from a security point of view. The control was insufficient, particularly on the north side of the Royal Docks. And once up a gangway, a thief could hide himself, or his loot, for as long as might be convenient. Eventually – possibly more suddenly than he had himself expected – the walls against which he had been prepared to batter his head indefinitely, collapsed. On November 6th, 1919, a letter was received by the Board from the Committee of Lloyd's, expressing grave concern at losses through thefts taking place not so much in the Docks as on ships within the Docks. Baker's reaction being formally requested, out into the open came his major project – a separate Police Force, within the Docks, operating exclusively on board ships where the existing

Force was without adequate jurisdiction. Such a Force, urged Baker, should be paid for in proportion to the use made of it by the Shipping Companies, whose basic problem this was.

The plan was passed by the Board to Lloyd's, who began at once to arrange conferences between all the major Shipping Lines. It was decided that the shipowners would act through an ad hoc Committee which would collect and pay to P.L.A. every six months, the cost of the Force within a Force. The manpower would be recruited by Baker, operating on the same terms as the P.L.A. Police, of which the Shipping Police, as it became known, would be treated operationally as a specialised component part. The new Force should have 1 Chief Inspector, 5 Inspectors, 20 Sergeants and 90 Constables. Its initial estimated annual cost was £35,000, including pension rights as well as wages. April 1st, 1920, was named as the day on which it should go into action. It should continue for a year anyway, termination thereafter by either side on the giving of three months notice.

That same spring saw a serious raid taking place along the Surrey Canal, which brought that area into sudden prominence. £2,400 worth of damage was done largely to the Authority's unoccupied property along the banks. Full police supervision would cost not less than £2,000 annually, as the two Rangers were not trained as police. As a first step, it was decided that all unoccupied property suitable for demolition should be knocked down without delay. Negotiations were then opened with the Metropolitan Police who ultimately arranged to take over patrolling of the towpaths, and also with contractors who constructed a high barrier between the Canal and Surrey Docks.

Dockland was troubled at this time by a spectacular rise in crime which detailed examination revealed was located almost wholly in the India and Millwall Group where vast quantities of spirits, mostly rum, were now being stored not in vaults but on quays. Very many dockers had embraced the habit euphemistically called scrounging in the Forces and, said Baker, a number of major professional criminals had been recently demobilised and were resuming their pre-war occupation.

The whole Force in 1920 was just over 1,000 strong – of which 116 were seconded to the Shipping Police and 29 ear-marked for the new extension to the Royal Docks, which the King was to open and name after himself. Baker was no doubt anxiously awaiting proof of the success of his bright new Force within a Force.

However, before this could be demonstrated, an outstanding piece of personal heroism occured when a Detective Constable named Berry saw to his horror that a horse pulling a van along Preston Road, which runs along the eastern side of the Isle of Dogs, had bolted, imperilling women and children by the score. Berry dashed without hesitating right in front of the terrified animal and grabbed the reins, swerving the van so that it avoided a woman and two children literally by inches. But the swerve had thrown him directly beneath the wheels of the van, which passed over his body. This being brought to the Board's attention, they solemnly added the sum of two guineas to the award of £10 made by the Carnegie Hero Trust Fund. And at the very same meeting, the Board made another award – to Supt. Seaton of the Royals Division, who had worked after office hours over a long period to prepare the Instruction Book then in full use throughout the Force. He received £100. One can imagine how D/C Berry must have felt.

And then came the news for which Baker and others were waiting. The statistics showed a tremendous drop in crime, plainly due to the Shipping Police. In one case, a crew member standing on the deck of a ship in Surrey Docks had surveyed an empty hold and told a Constable that this had been the first time ever that he and his mates had not had the whack they looked on as perks out of the cargo. The hold in question had been loaded with gin – and in contrast to the local tradition in such cases that not a stevedore went home sober, they had slouched unhappily away like the involuntary Rechabites they were, in the direction of the local pubs.

During the months that followed, crime continued to diminish markedly, especially on ships. But increasing trade naturally brought increasing opportunities – and temptations. And there was some irritating counter-balance in the difficulty of obtaining a conviction of a guilty docker at West Ham Sessions. This had now become virtually an impossibility, since juries then were made up of householders in the area which was populated exclusively by dockers, to whom the second great commandment (as it was known in Dockland) applied – "Thou shalt not shop thy mate". Baker beefed not unjustly about this.*

July 8th, 1921, was a day for the Authority to remember. It saw the official opening of the new Dock by His Majesty King George V. In the official documents we find: "Arrangements have been made with the Metropolitan Police who will detail a Force of some 450 men at the Gates of the Royal Docks and points along the route. Within the Docks, the Chief Police Officer is responsible for the preservation of order, with some 600 men at his disposal, which should be sufficient."

For the first time for several years, the 1921 Report mentions the annual cost of each Constable to the Authority for twelve months – just over £241 – this compares with the £367 per man for the Crown Forces. How much of this difference indicates salary is not clear. But one factor, minimal though it be, was the reduction in the Docks of the policeman's mysterious and esoteric boot allowance from 1/6d. to 1/–.

The Shipping Police continued a great success. In his 1922 Report, Baker remarks, "Pilferage by stevedores in the Port of London had been virtually wiped out". Despite this, however, the Shipping Lines Committee unexpectedly gave twelve months' notice to terminate the whole Force. The effect of this upon Baker may have been distressing – at all events, he notified the Board that his doctors had warned him that he might not last without incapacity to retirement age. He conceded that he could scarcely claim that his work necessitated an Assistant, but the Board might think it desirable to appoint someone who could learn the intricacies of the work in advance. The Board thanked Baker for his wise foresight, and advertised accordingly, which resulted in as many as 245 applications. 23 were short-listed and eventually, Major R. S. F. Macrae,

*With grave impropriety but some pride, the author would beg to record his notable triumph in face of the identical problem, decades later. Recalling that on the day before Sessions opened, any citizen could, on production of a shilling, demand sight of the jury list, he attended on the amused Clerk, paid the fee, and read the whole panel into a portable tape-recorder. This was immediately transcribed and checked with the National Dock Labour Board as well as P.L.A. Establishment Office. Then he let it be known among the jury in waiting that the Crown intended to challenge as many dockers as the rules allowed. It was necessary to do it only twice – subsequent dockers on being called declined to serve as they knew the accused. For the first time ever, P.L.A. got an unbiassed jury – and the author was promptly repaid in his own coin by the Deputy Recorder who threw the case out before it reached them! But the tactic worked – for the brief period remaining before those late and unlamented Sessions were abolished. After all, as someone was heard to observe, perhaps too loudly, at the time – "It is right that a man should be tried by his peers. But by his confederates?"

C.B.E., was appointed Assistant to the Chief Police Officer. at a salary rising to £750 annually.

1923 saw considerable retrenchment, and the Force's establishment was reduced to 962. But as the Shipping Lines indicated their wish to slide away, the resulting wastage had to be absorbed. In Surrey Docks, oddly enough, crime went neither up nor down – in Tilbury it dropped sharply. But the total increase in crime was no less than 40% – much of this being thought to be due to a combination of first-offenders in the ships and trivial pilferages discovered by extra vigilance at the Gates.

On January 24th, 1924, there was a change of heart among the Shipping Lines – the biggest ones strongly urged the continuance of the Shipping Police, though on a slightly reduced scale – 39 Constables and 2 Sergeants would do, instead of the original 107 men. The cost was re-estimated at £11,000 and on these terms, the new Force was reprieved – on a six-month notice basis.

A week later, Baker was told to consider the annual cost of the whole Force – £213,670 excluding the Shipping Police – and if necessary to re-think the whole, reducing strength if necessary. Baker emerged from a few days retreat with proposals for a much reconstituted Force, involving a reduction of 160 men and an annual cost saving of £35,000. There was, however, a long-term problem. Those departing would consist largely of those already past pensionable age, or those with less than five years service, who were entitled to nothing at all. Yet the Provident Fund stated that every Constable leaving the Force after his initial two-year probationary period was entitled to £42 – Sergeants to £50. Collection proving too great a problem, the Authority decided to bear this cost themselves.

Next is recorded a long and bitter dispute with the London County Council on the arcane topic of spark arrestors. These, it seems, were devices which had by law to be attached to steam-driven vehicles and visible from the road. Fire precautions, of which this was a basic one, had never been less than vitally important in Dockland, and several of these L.C.C. vehicles, if they had the devices, had not rendered them visible to inspecting Constables at Dock gates. Much mud was stirred up, in both senses, and the reader of the Minute Books is left hopeful, if slightly cynical.

Then suddenly the pages are filled with personalia. A Captain McLaglen collected £100 and many congratulations for teaching Jiu-Jitsu to the Force. And whether heroism or bolting horses are infectious, three separate carbon-copies of D/C Berry's courage came up – each man solemnly collecting his £2 from the Board. Special permission was granted to Insp. Boland 'to cultivate the banks of earth adjoining his house in Rotherhithe – but in his own time and at his own expense'.

Then up for consideration came the Authority's Firemen. There were 39 of these, attached to the Police but not of them, and they cost altogether an annual £8,500. Apart from actually fighting fires, they were the source of water supply to ships in dock, and acted as Gatemen during night hours. Now they were to be abolished, save at Tilbury where there was no Brigade to replace them. This reduced their strength to no more than eight, but the cost saving was only £1,600, as 16 new Constables had to be engaged for night duty.

In December, 1924, a series of timber thefts led to the detection of a P.L.A. Foreman, whom the Police duly charged. The defence involved an instruction unwisely worded by the Chief Accountant regarding document-handling, which the Gate P.C. had misunderstood and thought he was not entitled to check the Foreman through. The Court was caustic, and the Board angry. They directed that in future, not only should *all* prosecutions of any moment be conducted by the Authority's Solicitor (Mr. J. D. Ritchie, on a £2,500 salary, later to be General Manager) but they should not be initiated at all without his approval.

On January 8th, 1925, Stuart Baker formally retired, being replaced by Macrae at a starting inclusive salary of £1,200. He found himself at once faced with an awkward complaint against the Police, from the Dutch Consulate, alleging that a man on their staff had had his baggage turned over on his arrival at the Docks. Macrae was implacable. Indeed it had been – and the man detained until he had both established his identity and adequately explained the presence of a huge pile of brand new underwear inside! (And this before the creation of the Dutch-sprung "C. and A."!) No sooner was this settled when up came another – this one involving no diplomat but one, Charlie Wickens, a Tilbury greaser, who had been unable to think up a plausible explanation for leaving Dock with a bottle of fine Linseed Oil in his hip pocket. Taken next morning before Grays Court, he was released – the Bench indicating that they were satisfied he pinched the oil but would ignore it this once. Wickens set up an immediate complaint that the Police had refused to give him his oil back. He was told to get a Magistrates' order – if he dared! He did not.

But Macrae's early months in office were principally devoted to preparing the 1924 Report, in which he took the opportunity to hit out at property-owners who declined to prosecute thieves of their goods whom the Police had caught or even to identify the goods – so that the only possible charge was unlawful possession, which is very often theft of goods from an unknown owner. (This was a problem which the author did not have to face in the 1960s, as the celebrated golf-ball case of Hibbert v. McKiernan had established a residual legal ownership in the Authority – if only as ground landlords.)

Trained dogs were then thought of – Macrae was asked to investigate and report with costings. When the Board heard that the smallest capital outlay would be £275 and the lowest annual cost thereafter £325, the idea was dropped at once.

The year ended on an encouraging note, with an unsolicited tribute from the Union Castle Line who wrote at the end of a troublous strike, praising the P.L.A. Police for their courtesy and efficiency, and two men, Woodward and Mundell in particular for restraint and helpfulness.

Macrae had indicated that he intended to change the method of crime-analysis, which would mean a lack of comparative statistics for several years. And then, right at the start of the new year, he was taken seriously ill. Doctors prescribed prolonged rest and treatment in a warm climate and the Board, with expressions of concern and regret, granted him 3 months leave on full pay, for a start. It was, alas, too late. On February 25th, the Vice-Chairman informed the Board that Macrae had died five days earlier. Deciding to advertise for his successor, the Board directed as appropriate channels, The Times, Police Review (a weekly still in respected circulation) and the four leading national Indian newspapers. The age specified was between 35 and 50.

An item now records the successful prosecution at East Ham of a Mr. Alfred Edwards, who had been fined £5 (or 14 days in prison) for furious driving in the Royal Docks. The report continues: "This is the first case to have been brought under s.457(1) of the Port of London (Consolidation) Act, 1920". This, in effect, directed that roads within the Docks although not public places in law, should nevertheless be deemed to be public places for the purpose of a few limited offences, of which furious driving was one. This particular section had to be constantly re-amended as new Road Traffic

Acts were passed which were useless unless made applicable to the Docks. But in those days there was a fresh Port of London Act, not every year but in very many years. When the author was operating as Prosecuting Solicitor, the key section in this respect was s.7 of the Port of London Act, 1961, which applied to the dock roads all the necessary sections of the Road Traffic Act, 1960, every one of which had to be specified by number and title. This became tiresome after some time, inevitably, and eventually there was nothing for it but to tackle the enormous task or re-consolidating and up-dating all sections of all past Port of London Acts. This was ultimately achieved with everybody's co-operation but almost unaided otherwise by Miss Virginia Novarra, a solicitor brought on to the staff expressly to scale this legislative Everest, which she achieved with rare distinction, acquiring in the process a real and deep admiration for the Force as a whole.*

Policemen who had done conscripted war service, now concerned about their pension position, were reassured by the Board's resolving that those re-joining in 1919 could be treated as if they had been appointed in January, 1916.

In early June, a letter from the head of the St. John Ambulance Corps. reported the results of the current First Aid examinations, saying that the P.L.A. Police enjoyed a higher success rate than he had ever met with in his long experience – a fact which he attributed to their outstanding Instructor, Insp. Furlong. This exceptional standard in First Aid has become one of the Force's lasting traditions, and is enjoyed to this day.

Meanwhile, the Staff Committee were patiently sorting out 84 applications for the Chief Officer's post. They interviewed the final twelve and the Board duly confirmed their choice of Mr. W. J. Webster, then Police Commissioner, Rangoon. His starting salary was to be £1,100 plus use of a hired car and a telephone installed at his home. He took over on July 1st, 1926. It is interesting to glean his first – and wrong – impressions from an article he wrote for 'Police Journal' in 1930, later reprinted in abridged form in 'P.L.A. Monthly', Vol. 6, February, 1931, at p.99, where he confesses: "The writer on his appointment imagined that a pleasant part of his duty would consist in cruising up and down the River in a smart launch, but speedily learned that the River was policed by the Thames Division of the Metropolitan Police."†

It has already been noted that Supt. Seaton was a man well able to look after himself. With Webster safely in the saddle, Seaton applied for – and got! – a personal award of £200 for acting as Chief Police Officer between Macrae's death and Webster's appointment. He had of course written the 1925 report. Webster's own first – that of 1926 – commented that the best opinion seemed to be turning against the old idea that anyone can pick up police work without training, and recognising that to get the best out of the men, they had to be properly taught initially and their knowledge constantly up-dated and refreshed. In Webster's early statistics we may notice an informative item – the percentage of stolen property recovered by police work. It was 39% this time, but the normal was to become about 50%.

*This magnum opus was achieved in the room next to mine at Head Office, and I came to know that much of her stamina was due to a blessed sense of humour. When, once, I was ungallant enough to refer to her in a speech before her colleagues as "the girl who knows more about the Act than any one of you", Virginia led the laughter!

†It is also interesting to read Webster's description of his Force as "numerically inferior only to the Metropolitan, the City of London, the Liverpool, the Lancashire, the Birmingham, the West Riding, the Manchester, the Durham and the Staffordshire Forces, and as such, one of the largest in Great Britain".

In late summer, 1926, Webster was generously – and wisely – given authority by the Board to make a tour of all the main English Ports, expenses paid, in order that he might observe their policing and compare it with London's. No report is mentioned in the Minutes or in the Annual Report – it would have been interesting.

The Board Minutes and Annual Police Reports have for some time now become remarkably reticent on the subject of remuneration – a note on an allied topic does however include the information that an Inspector was getting £390-£420 per year, Sergeants £5 per week and the C.I.D. a plain clothes allowance of 7/6d. per week.

From the 1927 Report, we learn that the actual strength of the Force was 773 – twenty short of establishment – and the Force's annual cost, £204,000. Crime was decreasing but only 15% of stolen property was recovered. The year was notable for a sharp rise in cabin thefts, "but three experts in this field are now convicted and this should affect the topic in future".

The Force was continuing to run the Ambulances in all groups, as indeed they continue to do to this day. In 1928, an average year, they covered 1,245 accident cases. (It would be interesting to know, though impossible now to find out, how many later phoney claims for damages were spiked at source, thanks to Policeman/Ambulance Attendants having taken a signed statement from the potential plaintiff on the way to the hospital, often self-incriminating. And yet when this activity was threatened with discontinuance, in the period of savage cuts which followed Dudley Perkins' resignation, the dockers complained loudly!)

Early in 1928, a technical point arose over members of the public who wished to pass through Gates on to roads within reach which were not working areas. The Minutes state that the Dock Byelaws were "about to be revised, and new ones would contain a prohibition of even the most nominal trespass on the Authority's land.*

In early 1929, Supt. Seaton's age and approaching retirement were raised in the Board. Applicants were offered a £575-£725 salary ahd had to live in a house approved by the Authority as to its proximity to the Docks. Seaton's pension was £269, annually.

The Force that year cost the Authority £198,000, the actual strength being 754. The value of stolen property was beginning now to drop and the percentage recovered to rise. There is also for the first time a mention of that most valuable statistic, the detection rate, but this could be because it was as high as 61%!

The Shipping Police, small but effective still, suffered a slight hiccough when the 'Australia and Commonwealth' line sold out completely. But the buyer merely changed 'Australia' to 'Aberdeen' and, after an extension of time to consider its position, elected to join its fellow lines, and pay its share.

Meanwhile, remembering how they had been caught short when Macrae died, interviews were arranged and a City of London Chief Inspector named John George Shand was appointed not merely Superintendent in place of Seaton but as No. 2 to Webster, in terms.

1930 saw a paradox, for though there was recruiting for the first time since 1923 which added 14 to the serving strength, wastage dropped the total strength to 723. The Shipping Police, included in that figure, numbered 44. And yet, up in the fastness of Head Office, the Board were anxiously discussing how to save more than £10,000 per year on the Force. They worked out a plan involving the removal of one Inspector,

*Either it was overlooked, or the Dock Byelaws were never amended! I recall very clearly that those operative in the 1960s were ancient enough to include an express prohibition against any ship entering any Dock 'save with its sails furled!'

9 Sergeants and 38 Constables and combining three offices at the Royals into one, all in the building (later the Royals Divisional H.Q.) next door to the then Divisional Office, which had been the Seamen's Hospital. They re-graded office positions, allowing for the introduction of civilian staff on substantially lower salaries than policemen. Recognising the need for the occasional use at the Royals of a small launch, they contrived to devote to this purpose a launch freed by their alterations in the Harbour Service. Thus was the main theme retrenchment, bringing few advantages save that all the Force was now well housed, and the continuing battle against crime which was going splendidly. One case stood out – a carton of cigarettes had been stolen, and the empty carton filled with rubbish which the C.I.D. traced to a Camden Town piggery, which later revealed all the stolen goods, and achieved the arrest of three men who were later tried at the Old Bailey and imprisoned.

Inspectors in 1931 were getting £350 plus house and uniform, Sergeants £5 12s. 6d. per week and Constables £4 10s. Gates, when possible, were combined (London Dock Nos. 7 and 7a) resulting in a saving of two Constables and £432. The strength was now 668. Recruiting had been stopped almost as soon as it started. Training, by contrast, was being keenly pursued – young Constables were sent to local Courts as spectators. The overall cost of the Force was £190,000 per year – showing the Board's cuts to have been effective.

A young civilian clerk named Barton, who had been born in India, appeared as an Interpreter at the Old Bailey, and earned from Mr. Justice Rigby Swift a comment recorded by Webster, "I direct you to convey to the Port of London Authority my sincere gratitude for the loan of the most efficient interpreter I have ever had before me in any Court in which I have ever sat as Judge".

There was also a new field of activity. Diligent checks had long been made on those leaving the Docks, but those who entered were rarely challenged. Now a campaign was launched and in the first year of this, no less than 2,651 people were rejected, whether or not this related to the fact that crime dropped to the lowest figure for many years. But then came a severe blow – the London Shipping Police Committee gave notice to determine the entire scheme from March 31st, 1932. As liability, under the agreement, remained on the shipowners for two years after termination to pay the wages of all unabsorbed men, the Board was asked to start to absorb as soon as possible.

Finally, the year held the first personal note for the author – listing the transfer to C.I.D. of a young Constable named Chris Tipper. His progress will be noted as it occurs, but he was still serving when the author joined the Authority, and is still living happily in retirement at the time of writing.

The coming end of the Shipping Police caused the strength temporarily to exceed the establishment by 684 to 601. The total cost of the Force in 1932 was £185,000. No less than 6,000 were rejected at the Gates, crime continued to drop, and the detection rate to rise – it was now 59% of all crime. From Head Office came exhortations to economise. One official notice read: "Certain officers and men are offered the option of retirement during 1933 with increased pensions. 9 Inspectors, 14 Sergeants and 37 Constables have so far accepted." The early shades of severance? The last Minute of the year records the closure of the New Entrance at Tilbury on Sundays.

During the twelve months of 1933, the serving strength came down to 618 and the total cost to £160,000. Crime was still dropping – only 523 cases. Property stolen was a mere £90, of which a third was later recovered. Committees at Head Office diligently explored further cuts, a policy that included, but was by no means confined to, the Police. At the Royals, a large room in the erstwhile Seamen's Hospital was adapted for use as a Police Club, the work being done in their spare time wholly by policemen, and all at their own expense. A Sgt. W. H. Simmons, of whom we shall hear more, was made Inspector, as were others, including Det. Sgt. Chris Tipper.

In 1934, the total cost of the Force was only £153,000 although the strength was only nine less than in 1933 when it was £7,000 more. Crime cases were a mere 447. The shilling a day payable from wages by all those under the rank of Inspector who suffered illness or accident off duty was abolished, at an annual cost of £250. On the other hand, when the Board was told that the reduced strength was having the effect of reducing the benefits payable on retirement or death from the Provident Fund, it turned down flatly a suggestion that the Authority might make up the difference. Times were clearly very hard.

In the spring of 1935, arrangements were made for a contingent of 50 to assist the City Police at the Jubilee Ceremonies of May 6th, and the Home Secretary later sent twenty medals for distribution. The annual cost dropped a further £2,000, and crime cases to no more than 320. Webster's reports were becoming notably chatty – he tells of a well-known thief calling at the Police Headquarters on his way to apply for a job, to beg – successfully! – for the gift of an old pair of boots from the Force who had always given him a square deal. Webster's own salary was raised in July from £1,350 to £1,500. In September, he sent in a Report with plans to form a Police Reserve of all men retired but still under sixty, for use in the event of a national emergency. Though it was yet 2 years before Munich, the Board approved in principle.

In January, 1936, so shortly after the happy Jubilee, the Minutes are black-bordered as the Chairman records with deep sorrow the death of King George V who, he said, "had always shown such a keen interest in the Port, of which he entertained most pleasant recollections". The serving strength was now 593, the annual cost £147,000. Crime rose to 409 cases. The nation cheered up as early arrangements began to be made for the Coronation. 100 of the Force would be on Ludgate Hill and Sir Ion Hamilton-Benn would be in the Abbey. The Force resumed summer patrolling of the Surrey Canal, reducing one Gate by two men for this purpose. Sir David Owen, now General Manager, reported on the prospective Police Reserve, outlining the terms which the men should be offered. (Tull's summary of the Minutes reports that the whole idea proved ultimately abortive, but the Minutes are silent on the point.) Senior ranks applied for a rise, probably in view of Webster's, and were rejected. Young Det. Insp. Tipper received special mention for his work.

There is an atmosphere of distinct optimism in the 1937 reports which the reader, with the benefit of hindsight, cannot but find ironic. Crime was up to 432 cases, the strength was down to 571, and the recovery of stolen goods reeled back to 25%. The air was full of thanks and congratulation as the Coronation took place. But all was not well for everybody. P.C. Heard, a stalwart of London Dock Division, was found incapable on duty, clutching no less than half a dozen bottles of wine to his manly bosom. In due course (the quotation feared is checked!) "the Staff Discipline Sub-Committee heard Heard" (Ouch!) and his inevitable dismissal was ordered. By contrast, a routine enquiry triggered off a line of interrogation by a young C.I.D. man which unexpectedly cleared up nine undiscovered thefts of carpets from Cutler Street Warehouse. (The young man was Chris Tipper.) Pay rises were presaged, but turned out in the end to amount to allowances for good conduct and efficiency.

In 1938, crime again rose – now to 454 cases. The strength went down by three. Training resumed after Munich, not only for police but for A.R.P. Constables' pay was raised to equate with the new Desborough Scales. Long service awards were given shorter qualification periods. Pension rights improved a little. The Police Reserve was actively prepared. Slightly sinister communications are recorded as being received from the Government in secret, and later turned out to be from the Home Office about espionage precautions.

In 1939, the strength dropped to 565, though the cost rose to £149,000. There were seven complaints against the Police – people were becoming edgy as what looked like the end of the world slowly heaved itself over the horizon – four proved groundless, three disclosed lack of tact. The Police Reserve was to be offered uniforms and great-coats and £1 for boots. The style of helmet was altered to make it identical with the Metropolitan Police (not, of course, like the City, whose Roman style remains unique to this day) entailing a cost per helmet of 10/3d. instead of the earlier 8/9d. And then as expected, we were at war. Webster was at once appointed Security Officer for the Port of London. Shand retired and Simmons was made Acting Superintendent on a salary of £520 and a housing allowance. Sanction was given for the recruitment of 50 Temporary Constables for service in the Force for the duration of the war, only. They had to be 35-40 in age, of fair education, physically fit, and ready to undergo a month's intensive training before being sworn-in, when their pay would be £3 10s. per week plus uniform. The War Reserve men were summoned to serve until the Temporary men were trained, then released but on call to attend if air raids materialised. Thurrock U.D.C. took over responsibility for fires at Tilbury Docks, lowering the Divisional strength accordingly.

By April, 1940, there were enough Temporary Constables trained to release the last of the War Reserve men, who were effusively thanked by the Board for their efficiency, discipline, adaptability and loyalty. Initial training doubled in intensity and halved in time. The Force received War Grants from the Home Office, as did all Crown Forces – between 2/6 and 5/– per week according to rank, subject to annual review. (A rise by any other name would smell as sweet.) Establishment was reduced to 524, which included 34 Temporaries.

In January, 1941, sanction was given to recruit another 30 Temporary men – they had been flooding to enlist almost as soon as they finished training! Their pay was raised to £3 10s. weekly, plus allowances, increased by 5/– Proficiency available after 6 months and payable only on Webster's personal approval.

Early in 1942, the War Advance doubled. And then we learn that Webster had been suffering severely for some months and was now sent on sick leave on full salary for six months. In March, the Board directed that Simmons (who had now acquired an M.B.E.) should be made formally Acting Chief Police Officer as from February 1st, 1942. Webster was said to be available for consultation but then it is announced that he was leaving on attachment to the Military Mission in Pretoria, South Africa, for overseas Army service. Among the sequential variations in rank and allowances, Insp. S. F. Cox became Acting Divisional Inspector and was made Port Fire Prevention Officer. The Supt. of the Royals Division was now made senior to his equals in rank and was clearly marked as No. 3 in the Force. The mysterious boot allowance, earlier reduced to 1/–, it will be recollected, was restored to 1/6d! The War Advance was also raised and made to include Temporary Constables. The Minutes also contain a brief reference, otherwise unexplained, to Whole-Time Special Docks Police.

By now, Annual Reports were brief, informal and typed. By contrast, the printed Board Minutes increased in detail. Any policeman was permitted to do any work of national importance as long as it did not interfere with his duties – thus suspending the rule forbidding this, whose object has always been to protect the Constable from the temptation of commercial interest and loss of efficiency through tiredness. Out in Pretoria, Webster had been promoted to Colonel with a £1,200 salary – and the Authority sent him an additional £200 annually to allay his financial loss. Temporary Constables' pay and conditions were reviewed and varied. The five mile restriction, within which all police had to reside was now extended to nine miles. Revisions in Regulations and sundry allowances were applied as they came flooding in from Home Office.

In Spring, 1943, the Staff Committee was asked to consider the desirability of a P.L.A. Police Federation being formed – the men had not only asked for this but had submitted a draft constitution. General permission was given at once, and the first formal act of the new organisation was to convey its thanks and goodwill to the Authority. Following talks with the War Department, it was then agreed that the P.L.A. Police should undertake supervision of certain vulnerable points previously carried out by the Army. For this reason, it was decided to increase establishment from 523+41 Temporaries, to 527+181 Temporaries. All save £2,000 of the additional cost would be recoverable from the War Department.

To release as many as possible for military service from the civilian staff in Police offices, it was decided to employ women for this purpose. And then the Board passed a resolution which was to have a lasting effect upon its Police Force – indeed, that effect still remains. It is usually referred to by its official number in the 1943 Minutes Volume – Minute 186. And even at the time of writing, though the Social Contract has imposed its own terms upon all pay rises, that resolution will continue to bind future Boards as a matter of honour. That Resolution stated that the Authority would henceforth apply pay levels at all ranks exactly to equate with the Metropolitan Force, with small differences regarding sick pay, pension levels (which are governed by statute separately) and the like.

Arising out of the quasi-military responsibility mentioned above, disciplinary proceedings had to be taken against a Constable of long experience, whose name was Hancock. His dismissal was ordered and later ratified. Four years later, the whole matter was to explode into sensational life – more of which at its appropriate place in the story.

There was news in 1944 of Webster, who had written to say that he was about to end his military responsibilities and thus technically available to return to his post as Chief Police Officer. But discussions took place, most amicably, and it was finally agreed that Col. Webster should receive and accept six months notice and a pension of £581 each year. Thereafter, with effect from October 1st, 1944, he was to be appointed as the Authority's general Representative in South Africa at a nominal salary of £500. His duties, doubtless discussed, are not recorded in the Minutes. It was stated that no alteration should be made in the position of Supt. Simmons for the time being.

The war was now in its closing stages, and there was an increasing confidence, amounting almost to euphoria, noticeable in the Minutes. The Board authorised the issue of British Warms, dyed navy, instead of greatcoats, to Sergeants and above. The Force, with an authorised establishment of 604, was actually now down to 492. Recruitment was clearly called for, and three Sergeants were sent quickly on a Home Office course for Instructors. Advertisements brought a flood of applicants, and 29 were selected for Training. Simmons' report for 1945 records the crime cases dealt with as no less than 1181. Yet another runaway horse was stopped, at grave risk to himself, by a Constable Allen, whom the Chairman went to see in hospital and personally congratulated. And soon after VE day, men from the pre-war strength began to return.

Government discussions ensued. The War Department agreed that the then 144 Temporary Constables should be dispensed with shortly, and the Authority agreed to work out a new establishment, on the basis that it should include 80 Temporaries whose wages would be paid in the end by the Government. Inspectors went up directly to a top figure of £550 annually, and Superintendents to £850. Men left for C.I.D. courses at Hendon. A building in the Royal Albert Dock, at the back of No. 9 Shed, became the new Training School.* Annual Leave was increased by six days as negotiated with the new Federation. And though the Shipping Police was no more, a group of Shipowners asked the Authority for one Constable to attend on each ship during loading and unloading to buttress their cargo-watchers with powers of arrest. Of all those who left the Force for the services, only one in full health did not return – he was a Constable who, from the ranks, had risen to the position of Captain and naturally now felt he could and should get a better job.

During 1946, no less than 154 men passed through Training School, selected from an original 1,383 applicants. A Constable's pay in 1946 was £4 10s. per week during training and his first two years, plus uniform and sundry allowances. It then rose to £5 17s. Crime cases were back up through the 2,000 barrier to 2,262 (plainly, criminals, as well as police, had been demobilised!) and of the £9,000 worth of stolen property, only some £2,000 worth was recovered. The authorised strength was now 593, and of the 81 Temporaries, all but 16 chose to join the permanent Force. The establishment also included a special squad of barge-searchers, dispensed with during the war, although everyone is aware that a barge is much too vast an object to be efficiently and effectively searched! A further review at the end of 1948 was agreed.

During 1947, there were 135 recruits, making 288 post-war, and yet 66 vacancies remained. "Few Forces anywhere," commented Simmons, still glowing from his award of the King's Police Medal, "are able to attract sufficient recruits to maintain their authorised numbers." Nearly 20,000 vehicles were checked completely during the year at Gates, seven of which had stolen goods aboard. 2,211 crimes were reported and dealt with. But the real action was taking place up on Tower Hill, where the tricky problem of automatic dismissal for theft was under consideration. In the end it was agreed that any P.L.A. staff man convicted for theft of goods from the Docks would be dismissed at once, with appeals open to the Staff Committee. The former practice of merely transferring every convicted 'Perm' to the National Dock Labour Board list, enabling him to do the same work, would cease. Instances were cited of convicted thieves trotting from the court straight to the N.D.L.B., picking up an 'A' Ticket authorising them for Dock work, and attending the middle-day 'call', ending the day in the same gang as that in which they had formerly been!†

*It was later defined as the very first post-war School of its kind in the country. Its curriculum included Mock Courts, First Aid, Fire Fighting, and Drugs (Home Office permission being obtained for the Force to posses a chest of assorted samples in this field) in addition to all normal Police subjects.

†Agreements do not always last. In the 1960s there were instances known to the author of men convicted for theft of cargo turning up for work the next day as casual cargo-watchers over the very hold from which they had previously stolen and had been convicted!

On recruitment, Simmon urged that the lower age limit of 21 should be reduced for a while to 20, especial care in selection being promised. This the Board accepted. It was also arranged that the Force should be excepted from the Control of Engagement Order, 1947 – thus obviating any risk that some could be whipped away to do National Service.

By far the most important event of 1948 from a constitutional standpoint, was the civil action brought by Constable Hancock. He had, prior to the incident in question, served in the Force ever since 1920, and nothing of any kind was known to his detriment. Then in 1937, when he was stationed at Tilbury, a curious thing happened. For reasons never specified, he suddenly refused to wear the medal ribbons which he had worn with such pride up till then and was duly punished. (Indeed, he made this one 'leg' of his action when he issued his writ in 1944 – thus rendering it useless as the Public Authorities Protection Act, which imposed a 12-month limit within which proceedings had to be brought, completely protected P.L.A., as his advisers cannot but have realised.) But the main theme of his action was more substantial. It arose out of an incident as bizarre as that in 1937 at Tilbury. Hancock was one of a squad guarding the Royal Albert Dock Basin at 2 a.m. on November 6th, 1943. The patrolling Inspector told him to pick up his rifle and carry on – a purely routine order. To the Inspector's amazement, Hancock suddenly declined to pick up his rifle, though he had used it up till then. A "Sam, Sam. pick up thy musket!" situation ensued, during which the Constable became wilder eyed, alleging that the Authority had no power under the Firearms Act. Eventually he had to be put on a charge. So arraigned, he admitted the disobedience to an order and proffered a written explanation as follows: "The existing orders relating to firearms make the rifle a menace instead of a form of protection. The Authority have stated that we are not connected with Civil Defence or embodied Forces, or the compensations therefrom (sic). So, not being protected or provided for, I deemed the assignation a voluntary one. And as compulsion must have some Act which empowers it, I know of no such Act."

This was the more unexpected as Hancock had dutifully and happily shouldered his rifle ever since May, 1940, without demur. One cannot deduce with certainty just what prompted him to adopt without warning this strange point of view. It is a fact that his counsel as the action he brought had political views known publicly to be about as far to port as peripheral vision could decry. On the other hand, Hancock may have been no more than one of nature's eccentrics, and the whole affair one of honest iconoclasm which the Courts of the realm will always treat with infinite courtesy and patience.

Simmons' report was agreed, dating the carrying of arms as May, 1940, when invasion danger was imminent, and Webster had obtained not merely the authority but the rifles from the Home Office. The arrangements were identical to those in the Metropolitan Force. Mr. Justice Birkett (as the incomparable Sir Norman had then become) recited the facts in such a way as to raise them almost to the standard of literature. Then he said he had no hesitation in finding that the order given was both reasonable and clear, requiring obedience. But the Plaintiff had based his action on its being an unlawful one. The Authority were, he found, clearly within the provisions of the Firearms Act, 1937. Reading s.5 of that Act with s.28, he laid down clearly and for all time that the Port of London Authority Police had always been, was then and would ever be a police force within the meaning of that Act – a statutory body, acting in accordance with that statute. Judgment was accordingly inevitable for the Defendants –

not, in the event, with costs, upon the P.L.A.'s counsel, Sir David Maxwell Fyffe, expressly waiving them on his instructions which the Judge applauded.

Back in the Docks, an interesting and valuable creation had been that of a mobile squad, unattached to any Division, to be used for occasional blitzes without warning on Gates, when every vehicle could be and would be searched in full detail, and such specialised activity as meat thefts. (The squad came in time to be known as the Meat Squad so predominantly was its work in that field.) In charge of it on its creation was a very bright young Detective Sergeant who had displayed much initiative and won many commendations. His name was Gannon.

Ingenuity was displayed by the Board over regulations permitting police to volunteer for Reserve Forces Units – an arrangement which could have left the Force terribly undermanned. Finding the regulations unavoidable, they applied them – with the corollary that requirements resulting had to be met from Annual Leave!

Criminal cases were now six short of the 2,000 barrier. Upset by Gate blitzes, thieves were now trying to get goods out over dock fences whenever practicable – a task made easier by the shortage of beat men, for the Force was still 100 below authorised strength, though better off in this respect than many forces.

As the year drew to its close, Simmons indicated that he would like to retire within two years, on account of a disability. The Board decided to re-create an Assistant to the Chief Police Officer, at a £1,100 salary. Notified of this, Simmons made it clear that he would stay long enough to train this officer as his successor, in any event. (The Board Chairman, by the way, at this time was Sir John Anderson – after whom a war-time domestic air-raid shelter was named – soon to be better known as Lord Waverly.) The position, in the event, was filled from within the Force, by Divl. Insp. S. F. Cox.

1949 saw an authorised strength of 594 and an actual strength 104 below that. Recruiting was difficult, but the Oaksey Report on pay was expected to help when it emerged. No less than 903,497 Passes were collected by Gate Policemen from outgoing vehicles, over 22,000 of which were searched in detail – several being found to have stolen goods on board. Crime was down to 1,744 cases.

The Oaksey Report emerged in time. Superintendents were to rise to £1,025 – Assistant Chief Constables to £1,200. Chief Constables were to go up from £1,450 to £1,600. Lower ranks were to be dealt with later.

It was just at this time that a new General Manager was appointed in succession to Mr. Theo Williams, who had retired. This was Mr. Leslie Ford, later knighted during tenure of that office, and a man whose heart was very much with his Force.*

Following the Metropolitan Force in matters additional to that of pay, the Board allowed open-necked tunics with shirt and tie to replace the old high-collar uniform for summer wear.

The year contained one small personal tragedy. A Constable was found drunk on duty and was duly disciplined. £2 plus a doctor's fee does not seem harsh. But in years to come, the author came to know that particular Constable well. He was a fine man, wise in experience, and it seemed surprising that he was never made Sergeant.

*This I knew personally because he came from Cardiff, where in 1949 I was practising as a solicitor in partnership with my father who, as a young lad many years before, had sat next to the young Leslie Ford at school. I am glad to say that at the time of writing, Sir Leslie is well, and as ebullient as ever.

To disclose his name would be outrageous, but it is a matter of sad regret that years of loyal service were thrown largely away through one early slip.

Vacancies rose to 111, and Part 2 of the Oaksey Report was awaited eagerly by all concerned. Meanwhile, the figure covering those refused admission to the Docks is seen again in the Annual Report – obviously, during the war, only those expressly authorised could enter at all – during 1950 it was a mere 651, most of that figure divided equally between people wanting to take short cuts and trollops anxious to visit ships for business reasons. Two plain-clothes men still patrolled the Surrey Canal, warning and escorting to safety some 204 children. Crime was a trifle up, at 1,856 cases. One alert Gate Constable thought the deformity of an apparent hunch-back a little unusual in shape and position and, putting aside his instinctive sympathy and ignoring the harsh words of those passing, required a search – to find that the hump was plastic and contained assorted goods, mainly chocolate and nylon stockings! This 1950 Report was the first signed by Mr. Cox, who formally took over the previous August 1st, on Mr. Simmons retiring.*

Early in 1951, the Second Part of the Oaksey Report emerged, with its recommended rises, and the position eased slightly, all round. No less than 86 future Constables passed through the Training School. The upper age limit was raised, temporarily, to 29, plus fifty if admitted from the Forces up to 34. 24,687 vehicles were searched from end to end – stolen goods being found on 32 of them. Criminal cases investigated were 1,958. The use of a launch in the Royals was discontinued, as it was now easier and quicker to move from one end to the other by car. All traffic police were now fully equipped with powerful motor-cycles. And up at Trap One, the vacancy for a Deputy Solicitor was filled by a man who never spared himself in the service of the Force he came to value so highly and love so well – Dudley Perkins, then aged 40, and already known to almost every household in the land for his matchless "Can I Help You?" But despite this radio experience, Mr. Perkins was not, as he would be the first to agree, directly responsible for a major step forward taken just after he joined the staff at a cost which today seems quite ludicrously small – a mere £7,000 – which was the equipment of the entire Force with a V.H.F. radio-telephony service.

We now find the complete range of police pay set out in a Minute which refers back in terms to Minute 186/43 – that which gave an undertaking that the P.L.A. Police would always equate with the levels of the Metropolitan Police. Summarised, it reads:

Constables: £7 13s. 4d. on appointment, rising to £9 13s. 7d. per week.
Sergeants: £10 7s. on promotion thereto, rising to £11 4s. 3d., weekly.
Sergeant-Clerks: £11 10s., rising to £11 15s. 9d., weekly.
Inspectors: £675–£720 per year.
Chief Inspectors: £830 to £880 per year.

The last Minute for 1951 records the purchase by the Authority of a large old house on Blackheath, for £2,800, which was to become the main transmitting station for the V.H.F. system and, it was hoped, also a Hostel for unmarried Constables.

*Whatever Disability prompted Mr. Simmons to retire, it must happily have receded, for although I did not meet him, we exchanged letters, and it was while I was in Eric Ellen's company, engaged in researching the final part of this volume, in March, 1977, that news of Mr. Simmons' death reached us.

Increasingly, now, personalities appear who were to become the author's friends and colleagues. Ivor Hughes, a stripling of 24, joined the Solicitor's staff, while in the Docks, Peter Gannon, still head of the Mobile Squad, was made an Inspector. In January, 1952, no less than 102 members of the Force, including the Chief Police Officer himself, received Long Service and Distinguished Conduct Medals – affectionately mocked as the 'N.F.O.' (standing for Never Found Out) but worthily won and always worn with quiet pride. At the same period, a raw, young recruit entered the Training School, whose name was Eric Ellen, of whom we shall hear more. A month later, a beautiful Princess, up a tree in Africa, learned that her father, who had learned to walk with death as a friend, had passed away in his sleep, and she was Queen.

The use of the open-necked jacket now became an all-year-round condition, and the old high-collared ones, basically the same as those worn maybe in 1802 and certainly in 1829, the neck-piece reinforced to combat garotting from behind, became used only on occasions of high ceremonial.

On Shooter's Hill, an extra £1,000 was allocated for the building of an underground chamber to house the master radio station and the auxiliary generator set to guarantee its life. In his report for the year, Cox recorded 71 vacancies, but noted that the actual strength of 522 was the highest since December, 1938. Moreover, there were at the time of his Report only 88 men who had been in it in 1938 – 434 being post-war entrants – virtually a complete new Force had assembled since 1945. More than a million Passes were scrutinised at Dock Gates. Crime was again down a fraction – 1,911 cases.

In 1953, the actual strength dropped to 512, even though no less than 52 recruits passed through Training School. The Discipline Regulations came under discussion – they were basically the same as those of the Met., save that for long and not very comprehensible reasons, the Chief Police Officer was permitted to punish without confirmation to a slightly greater extent than the Commissioner – although one is speaking about no more serious a penalty than the official caution. Crime dipped notably – a mere 1,519 cases. And the big event around which everybody's year revolved was, of course, the Coronation. 116 members of the Force lined Northumberland Avenue.

But there were other developments – for instance, the retirement of the India and Millwall Dockmaster meant that half of Bridge House was available for conversion into the new Training School and the whole into the new Chief Police Office. The total cost of this was almost £9,000, as it entailed building a new house for the Dockmaster's successor. The old Headquarters became the India/Millwall Divisional Office. It was further agreed at this time that the Chief Police Officer should have either a special allowance of £150 annually, or a house bought expressly for him, as it was clearly necessary for him to live within range of the Docks.

The year was futher marked by a spectacular incident centring on P.C. Brooks, a very brave man, though the incident in which he figured is described differently in the Minutes from the account in the Annual Police Report, which is likely to be more accurate. The Minutes merely congratulate Brooks on his bravery in diving into Millwall Dock to rescue a Chinese seaman. The Report identifies the Chinaman as an escaped prisoner, trying to get away, with an opium pipe clutched to his bosom! Moreover, the double leap into the murky waters preceded a fight between pursuer and pursued in the water which lasted fully 30 minutes – it makes one shiver merely to contemplate it!

In 1954, the Force was 90 under its authorised strength. But the offer of housing was a recruitment factor of value. And the large house of the edge of Blackheath, the conversion of which was almost complete, would hold some 30 single Constables, with a married Sergeant as Warden, accessible to all Divisions except Tilbury. £2 was decided as the fair weekly charge for food. Meanwhile, the Senior Ranks received another pay rise – Chief Inspectors could go up to £955 and Superintendents to £1,230. Moreover, modifications were made to rank structure – the old Sergeant/Clerk being abolished, and Superintendents now having two grades. Cox had found, and the Authority had bought for him, a house in Southgate. Statistics disappear for a while and then recur. Crime was always with us, of course – 1,619 cases in 1954. 191 children were warned about the dangers of the Surrey Canal towpath, but perhaps not enough about the dangers of selecting one's companions, at any rate for one poor little fellow, who was pushed in and held under by his playmates until he drowned. 374 people were refused admission to the Docks, and 1,154,213 Passes were checked at the Gates. The list of commendations reveals that Chris Tipper is now Detective Superintendent. His Chief Inspector was a young man whose early progress was notable for the commendations it attracted – a man who was later to become Tipper's successor and my valued colleague, Ken Cater. Finally, the Report reveals another new development – the introduction of four women Constables. 54 Coronation Medals were distributed.

Contrary to expectations, with the Hostel now running, the strength declined to 480, and the working week was reduced from 48 to 44 hours by the grant of an Additional Rest Day once every two weeks. Since this was based on notional full establishment, it was never able to be taken as such, but attracted overtime rates for its length. There were also allowances which, if diligently studied, could raise a bright young "Aide to C.I.D." into a weekly income bracket equivalent to a Uniform rank of some stature. 39 recruits passed through the Training School, almost a million and a quarter Passes were checked, 1,686 crime cases were investigated, a great deal of valuable bullion was escorted, and the Authority's relationship with its Police Federation was referred to by both as "cordial".

1956 was a year of much development and great potential for the Force. Crime cases totalled 1,765 – 187 people were refused admission to the Docks – 116 bullion escort journeys were made – 183 children were warned off the Canal towpath. All these statistics are familiar now to every reader. But behind them, things were moving. For a start, there was Departmental status. A vacancy for Senior-Superintendent – the de facto Deputy Chief Police Officer – arose. The Minutes are quite specific – the very best man for the job would be Det. Supt. Chris Tipper. But "it would not be in the best interests of the Authority to appoint him, as this would entail his transferring from C.I.D., for which he has special qualifications and vast experience". After much consideration, it was agreed by the Board on May 3rd that there should in future be *two* Senior-Superintendents, one Uniform and the other C.I.D. but the former always being the de facto Deputy Chief Police Officer. In this framework, Supt. Brown was then made Sen. Supt. and Chris Tipper "Det. Sen. Supt. and Head of C.I.D." That young constable had reached the top of his particular tree.*

But the outstanding event of the year was the complete Review of the Force by the General Manager, and the Board's consideration of it, a few days before Christmas.

*And it is my especial pleasure to record that at the time of writing, he is still fit, well and happy. One of my great friends, Eric Philcox, retired Det. Inspector, sees him regularly and, through him, Chris and I exchange cheerful good wishes.

The Force, said Sir Leslie, had for some years enjoyed an actual strength of about 500, as against an authorised establishment of roughly 600. On the other hand, not least because of modern aids - radio, vehicles, etc. - efficiency had soared. But if, instead of doing overtime, the men were allowed to take the leave they had been granted as necessary to their health, the authorised establishment would have to be as high as 661! It was, said Sir Leslie, desirable to bring the Force's rank structure more into line with that of the Crown Forces, and this would be assisted by the creation of two grades of Sergeant - First and Second Class. Costwise, he reflected that in 1938, this had been just under £200,000 and now, in 1956, it was a litle over half a million. He thought it would be possible to take such steps as would abolish overtime and provide adequate Docks security with a new establishment of 584. This involved a reduction in Constables from 395 to 349. To all these matters, the Board agreed. The new, slim-line Force took its belt in another hole and hitched its navy-blue trousers for action.

There was no recruitment in 1957, although 14 men in course of training entered the Force, which then had a total serving strength of 476 - precisely 108 short of even the new establishment. Pay rose in accordance with Minute 186, and that alone increased the cost of the Force by no less than £11,450. On the other hand, modernity was not all-embracing; the Board in April approved allowances payable to Sergeants and Constables who used their own pedal-cycles in the performance of beat and patrol work. (They were increased from 6d. per day to 7d. - at a total annual cost of £60!) Passes checked were just over a million and a quarter. Crime stayed at the same level - 1,761 cases.

The active sensation of the year came when a Mr. Scotchmer, a P.L.A. Diver, in the course of his work beneath the black and turgid surface of the West India Docks, encountered what felt to him rather like a huge acoustic mine. So indeed did it turn out to be - a hefty German 2,000 pounder - and still alive! The Navy attended, the dicey business of defusing by touch under water was successful, and the mine was gently towed through the lock and out down river to the estuary, where it was exploded.

May, 1958, saw the retirement on pension of the Chief Police Officer. Mr. Cox had served as such for eight years, and altogether in the Force for 45 - a fine record of loyal service. Many of the older members of the Force in the author's time knew him well, and he was widely admired and liked - not least for his habit of dropping casually in on his men, even at Gates, and getting to know them. He was also insistent on knowing about everything that was going on - there were few reports of any kind which he did not read, and usually initial. He seems to have been appreciated most as a 'policeman's policeman'. The Board recorded their appreciation of his long and loyal service and tendered their best wishes. They advertised for his successor. (The Sen. Supt. had but a few months to serve and was thus scarcely eligible.) Six applicants were short-listed and the mantle of Capt. Robert Bartlett and all his successors fell upon the wide shoulders of Thomas J. Oliver, O.B.E., then aged 49.

Readers will appreciate that the author came to know Tom Oliver closely over the years which followed. He was not an easy man to get to know, being intensely shy by nature. He had begun his police career in Birkenhead and had proved himself a fine administrator, particularly in service with the Control Commission in Germany after the war. At the time of his appointment, he was Civil Defence Officer for Kent.

He had been orphaned as a child, and brought up in Institutions. To know this was to understand a few personal foibles which, unexplained, were not perhaps particularly endearing. Like many a shy man, he had erected between himself and the world a thick barrier of formality which was really very difficult to break down. Inside was a warm-hearted, generous, kindly, intensely nervous man, of whom the author grew very appreciative as he got to know him well.

In his relationship with the Force, his lack of self-confidence made him nothing like as popular as he could and should have been, had he let himself be better known. He was a natural worrier, lacking not the mind to decide but the confidence which brings a decision, right or wrong. Tom Oliver was apt to cling to the merits of both sides, which entails vacillation, and was too inclined to follow someone who, though probably less able and certainly less thoughtful, would spring to a snap decision and follow it.

His men, sad to say, hardly knew him. Some of them used to joke that they had seen him only when functions involving P.L.A. were shown on television. It was his especial bad luck to succeed one whose forte was contact with his men at all levels. His withdrawn nature hid from them how intensely proud of them he was, how loyally and how hard – but how clandestinely – he fought for their interests. Those who did know him well invariably liked him warmly; too many knew only the slightly distant, cool, scrupulously correct, honourable, formal Chief Police Officer.

His Force was 488 strong, against an establishment of 584. Passes checked, crossed the million-and-a-quarter barrier. Crime was back to its barrier – at 1,993 cases during 1958. The early effects of the Clean Air Act were demonstrated when the City, as Port Health Authority, with the P.L.A.'s co-operation and evidence, successfully prosecuted the owners of a vessel seen to emit volumes of dirty black smoke in the Docks.

In September, Supt. Brown retired, to be succeeded by Harold Hartley – inevitably long known to the Force as 'Plum-and-Apple'. At once, though seen by few, material changes took place, and the Chief Police Officer saw only what his Senior Superintendent decided were matters concerning him – he operated a filter system, which is one way of working. Hartley's intention could hardly have been to increase the new Chief's essential remoteness from his men. It was, alas, undoubtedly one of its effects.

1959 was the Authority's own Golden Jubilee year, full of exciting occasions, climaxed by the visit of the Queen and Prince Philip to the Docks. For a trial period of twelve months, the Board allowed the upper age-limt for entry to the Force to be raised from 34 to 40 for ex-Service men – a particular bait for N.C.O.s. And to some extent it worked. By the end of the year, there were only 74 vacancies, there had been 1,420 applications and 36 men fully trained. 446 children had been warned off the Canal towpath, and crime was back through the barrier, at 2,194 cases. The detection rate came back into the regular statistics with an almost incredible 87.5%. Even allowing for the case-load being materially less than that in Crown Forces, it was a staggering result.

In 1960, the topic to the fore was that of premises. Surrey Divisional H.Q. had long been a house in Lower Road, with a hut in the garden serving as Muster Room. Mr. Oliver pushed hard and secured a Board decision that the former Dock General Offices would be converted into an adequate H.Q. and Police Club, and the house in Lower Road was to become the Training School. At the Royals, canteen facilities were much improved. Meanwhile, vacancies were down to 66, with 518 actual strength. Crime was up to 2,237 cases and the detection rate had slid only to 82.2%. The new Chief also got through the acceptance of new lightweight uniforms for summer wear which the Force greatly appreciated, though one wonders where the credit went.

Whenever pay levels in the Met. Force rose, so did the P.L.A. in faithful accordance with Minute 186. A new and fairer system of examinations and promotions was one of Tom Oliver's changes, operative from March, 1961. The strength moved up four to 522. A testimonial on vellum was awarded to P.C. Peter Kyle (later a stalwart of the Mobile Squad) who saved the life of a docker drowning in Blackwall Basin. "Upon hearing the Chief Police Officer," says the Minute, "the Board were pleased to add their cheque for ten guineas." The question of powers came up again - Oliver was pressing hard for operational jurisdiction throughout the Metropolitan Police District. A small event during the year up at Head Office was the appointment to the Solicitor's staff of one, Glyn Hardwicke - it is a happy coincidence that the very same Minute records the promotion to Inspector of a bright young Sergeant named Eric Ellen. Crime cases were down slightly to 2,221, but the detection rate was back up to 84%. Improved pay and conditions lifted Force morale.

1962 was a year of quiet progress. The Police establishment was reviewed and fixed at 601, with 537 actually serving. Crime cases rose to 2,245, and it appears that Mr. Oliver had noticed one reason why the detection rate was artificially high - it had included heaps of little Byelaw convictions, mostly pleas of guilty. The rate was now recorded as 62% - but of indictable cases only. It was still a very high figure. By s.10 of the Port of London Act, 1962, the jurisdiction was enlarged to the extent that the Force had, on top of the one mile range a 'pursue and follow' jurisdiction anywhere in the land. A curious item in the Schedule of an Act apparently applying only to Scotland enabled our men to (and therefrom always did) serve all summonses on defendants in the Docks area, formerly precluded by the 1839 Act. Shirt-sleeve order at the Chief's discretion was permitted during intensely hot weather. But the Minutes are marked by a not of unintended hilarity, here quoted without comment: "It is proposed that the six lady typists presently set against the establishment of the Constables should be substantively authorised, experience having shown that such staff in such positions cannot be regarded as providing effective replacements for Constables in Police Offices." Ah well!

Meanwhile, in Head Office, Mr. Dudley Perkins called his staff together and told them he was being elevated to be Deputy General Manager, later to succeed Sir Leslie Ford, being himself replaced by a young man from the Treasury Solicitor's department of terrifying intellectual brilliance, Geoffrey Robinson.

1963 continued the quiet, steady progress of its predecessor. Against the new establishment of 601 (and I speak not of typists!) the actual strength was 563, leaving only 38 vacancies. There were three Surrey Canal fatalities - but all turn out to have been elderly suicides, and the child-warning routine went patiently on. Crime went up to 2,264 cases and the detection rate dropped to a realistic 60.7% - still far above national average and more than double that of the poor Metropolitan Force, whose conditions were very different. Another restored statistic tells the reader that £38,000 worth of property was stolen, and £19,000 worth recovered - the 50% figure regularly indicating efficiency and ordinary luck. Another Minute raises the reader's eyebrow - "A trial among the Force of 3 Gannex overcoats having proved favourable, this cloth will be used for all police greatcoats in future." (And I wager the same question flashed through the reader's mind - but in fact he didn't come to power until 1964!)

In 1964, there were 568 men serving including 8 in training, and thus a mere 33 vacancies. No less than 28 complaints against the Police were made, but on each being scrupulously investigated, not even so much as a lack of tact was found. 1,161,006 passes were checked at the Gates. Crime cases slid nearer the 2,000 barrier, with 2,036 investigated. The detection rate had settled now at 50%. A national competition was started among all Forces contributing to the Hove Convalescent Home – of which the P.L.A. Force was one – and it is with some pride that we were found to have reached our target of £1,800 first in the country.

1965, with 570 serving and only 31 vacancies, saw a very pleasurable event with the opening of the new St. Katharine Dock House. Into its ground floor moved the whole of Police Headquarters, also the entire London Dock Division, together with the Training School and the 24-hour Information Room, with a console of coloured lights looking for all the world like a cinema organ of the 1930s. On the first floor was a truly magnificent Police Club, with dining facilities to suit. Here it was the author's pleasure to lunch daily with the senior officers, so that all the current cases and their attached problems were able to be ironed out almost as soon as they arose. Here, too, it was the Force's pleasure to entertain to drinks and lunch visitors from very many Forces in Britain and from abroad. The reader may be surprised how much goodwill was spread right across the nation in this way, and every case involving our Force with that of another area was able to be discussed in pleasant surroundings and on the friendliest terms. Here, too, it was the author's joy to meet and come to know well top-flight detectives not only from Scotland Yard but around the world.

At about the same time as this major improvement in amenities up river, a brand new Divisional Headquarters was opening at Tilbury. One sad note was struck by the sudden collapse on duty and death of Chief Insp. Barber – a fine officer and a great loss. A number of men were sent to Courses such as those on scenes-of-crime and crime-prevention, at Hendon. Seven complaints were checked and all proved either phoney or too trivial to warrant action. Crime had dropped markedly to 1,674 cases. The detection rate had risen to 58%. Of national significance was the sad passing of Sir Winston Churchill – the true father of the Authority even though the flamboyant mountebank Lloyd George grabbed the credit for putting the Act of 1908 through Parliament. 60 men from the Force were able to assist at the Funeral, and each of them was later presented by the Board with a Churchill Crown – a charming gesture, typical of those who led the Authority at the time, Lord Simon, Lord Cottesloe, Sir Leslie Ford and Dudley Perkins.

The Blackheath Hostel was re-examined in the light of its running costs and the reluctance of new recruits to live there. The residential load had been 21 – now there were but 14, and a staff of eleven! It was closed on economic grounds, and the house was bought by Greenwich Council for £25,000. The other thing to disappear was the compulsory swimming qualification, which had always attached not merely to those working in the Docks but to everyone under 40, even if they were unlikely ever to glimpse dock water. Many a good man was dismissed because he could not swim 50 yards within his first six months* No such condition was imposed upon entry into,

*I take the opportunity to confess the devious trick, the perpetration of which alone secured my own continuing employment. Able to swim, though not in ice-cold water such as the Baths where employees were tested, and coming from Cardiff where the superb new Baths had a Heating Engineer whom I happened to know, I contrived to have the entire Olympic Pool heated 'by accident' to 80 degrees, one morning, and completed my fifty yards in comfort before witnesses who then swore prepared affidavits which, added to one of my own. I successfully submitted to the Establishment Officer!

for example, the Royal or Merchant Navies. It took some years of quiet effort, but we finally pushed it through, and its effect cannot but have been generally beneficial!

A tragic incident at this time may usefully cast a light on the much maligned routine of 'the man at the Gate'. Routine it may have been, most of the time. Not always. Take for instance P.C. Wally Bromley – a 28-year-old, likeable lad in his third year of service – who was on duty at 14 Gate, Millwall Dock on the afternoon of June 18th, 1965. It was 4.30 p.m., on a warm, sunny day, his wife was expecting a child, all life seemed before him* Minutes later, he was fighting for that very life. The Police Box at 14 Gate was a brick-and-glass structure. A lorry turned into the Dock entrance too quickly, and half its 12-ton load of timber planking slid sideways, crushing the box almost to smithereens, and Wally Bromley with it. Within minutes, not merely policemen of all ranks, but dockers, passers-by, the lot, were all digging madly for the man under it all. After 25 minutes, a Police Ambulance carried the freed but shattered P.C. to hospital. In Poplar Hospital he was to go through weeks of pain, discomfort, surgery, flowers, fags, elation (one new-born child), despondency and concern. The price – a broken pelvis and a punctured bladder, principally. Then the long, slow climb back towards recovery, convalescence, and finally a spell of light duty. Eventually, when it was clear that he would never again be properly fit, and five years after joining, Wally Bromley resigned, to take a local office job. And if lorry-drivers in pubs are heard to shoot their mouths off about 'those bleeding layabouts in the Police boxes', Wally's may be the face quietly smiling behind his pint pot in the corner.

The establishment in 1966 was 602, and the actual strength 569. Nice, worthy, P.C. Paddon died after a long illness. 1,083,205 Passes were checked at Gates, 1,698 crimes were investigated, and the detection rate was 55%. £140,000 worth of goods were stolen, half of which were later recovered by police and restored to their owners. But the morale of the Force was sadly down as a Labour Government pushed through their Ports Nationalisation plans. The Federation Collective Board studied the problem and the prospects in detail and produced an admirably realistic Report. Having first dealt briefly and reasonably accurately with the origins and history of the Force,† they analysed the four possible effects on the Force of nationalisation – (a) Regional Dock Forces (b) National Ports Police Force (c) amalgamation with British Transport Police and (d) amalgamation with Crown Forces. Of these, with which the Report dealt in detail, the only acceptable one was said to be the last cited – although with a proper realism, the Report wonders whether it would be as acceptable to those Forces. The B.T.C. amalgamation is wholly rejected – neither their organisation, their efficiency nor their conditions were up to P.L.A. Police standards, and the effect would have been to bring the 500 down to the level of the 1,500 in the larger Force. They viewed the prospects of a National, or a Regional, organisation with sanguinary caution – it might be satisfactorily set up – it could be – but it was scarcely likely to be. Naturally, it was logical, though not certain, that Docks areas would always need to be policed by specialists, but the continuance of the Force in its past and present form was not in the least likely, and unhappy rumblings over the beer mugs and coffee cups were rightly

*The incident is vividly recorded in the Police Federation Newsletter No. 2 of February, 1968, to which I am indebted.

†As had been many before them, they were understandably misled by a recruiting pamphlet produced in 1956, which hopelessly confused the military Centinels with Colquhoun's Second Force. Until my research showed this to be codswallop, as shown supra, I too wrongly accepted it!

to be expected. The author, constantly canvassed for his views on the prospects, tried hard to maintain an optimistic forecast, despite his own serious misgivings, but it must have shown itself a bit threadbare at times.

Each Annual Police Report from the earliest ones had included a bevy of summaries under the mild heading of Some Interesting Cases, and by this time, with the Prosecutions Department at its zenith,* the only problem would be one of selection. But if one started telling such tales, however vivid, however true, there would be room for little else. However, on March 3rd, 1966, an incident took place which was reported to the Director-General (by the author personally) immediately it had concluded and related by him at once to the Board, in whose Minutes an account in some detail proudly appears. This does surely provide an opportunity to insert just one example of the work of the Force and the co-operation with other Forces – in this instance the Metropolitan.

The staff of the Authority who served far away from Tower Hill had to be paid weekly. Tradition, not to mention the old Truck Acts, precluded safe payment by cheque. Therefore, each week a police van, with driver and escort, picked up a staff member with bulging wages bags at Head Office and locked him in the back for the 300 yard journey to the entrance to Tower Pier, where a launch awaited him. On March 3rd, 1966, the routine was without incident until David Taylor, the carrier, stepped from the back of the van. At this moment, four thugs dashed at him across the road, each armed with a steel bar bound for better grip with insulating tape at one end. One snatched the bags and threw the surprised Taylor against a wall. Another bashed the unarmed escort P.C. Jon Urwin, over the head with his bar, and spent a moment kicking his semi-conscious body with heavy boots. Two thugs then lost themselves among the tourist crowds which thronged Tower Hill, and the other two re-crossed the road to where a stolen Jaguar was now slowly moving off. All this had taken but a few seconds, and the police driver, P.C. Stanley Baldock, hearing noises, had grabbed a pick-axe handle which foresight had led him always to take along, and ran at the Jaguar, getting there as the two thugs hurled the bags in the back and jumped in. Wisely, he went not for the men but for the windscreen, which he shattered with one blow, before changing his grip and managing to smash both off-side windows as the car gathered speed. In the road, P.C. Urwin staggered to his feet, pulled out his truncheon and hurled it at the car's back window, which it hit and smashed. Meanwhile, young Taylor was bravely but dazedly dashing across the road to help, when one of the men in the car hurled his steel bar out of the window. By mischance it caught Taylor full in the face and pole-axed him. The Jaguar paused at the top of the hill to pick up the remaining pair of thugs and sped eastwards. Back at the van, Baldock was using his radio to spread the alarm in all directions. The Jaguar soon swung into Prescott Street – at which moment, the luck turned. For in that street is the Co-operative Bank, which at that very time had been the subject of a hold-up and robbery by an unconnected gang, and the street was saturated with Met. Police cars and men. Seeing a Jaguar screaming towards them with smashed windows, they realised what had happened and

*We were but three – my Personal Assistant, the incomparable Ivan Owen, one secretary-bird, Linda Mann, then later Valerie Chinnick, and myself – and this is a history of the P.L.A. Police, not of its Prosecutors – but we were by now clearing some 200 cases a year, in court almost every day of the week, with tremendously detailed reports, of which I kept personal copies. Each case was reported to the Director General with a copy to the Police, and I am still amused to see my own slightly racy narratives appearing in chunks among Interesting Cases annually!

one car started off in lightning pursuit of it as it passed. A chase followed worthy of any television series, which ended with the Jaguar becoming blocked in a lane. Hastily evacuating the car, the driver and the thugs dashed into a nearby Builders' Yard, leaving the wages bags behind, still unopened. Four reached the end wall before the pursuing police and were away over it. The fifth man, too late, hid among the piles of tall timber in the yard, where he was quickly found and arrested. He claimed plausibly to be an innocent passer-by, caught up in a running group whom he did not know from Adam. But the Police now on the scene included Det. Insp. Philcox, whose search of the arrested man revealed a pocketed ticket for the big car park which lies almost opposite the site of the robbery. We took the suspect there at once. In the glove-box of the man's private car was a roll of insulating tape – its outer end torn roughly. This end was placed alongside the tape which had bound the steel bar thrown at Taylor from the car. The two ends were a perfect match. Later at the Old Bailey, the thug received a salutary sentence of imprisonment. P.C. Urwin later transferred to the Tilbury Dock Division. Stan Baldock is retired and works as an exchange clerk in a London Bank. David Taylor is now with the Thames Water Authority. I cannot of course suggest that the incident is typical of everyday P.L.A. Police work! But it shows one aspect of it.

But now the tide of change was beginning to flood over the Port of London. Operationally speaking, the most significant item was the advent of the first of the U.H.F. Personal Radio sets, which proved themselves invaluable not only physically but psychologically – it is well-known how the sense of isolation on, say, a night patrol vanishes when the officer can be in audible contact with his Headquarters all the time at the touch of a button, and constant in his ear is the evidence that he is one of a team, each in touch with the other, and that the Control Room knows the whole picture, including his part in it.

The other event of overall interest in 1966 was the receipt of a formal request from the British Waterways Board for the P.L.A. to take over the policing of Regent's Canal Dock. Mr. Oliver was asked to work on the costing of such an exercise. The Dock in question was a small pocket between the London and the India Docks, so riddled with crime that in most years more goods in value were stolen from there than from the whole of P.L.A.'s five groups put together! For this, at least in 1966, the unhappy British Transport Police were not to blame, for they were no longer operative there, and the only security was provided by one of those private organisations, who have their place, but not in a situation such as holding the Gates of a Dock. Because under no circumstances could such a body have or acquire police powers to stop, search and detain, which has been shown earlier to be a privilege necessary to only a few full Police Forces. Without such powers, the only thing that such a Gateman could do, apart from preventing unauthorised people from trespassing inwards, was to check goods carried against a pass or similar document. If he found aught wrong, he could do nothing except ask the carrier to wait, while the Police were summoned – to which the thief's reaction would be an abrupt departure as soon as his laughter had died down sufficiently. Until he actually set foot outside the Dock, the Gateman would not have even a citizen's power of arrest.

Legally, while Regent's Canal Dock was obviously part of the Port of London, physically it lay outside the P.L.A. Police's existing powers. True – an attempt could have been made to provide such jurisdiction in the next available Port of London Act – indeed, such provisions were in due course inserted in Miss Novarra's magnum opus in case such a request from any source arose in the future. But in fact, when the costings were worked out, it emerged that even were this plan legally possible, it simply was not economically viable. The Authority would have to charge the Waterways Board more than the continued existence of the Dock was worth to them. The end result was that the business in the Dock was transferred and run down, and the unsalubrious little pocket eventually closed. It was no great loss, even to British Transport, having for many years been no more than a small flag-waving outpost of their empire. But it had long been a thorn in the Authority's side, politically and also criminally – it was well known that one easy route for stolen goods out of the P.L.A. Docks was to have them placed quietly on one of the many barges, much too big to be thoroughly searched, which emerged from a convenient lock into the River destined for a call at the Regent's Canal Dock whence, in the fullness of time, it could be removed by or on behalf of the thieves.

At about this time, too, the Authority received a submission from their proud and active Federation asking for recognition that was not merely *de facto* but *de jure*, analogous to that enjoyed by Crown Forces under s.44 of the Police Act, 1964. This Act did not, of course, apply to the P.L.A. Police save for the single instance of an assault under s.51, this being on a Constable (which our men were) as opposed to a member of a Police Force (which, in the context of the 1964 Act, they were not).

The Federation's existence rested solely on Minute 34 of 1943, and while it was entirely content to rely on the integrity of the existing Authority, the moves towards nationalisation might result in an Authority differently constituted and much less reliable from the Federation's point of view, and they might thus be left with nothing on which to base their very existence save for an old Minute which might not even bind a future Authority. The Board replied, saying that while the point was appreciated, the Police would be no worse off than any other section of the staff – they offered a fresh assurance both as to the Federation's existence and to the effect that no steps would be taken affecting their status without their consultation.

The Federation could not and did not let the matter rest there. Back went another submission stressing that nationalisation, then almost inevitable, would probably be followed (as the Bill indicated) by a National Ports Police Force. Two forces such as the P.L.A. had been in an analogous position in recent years, only to find themselves totally abolished.* Morale, the submission continued, was at its lowest ever. No change in the negotiating machinery was requested – things were admirable just so long as the Authority's existence and nature remained. The assurances offered could not of their nature guarantee that. The Authority bowed to the indestructible logic of the submission and conceded that statutory recognition was vital. Appropriate instructions were passed to Miss Novarra. At the same time, arrangements were made to cover the new Superintendents' Association.

Another small development took place at this time (the Minute was in the end dated March 23rd, 1967) which gave profound pleasure not only to the Federation, who had urged it, but to the author, who had been niggling away at it for several years – this was to change the ancient title of Chief Police Officer to the modern Chief Constable. I had seen how the old form had wrongly conveyed an impression of lower status among gatherings such as A.C.P.O. (The Association of Chief Police Officers –

*Though not certain, I take this to refer to the Airport Police for one, but cannot trace the other.

and the irony does not escape me!) And suddenly the time became ripe, the proposal was made, the reactions to it from those who had in fact urged it were formally canvassed and proved universally favourable, and the change was effected. (The Federation had gone further, successfully, urging that Senior Superintendent should be amended to Chief Superintendent.) In all conscience it must be said that Mr. Oliver's genuine humility had made him the last, rather than the first, to press the change.

Later – indeed, in 1968 – the London Docks Group was finally closed, and the staff's general despondency grew ever deeper. It seemed now that blow after blow was raining down on to the Authority's head, battering not only the optimism for the future, but the quite extraordinary cameraderie – the spirit almost of family – which had been an essential element of it, the foundation for its vitality and inner pride.

To the Police, it meant the reduction of their organisation by a complete Division. The Force was closely scrutinised from a strict medical standpoint and large numbers (in 1969 about thirty) left on health grounds each taking his pension. Behind this was the fact that everyone knew, despite all official denials, that the Surrey group was going to be next to close down. One symptom of this was the stopping of all recruitment – recognised at once as the preparation for the absorption of the Surrey Division men. Not that the Training School closed – for the criminal legal world was at this time undergoing its most traumatic change for 115 years and the author had the privilege of giving lectures which in the end covered the whole Force, on the Criminal Justice and Criminal Law Acts of 1967, the Theft Act, 1968, and the Port of London Act, 1968 – Miss Novarra's masterpiece having by now leaped all its Parliamentary hurdles in triumph!

A violent raid on a bank which had a branch just inside the gates of the Royal Albert Dock increased at a stroke the stolen goods figure by £88,000. But still the detection rate for the 1,604 criminal cases stayed at 48%.

In 1970, what was known widely as Devlin II – the second stage of Lord Devlin's Committee report on Docks Operations – came in, radically altering many operating methods which had scarcely wavered for 150 years, not least when viewed from the police aspect. For instance, 'rush hour' now fell at 2 p.m. as the new shifts changed over and active periods at Gates markedly increased. Surrey Docks did close, as expected. Morale in the Force dipped yet further as the 88 men from across the river had to be absorbed into Divisions which were themselves almost visibly shrinking. There were now no more than 37 constables in the entire Force under the age of thirty.

A veritable campaign of stealing mercury began – a most difficult crime to bring home to anyone, for stolen mercury blends with unstolen mercury into one smooth sinuous blob. In this instance, the C.I.D. knew exactly who was behind the whole campaign, but that there was no hope at all of obtaining any evidence to link him with it. On the other hand, one dramatic attempt to steal an entire container and its contents (hundreds of thousands of razor-blades) was triumphantly foiled, although not quite in the way it had been diligently planned. The subsequent trial of six men at the Old Bailey was likewise somewhat traumatic, as it involved allegations of curruption made in open court not only against the police but against the prosecuting solicitor! (Happily these were able to be completely disproved and all were withdrawn as openly as they had been made, but it took years off the author's life for one – and one day that story will be told!)

On the good and optimistic side, however, a new, exciting and tremendously valuable organisation had come into existence – the International Association of

Port Police. Part of its foundation had stemmed from Canada at a time when the author was visiting Toronto, and the ground was thus able to be slightly prepared for the Chief Constable to be sent abroad for the Association's first highly successful formal meeting. Of this more later.

The other event of moment in 1970 was the unexpected calling of a General Election. The timing of this entailed, among other things, the Ports Nationalisation Bill, which had lacked only the formality of the Royal Assent to become law, becoming overnight piles of waste paper, fodder for the shredder. And the resulting change of Government meant its future abandonment, at least for years ahead, so that almost every port in the country, having prepared itself for the trigger to be fired, felt itself to have stuck at half-cock.

But now developments were pressing hard upon the Authority and on its Police Force which are clearly more suitable for the final section of this book, if they are to be seen in proper perspective. The Chairman and Vice-Chairman, both so admired, so respected – to say loved would not be putting it too high – Lord Simon and Lord Cottesloe, both came to the end of their long and devoted service. The incomparable Dudley Perkins, whose heart had never ceased to beat in unison with that of his men, had become first 'not at all well' and then seriously ill – small wonder with the stresses which he had been forced to shoulder. Finally he was persuaded to bow to the advice – one might indeed say orders – of his doctors and tender his reluctant resignation from office.

Even Trap One – the impressive custom-built pile on Tower Hill whose own tower, clutching the statue of Old Father Thames to its bosom, had been visible from high points all over London, marking the centre of administration of England's greatest port – had now been sold. St. Katharine Dock House, which had won several architectural prizes and, more slowly, several hearts, had likewise been disposed of although a chunk of the upper floors had been leased back to house the Boardroom and chief executives. The rest of the staff was scattered throughout what was left of London Dock, the Indias, the Royals and Tilbury – the last of which alone, with its inspiring new extension and provisions for containerisation, faced the future with a head lifted, albeit slightly scarred by industrial unrest. But Tilbury, for all its pristine glory, was down in Essex, and the eyes of the Authority's leaders seemed to be fixed further out still, at Maplin. The old, proud Port of London was but a pale shadow of its once glorious self.

And yet the problems of security remained. In 1972, Police Headquarters moved to the Royals – twice, in fact – once to the area of the dusty flour mills on the south side of the Royal Victoria Dock and then to a house looking out on Gallions Entrance at the eastern end of the Royal Albert Basin. But still many millions of pounds worth of goods passed through what was left of the Docks in a reduced but never-stopping flow. Indeed, in 1973 they totalled 10 million tonnes, valued at £300,000,000 – and that's excluding oil. Losses through theft, that year, amounted to 0.005% – one half penny in every £100. This surely speaks for itself.

The Force faced the future, too, with a new man at the helm. Tom Oliver was 63 in 1972. The retirement for which he had worked so long and so patiently, had been reached at last. His last day in office was March 31st. Quiet but cordial and genuine good wishes saw him off on Maundy Thursday as he diffidently laid aside his professional burden. He went home, as usual, alone.

On Good Friday, he was not at all well. It was an aneurism. On Saturday, an ambulance took him to hospital. Easter Sunday saw him having been successfully operated on – recovering and happy. His wife, Do, was told by him and by the staff that the danger was over and she should go home for a good night's rest. Barring accidents, Tom was getting well again.

By Easter Monday, he was dead.

PART FIVE—THE FRONT DOOR OF THE KINGDOM

The Wright Report — Consequent and recent developments. Present and future considered.

PART FIVE—THE FRONT DOOR OF THE KINGDOM

The sad event of Mr. Oliver's death was directly followed by a number of developments which were the direct consequence of matters that had been quietly taking place for several months before it, unknown to many.

The Wright Report

During the autumn of 1971, the Authority decided that a complete up-to-date survey of their Police Force was necessary, as well as detailed research into the question of whether it should continue to exist at all. Seeking a man who could carry out this formidable task with speed and thoroughness, they made enquiries which led them to Mr. Kenneth Wright, then – and still today – Security Consultant to the City Corporation. Mr. Wright, who had first entered the world of security almost by accident, was greatly gifted with the perspicacity to recognise and identify his natural niche as soon as he saw it. Fortunately, he was also a man with a great sense of history and of the importance of tradition. Above all, he approached the task of this commission with an almost bottomless fund of goodwill towards the men who would be most personally affected by his ultimate decisions, yet fearless in expressing what he believed to be just and right – a man over whose eyes it would be immensely difficult, even if it were possible at all, to pull the proverbial wool.

He began by assimilating the basic history of the Force – the author had the pleasure of more than one long session with him in those early stages. Then, based thus firmly, idealistic but with both feet firmly on the ground, he set out to observe the Force from every angle, not least (one might say especially) that of the thinking policeman within it.

His initial report is dated January 31st, 1972. He began by facing frontally the question of whether there was any practical alternative to the existence of the Force. He asserted that any alternatives would involve throwing the Docks literally open to the public, which would at once render them almost impossible to operate. The vast existing problems could not, he said, but be seriously exacerbated if the public were given access to quays and loading bays, and the Authority would be unable to shrink from those problems, not least because of their responsibilities to the users of the Port. The Crown police forces not only would not – but could not assist. Standards of security would inevitably fall dramatically. To farm out security work to commercial firms would be easy and economically cheap – a mere £350,000 per year at most–but no such firm could even begin to do an effective job in the docks, for it would lack not merely the resources but the powers of police. While the Force's establishment should undoubtedly be streamlined, its continuing existence was nothing less than vital. He had quietly explored the position with the heads of all the major shipping lines and cargo-handling firms, so that the statement was more than a mere confident assertion – it was known fact.

This opening must have seemed like fresh air rushing into the stifling gloom into which the Force had descended. And his 22 major recommendations which followed, each argued out logically to the point of incontrovertibility, showed the immense thoroughness and also the understanding with which Kenneth Wright had discharged his trust. The more significant of them were briefly as follows:

If manpower and overtime problems were to be avoided, the police establishment had to be related directly to those tasks which really needed to be done. The gate-manning schedules afforded chances for dramatic economies. Routine administration should be decentralised, dock police stations being authorised to deal with P.L.A. Departments direct. The H.Q. Operations and Research and Planning Sections should be abolished. Refresher Training should be discontinued. The Mobile C.I.D. should be reconstituted. The Supervisory Officer ratio should be reduced. The organisation should be merged into a single operating Division, based initially on the Royal Docks. The C.I.D. were wasting much time dealing at length with enquiries foredoomed to be fruitless, and its establishment should be radically altered – the rigidity of its structure should be broken down, for a start, officers being posted to C.I.D. on short-term appointments.* Beats and patrol activity should not be too inflexible – officers in charge of it should have considerable latitude in deciding how to deploy their manpower. Duties at Cutler St. Warehouses, by contrast, should be farmed out to a commercial security firm, with a saving of up to £11,000 per year, at present being wasted. Similarly, less time should be spent on Surrey Docks. The continuance of the ambulance service was a political decision but its use seemed hardly economically viable, despite its benefits.

In summary, the effect of all the recommendations would entail a future establishment of 44 Supervisory Officers and 273 Constables, against the existing 76 and 376. The annual cost of the proposed Force would be £954,000, as against the present £1,314,000. The current under-manning allowance should continue to be paid, as the loss of regular overtime would be a hard blow for many of the men and the potential annual saving was no more than £21,000. Mr. Wright then made the telling observation that if every officer of fifty or over accepted voluntary severance, the actual strength of the Force would be reduced to almost exactly the recommended establishment, rank for rank.

It was this type of considered observation which gave this Report its dynamic quality. Mr. Wright ended with a detailed survey of the steps, in their order, which would be necessary in order to put his recommendations into effect. This would naturally involve consultation with Dock Managers on their gate-closing policy, and re-framing the terms of the Pension Fund. "A policeman is in any event past his best after the age of fifty and should no longer be expected to work long hours in dirty weather, or to tackle rough customers," he commented. From this age-limit he suggested that the Chief Constable alone should be exempt – he should be offered a five-year contract

*I confess this was the one point in his Report on which I found, and still find, myself in total disagreement with Mr. Wright. Based on long personal experience, I know that in the docks more than anywhere, C.I.D. effectiveness depends on a personal trust and rapport between dock-worker and detective which can only be built up slowly and with greatest care, without which it cannot be created at all, much less grow. I recognise that the principle advanced by Mr. Wright is correct as regards all large urban areas – in Dockland it happens, for all the theories, to be unworkable. I know because I have not only studied it long and closely – with the co-operation and help of docks detectives, I have personally practised it. Its existence explains why certain men, otherwise most able, never could and never can become wholly effective docks detectives. The dangers in the system are real and must not be under-estimated. But the link upon which docks C.I.D. work can and must be based is one of long-established personal trust between the policeman and the dock worker, and no man, however worthy, however able, who cannot win that trust, can ever become an effective detective in Dockland.

with an age-limit of sixty. In conclusion, Mr. Wright saw the Force settling down at an ultimate establishment between 250 and 275, "pending the closing down of all the up-river docks".*

Mr. Wright's closing paragraph cannot but be quoted in full:

"*I therefore strongly recommend the retention of the P.L.A. Police Force*, albeit in a streamlined version of the present establishment. If the Force were to be disbanded, it could never be revived – it would never be the same Force – it would have lost its sense of loyalty to the P.L.A., its expertise in the Docks, and all the traditions of which it is so rightly proud today. In my opinion, the P.L.A. cannot afford to do without its police – indeed, I believe that much more could be made of the Force as a sales aid – one of the outward and visible signs that the Port of London gives the best of service to its users. Any reduction in the security levels provided in the Port will appear as a reduction in the value of the port users are getting for their money. The P.L.A. therefore stands to lose goodwill if security and safety in the Port of London deteriorates. If losses and insurance premiums combine to make London an unduly costly port – and if chaotic conditions and over-frequent accidents combine to make working in the port unduly difficult and expensive, the P.L.A. would surely lose more than they would hope to gain by economising on security. It is future revenue that is at stake here, not present costs. I conclude that the P.L.A. would be wrong to abdicate the responsibility for good order and security in the docks, and I base this conclusion not on moral or social grounds – although these are important enough – but on an assessment of the commercial advantages to the P.L.A. of keeping their docks running smoothly, and of being seen to be coping with the crime that is rampant in all docks."

It is an undoubted fact that the Authority, in accepting the Wright Report in principle, did so because of these concluding arguments. To a great extent, therefore, the men of the Force owe their continuing existence to the activities of Mr. Kenneth Wright. If the men could have seen so much as that closing paragraph (which I do not suggest was practicable) many unhappy general misgivings might have been exorcised. Unfortunately, for all the confidence that Mr. Wright inspired in those with whom he worked so closely and understandingly on the preparation of his Report, the majority of the men knew only that 'some chap from outside' was considering the question of their existence. They could have lived and worked without this serious worry only if they had been fortified by complete faith in the Authority's management. And this – which had indeed once existed – was, in 1972, a thing of the past.†

Mr. Gannon Takes Over

For reasons which are understandable, the Wright Report was not generally distributed. Mr. Oliver's approaching retirement was known, and naturally he was given

*I well remember the shock of seeing the conclusion implicit in the phrase quoted, during my own first perusal of the Report. It seemed clear that Management were at this date actively considering the total closure of all their docks above Tilbury, not if compelled reluctantly by a series of possible economic disasters, but as a pre-planned policy. But since this has not yet come about and shows no immediate signs of doing so, the policy has either changed or I must acknowledge my conclusion as wide of the mark!

†I make that observation irrespective of the justice or injustice of it, as a plain statement of fact.

an opportunity to read, even to comment on it. But the Force as a whole have never seen it to this day, which is a pity, as there is much in it which would do the hearts of the men much good. Certainly in its early existence its distribution was so restricted that when one of its most sernior officers went to attend upon management one day, he had never seen it. And yet that officer was at that time in charge of the Tilbury Docks Division. His name is by no means unknown to readers already. It is Peter Gannon.*

He was at that time looking forward to, and had indeed made plans with his family for, severance and retirement, and was amazed to be asked if he would take over as Chief Constable in succession to Mr. Oliver. After some discussion and consideration, and not without some misgivings, he accepted it, and at a probationary salary – which was later caught in the Government's wage freeze so that he remained perforce seriously underpaid for his rank and the responsibility it entailed, once his initial experience had been gained.

Having accepted it, Mr. Gannon was given his first sight of the Wright Report! He was told that his duties at Tilbury would be handled by others and that he was to devote his immediate future to producing a full detailed plan for the short and longer term future of the Force, for which initial task he was given precisely two weeks. He has since told the author that the first week was spent in reading the Wright Report until he knew it almost by heart while his subconscious mind was busy applying it to the particular problems. At the end of the fortnight he duly produced his initial plan, which was accepted.

Meanwhile, during the final weeks of Mr. Oliver's tenure of office, his successor-elect sat with him in his room and saw at first hand the day-to-day matters that arose and how the Chief Constable dealt with them. Finally, on the evening of March 31st, the two men shook hands with what Mr. Gannon was later to refer to as a new and deep understanding and what was undoubtedly a mutual respect. One fact is perhaps worthy of mention – Tom Oliver's unshakeable certainty that his successor's future plan was inoperable!

As we already know, the new Chief's earliest duties were those associated with the personal tragedy of his predecessor's sudden death. But at the time he assumed office, the authorised establishment was 473 – the actual strength being 399 – and during 1972, the former figure was reduced to 314, the latter to 278. Not without reason was Mr. Gannon to define his first year, in his 1972 Annual Report, as "a year of departure and rationalisation", bearing in mind that 121 of his men had left by voluntary severance. Relevant to this was the immense advantage, hard won by the Federation's negotiators, of their service ranking equally without deduction, on transfer to any Crown Force. The earlier lack of this agreement had made a transfer plan simply not financially viable – the number of years service governs the amount of the man's ultimate pension. Henceforward, every Crown Force in the Kingdom was open to the man who wished to leave P.L.A. – with the sole exception of the City of London if he was less than 5 ft. 11 ins. tall!

*For the record, this is not strictly correct! Mr. Gannon was christened Douglas and two other names but neither of them was Peter. However, from his earliest childhood, it is as Peter that he has been known not only to his friends but even to his family. I am not sure that even he is certain exactly how and why this habit began! Thinking of another man who once also acquired that name though not christened it, the precedent, may however, be thought no less than auspicious!

During the summer of 1972, Mr. Gannon was able, if nothing else, to assess the size and depth of his problem. £137,516 worth of goods were stolen, of which £52,404 worth – 38% – was recovered. There were 942 criminal cases, all different branches of theft but 46.

The Chief Constable pressed the Authority to back his request to the Home Office for the extension to the Force of the right to win entry on merit to the Police College at Bramshill – probably one of the finest conceptions in the history of the service. This was to bear fruit in due course, as will be seen.

It is interesting to note Mr. Gannon's observation that docks' criminals were electing to go for trial whenever this was legally possible, not becaue they might pull the wool over the eyes of a jury, which is the normal reason, but in order that they might use the time between committal for trial and the trial itself to apply for and secure voluntary severance, with its usual generous terms. Another trend was less amusing – those found guilty of theft in the docks and imprisoned without first being able to obtain severance were invariably allowed a day out of gaol in which to present themselves under escort before the Port Labour Board who would almost invariably grant them reinstatement on the list of registered port workers, effective upon their release. And this must be measured against the statistic that all major crime in the docks was being dealt with by a C.I.D. of precisely nineteen men, between them providing a twenty-four hour service, seven days a week.

A more cheerful aspect of Mr. Gannon's work, which assumed a fitting prominence in his reports, related to an organisation mentioned earlier as having been founded in 1970 under the title of the International Association of Port Police. Of this admirable body, Mr. Oliver had been made Vice-President, and his death was followed by a request that Mr. Gannon should take his place. In due course, Mr. Gannon became President, and in 1974 the Association's Annual Conference was held in London where it was addressed by some of the world's most distinguished policemen.

Its foundation rests primarily upon the simple truth that if law enforcement makes sense, then good law enforcement makes better sense, and since ports throughout the world were dealing with parallel problems and difficulties, then international co-operation, consultation and communication could serve but to improve the operational effectiveness of all individual units. It is undeniably, as the Association claims, of the greatest value for a port police chief to know and to enjoy already a personal rapport with a man facing similar problems on the other side of the world, who is much more to him than a name and address in a handbook. Increasing technology has made it more vital than ever for those fighting specialist types of crime to get together and help each other. And although the Association began in Canada and the United States, its membership is now truly world-wide and a consultative status with the United Nations has recently been gained.

Mr. Gannon indeed took many practical steps to further this theme, which have been hailed by his international colleagues as outstanding. He founded, and became first Chairman of, the British Association of Airport and Seaport Police, and similarly in respect of a European Association. His then Chief Staff Officer, Eric Ellen, of whom more anon, became Secretary of all three organisations, and is currently in his second year as President of the parent one – an unprecedented honour. It is no idle boast but simple fact that the Port of London Police are accepted in these international circles as the finest in the world, holding the best record for losses of any such forces –

0.005% of the value of goods passing through the enclosed docks – which amounts to ½p in every £100.

Mr. Gannon was soon well and truly in the saddle and introducing personal initiative in a range of projects which were to make the period between 1972 and 1975 the most active and intense for many years. As the Authority was giving the outside world a general impression of thrashing about, hitting here and missing there, so in its police activities it seemed to be achieving a succession of hits.

One faculty which Mr. Gannon had with which not all men are blessed, at least which survives when they reach a position of command, is the ability to delegate. This of course involves repeated judgment of his aides and subordinates which, if it is correctly attained, frees the commander's mind to concentrate on matters in perspective. As his Chief Staff Officer Mr. Gannon had no hesitation in selecting the eager young officer whose progress has not gone unnoticed – Eric Ellen. He did so knowing that if his judgment was accurate, the problem of succession could be solved. Happily, Mr. Ellen showed a marked ability for administration and a facility for working in harness without losing that drive which had been shown by his gaining an extra-mural LL.B. whilst a serving inspector. And in 1973, Mr. Ellen was selected for application to enter the Senior Command Course at Bramshill with the encouragement of the Authority – he obtained his place with 21 others from among a total of no less than 122 applicants. He was to complete the course with notable success – there is no higher qualification in the police service throughout the world.

In 1973 also came confirmation, if any were needed, of the correctness of Mr. Wright's recommendation that the Force should continue to exist as a professional, properly trained, mobile and equipped entity with proper and adequate legal powers. For a similar study was made by the Mersey Docks and Harbour Board in relation to Liverpool Docks which up to this time had been guarded by a curious amalgam of a section of the Liverpool City Police, a commercial security firm, and private watchmen. Having reviewed the alternatives, the consultant advocated the creation of a new autonomous Docks Force (which took place and exists today) saying: "There could be no better model to follow than that of the P.L.A. Police Force which is in any case outstanding in the qualities required at Liverpool." The costings with which this view was backed are also interesting. It was found that the cost of employing each commercial security guard was £5,000 per year based on an 8-hour day shift, and £8,500 on a twelve-hour shift. By comparison, the employment of a 13-year-service constable (the average P.L.A. service, although the Metropolitan constables are available on hire based on a five-year-service man's cost) was £5,288 annually. Thus it was clear that the establishment and maintenance of a separate Force made financial, as well as social and moral, sense. And it may be noted that back in 1967 on another topic, in the course of an adjournment debate in the House of Commons, Mr. Roy Hattersley, then Parliamentary Secretary to the Minister of Labour, had said about the P.L.A. Force, "They are in parity of pay because it is our absolute belief that no distinction can be drawn between the importance of their service and their importance to the community as a whole".*

Mr. Gannon's expressed aim was to modernise without increasing the costs beyond the benefits derived from the measures taken – bearing in mind particularly that some 95% of costs in the Force is attributable to salaries. Recruiting and selection

*See Hansard, 1967, Cols: 358/368.

procedures were overhauled, and the national standards for entry into the service were introduced. All transport in use was up-dated, vehicles being chosen for effectiveness but with economy in mind. A small and select Special Branch team was created within the Force, its members combining these duties with their normal ones. An effective liaison was thus achieved with Government, Metropolitan and County Forces, and there was a ready-made protection squad for visiting V.I.P.s.

Crime Prevention was also given special attention. This group, all of Inspector rank, similarly combined these duties with normal ones, surveying premises and advising on security in them, encouraging staffs of tenants and customers to be aware and vigilant. And at long last, a link was established with the Authority's own Engineers, precluding any repetition of the lamentable incident when a new Shed was built and won architectural prizes in the India Docks although the best part of one wall from first floor level up to which ran a vehicle ramp, was a glass window! A serious gap had at last been filled. Future shed design would take security into consideration.

Some indication of Mr. Ellen's staff work may be seen in the remarkable fact that the entire Force was managed by a select staff of no more than six, whose achievements included the introduction of a specially written handbook of instructions, the evolution of a new style of Annual Report, a new system of staff appraisal, a pro-forma report system and a refreshed service record system, not to mention the basic handling of all prosecutions.*

Another major concern related to the risks which, particularly in target areas such as Docks, have recently so strongly increased. Mr. Gannon, in consultation with the Metropolitan Police and the Government generally, formulated contingency plans against the possibility of terrorist attacks on docked ships. The matter also received the consultative attention of the International Chamber of Shipping – particularly regarding vessels carrying explosives. A very detailed survey was undertaken, and regularly up-dated, of vulnerable and key points – over and above which Mr. Gannon was regularly involved in important meetings dealing with classified information under the auspices of the Defence Department. The times were often apprehensive and occasionally no less than fraught.

The Second Wright Report

One might have thought that after the complete and exhaustive investigation on all security questions resulting in the Wright Report of 1972, so effectively followed through by the Chief Constable ever since, the existence of the Force would not again be challenged for at least a decade. And yet as 1974 passed into 1975, the same consultant, Mr. Kenneth Wright, was asked to re-investigate and re-assess those very same questions of principle upon which he had so fully pronounced three short years before. Happily, he had at this time to do no more than check that he was fully up-to-date and confirm

*I record this with mixed feelings, admiring the drive involved but deprecating the activity as one with which police should have nothing to do, as long as the accusatorial system, with all its defects, remains with us. Police work should be restricted to the investigation and the collecting of evidence, everything else being handled by lawyers. It is stupid and unreasonable to place the police on one side in a contest and require at the same time that they should exercise the dispassion of someone not party to the contest. Of this, after decades of study and experience, I am wholly convinced.

that his conclusions had not varied. Even so, he understandably expressed surprise that he was asked for his preliminary conclusions literally within days. Valiantly he managed to comply, being even more clear and emphatic than before that the existence of the Force was so desirable as to be virtually essential. He was able to point out that while the cost of security, as with everything else, had doubled in three years, the efficiency of the commercial security organisations had improved not at all, leaving the credibility gap wider than ever. Any replacement of the Force by any other type of organisation would involve an extra burden being thrown upon the already overworked P.L.A. executives by reason of the disciplinary problems which, in the light of new legislation, would be immense. H.M. Customs would demand extensive strengthening of many dock buildings if the Force were disbanded, port users would be seriously inconvenienced in many ways, and the services they received would cost them much more. The general situation was even more unfavourable to the idea of radical change than in 1972, he stated.

Within a very short time, this was followed by his full re-survey. The optimum strength, he could now say, was an establishment of 283 men, which would eliminate overtime on the existing huge scale. Below this figure, however, he felt it would be dangerous to go, the Force at that level being so thin on the ground that a security emergency, or even a flu epidemic, could not but create terrible problems. The aspect which he found most hightly in need of change was that relating to dock gates. He recognised that these were located when not only was the economic climate different, but so also was the volume of traffic. To a man on foot, it was important that there should be as many points of ingress and egress as was reasonably possible. To a man in a lorry, it was of relatively small moment that he had to travel a mile or more further, to enter or leave the dock. Earlier, Mr. Gannon had advanced the possibility of creating within the main docks a circular access road to all parts of the Royal Docks, serving a single entry/exit gate, saying that the manpower savings which would result would quickly recoup the initial capital outlay. As it now was, remarked Mr. Wright, Gates were kept open in many instances without any real need, and were cruelly absorbing of police manpower. Indeed, it was consequently most unjust that the Police department should be blamed for failing to reduce their costs when so much of these depended on commercial decisions outside all police control and contrary to police recommendations. Mr. Wright said that in any event a proper census of traffic should be undertaken and a resulting 'gate policy' formulated.

Looking to the immediate future Mr. Wright noted that as he had forecast in 1972, the Force had become a little staid and elderly – no less than half the total actual strength now fell within the 40/50 age bracket. Only nineteen men in the whole Force were under thirty years of age! He felt it important to introduce new blood as soon as possible, and also to make promotions among the senior ranks. The supervisory officer/constable ratio had widened in three years, however, as he had planned, from one-to-four to one-to-six.

Mr. Wright also touched on the particular problems of the C.I.D. of the Force. He recalled his recommendation that a Headquarters Squad be formed to co-ordinate the drive against crime and to tackle special problems in strength. He noted that this had not been implemented, although the total C.I.D. was now 22, against his recommended 23, as this number was divided amost equally between the three dock groups, each dock being virtually independent, detective-wise. This, said Mr. Wright, made the Detective Chief Superintendent a 'king without a kingdom'. The work could never justify the rank in itself but, he conceded, it was essential to have someone holding it, as otherwise the Force would be outranked in questions involving co-operation with other Forces – indeed, even if the present Det. Chief Superintendent were to retire, a similar appointment would have to be made, for the rank, which the work could not be said to warrant, served to remove a potential source of friction. The logic of this is unforced, the facts clear. A slight mystification remains.

Concluding his report, Mr. Wright bears tidings. "I learn with regret," he says, "that Mr. Gannon intends to retire this year. To my mind, he has made a most constructive contribution in the service of the Authority, and I can testify from my personal contacts with high-ranking officers of many Forces that the name of the P.L.A. Police stands higher today than ever before, not least because of Mr. Gannon's qualities." It is a great pleasure for the author, who knew and worked closely with Peter Gannon over twelve years, to endorse this exceptional tribute which comes originally from someone uniquely qualified to make it.

Mr. Wright continued by stating that Mr. Gannon was showing, in his choice of retirement date (August 31st, 1975) the same public spirit that he had shown in accepting the post when he could have retired on generous terms of severance. Certainly, he had but to soldier on until the end of the existing freeze in order to retire with a materially higher pension, but, observed Mr. Wright, his retirement now would ensure that the one officer uniquely qualified to succeed him would not be forced to leave the Authority in order to gain advancement elsewhere. The observation is mentioned here only insofar as it might be thought necessary to remove even the slightest suggestion (which Mr. Wright in no way intended to convey) that the man waiting in the wings had done anything to pressurise Mr. Gannon into advancing his retirement. For there was but one person in the land equipped to step modestly and without any assimilation period into his predecessor's shoes – and that officer was by this time the officially appointed Deputy Chief Constable. To look outside the Force would have been folly. It was one which the Authority did not commit. At their command, after a few months devoted to making the hand-over even smoother, Peter Gannon handed over his baton of office to Eric Ellen.

Looking back over Mr. Gannon's remarkable tenure of office, it is clear that Mr. Wright's tribute was indeed not over-stated. Much stemmed from Peter Gannon's absolute lack of fear, and his willingness to accept responsibility for all his actions. Naturally he was not always right, but he was never less than resolute. He declined in terms to 'take stick' from masters or men – making it clear from the start that if he felt he was being unjustly treated from above or pressured unreasonably from below, he would resign without hesitation. In fact, where Mr. Oliver had regarded his Federation officers with open apprehension, Mr. Gannon positively welcomed them. Once properly in the saddle, he not only had a weekly Senior Officers' Conference at which a new and invaluable frankness and lack of formality prevailed, but to these sessions he invited the Federation's Secretary (the restrained, courteous and reasonable but tenacious Sgt. Wilson to whom the lower echelons of the Force owe perhaps more than they realise) to attend them as an observer. To the Federation itself, his attitude was firm and handsome – "Ask me for anything you want and, provided only that I consider it reasonable, I will take it to management and advance it as strongly as I know how. If they turn it down, you will know it won't be my fault, and you and the rest of the Force will just have to accept it". Thus did everyone know just where they stood with

Peter Gannon, and upon this as much as any factor his real and undoubted success as Chief Constable was based.

Mr. Ellen in the Chair

Following Mr. Gannon could not have been easy, especially for someone of an essentially retiring nature. But if there is one thing that Eric Ellen does not lack, it is courage, and if there is another, it is administrative ability. He formally took over on September 1st, 1975, and it is of course much too soon to assess the mark he has made. But the author has had the benefit of talking with him expressly about the present and the future of the work, as well as the recent past. From the beginning he found, as had Mr. Gannon, that Mr. Wright's most thorough surveys were of great assistance to him. But as he felt his own way into the job, he began to be aware of the dangers of what might be called tunnel vision. From the base of Mr. Wright's position, such thinking is inevitable and right. But once the course is charted and the objectives clear, the Chief Constable reached the view that it was desirable that he should re-cast the mind more laterally – to think out the problems in a new way, not implying any earlier error, but because those problems' bases were themselves changing.

It was hardly kind of management, almost as the new Chief Constable sat down at his desk, to require him to provide yet another justification for the Force's existence as if there had been no prior consideration of the matter at all. But Mr. Ellen, probably wisely and certainly boldly, did not embark on a long and detailed exposition. He did the whole thing in one page and four succinct paragraphs, the first of which may be quoted in its entirety: "The continued existence of a unified Port Police Force is absolutely essential to the Port of London Authority".

He went on to comment that every single major port in the world maintains a port police system, that the Third World was studying British methods, and that the eastern bloc was seeking their advice on the more effective protection of world trade. Within the three months immediately prior to his Report, two complete Forces had been freshly established in the United Kingdom – at Liverpool and Felixstowe. Other smaller ports were considering emulation and, as he put it, "to consider dispensing with a Port Police system in London would be to fly in the face of all the evidence both national and wider". He cited Liverpool in particular on the matter of finance – that new force, 250 strong, was costing quarter of a million pounds less than the former inefficient piecemeal security control. Further – the calibre of man pursuing a police career is markedly higher than that available even to a large commercial security organisation; more 'security men' had been charged with criminal offences in Liverpool than any other single group of offender. He went on to urge that reason, and not finance should be the criterion for action on security. "In attempting the impossible – that is to quantify the effectiveness of a police force – it is wrong to cost it without estimating the cost of the alternative. For example, in the field of container security, where London has an international reputation, there need be the loss of but one container for the resulting liability to be £80,000 to £100,000, to say nothing of the untold damage caused by the loss of customer-confidence which the Port can ill afford."

He insisted that to lower the level of security below that of competitor ports would be to invite a situation such as existed in New York, where over a hundred complete containers were stolen each year. He ended strongly and confidently, pointing out that even a brief study of several aspects, which he cited, would serve but to prove further that "London has always led the rest, and this is no time for retrograde consideration".

If he had not knocked the doubters senseless, this "Shut up and don't talk nonsense!" line patently did still them for the time being! Metaphorically dusting his hands, the new Chief Constable proceeded to get down to work. And of all the major topics crying for his primary consideration over and above the day-to-day running of the Force, he assessed that which needed thought and action most as the matter of the security of the container.

The 'container revolution' as it was called in its hey-day, had begun a little more than a decade before, and its roots in Europe extended back scarcely beyond the late nineteen-fifties. From a police angle it was something that at first blush should have made security more simple – goods in quantity being securely packed inland, carried by road or rail to the Port in a sealed container and lifted bodily into or onto a ship designed expressly for the job, taken overseas and passed through the landing Port to its ultimate destination without intermediate disturbance – the idea would be impeccable, were it not for the criminal mind. Happily, the criminal is among the less mentally acute members of our society, save for the financial fraud, and the criminal mind is one in which cleverness has been switched for ersatz cunning. This is why the police will always start one-up on the criminal, albeit this is an advantage quickly lost by the handicaps of procedures and safeguards, for it must be remembered that the English system of criminal justice is the greatest in the world – from the point of view of the experienced criminal!

But a second glance at the container system will suffice to see that it depends upon the container being securely sealed at the time of its initial packing and remaining so until the destination is reached. And as the strength of a chain will always be that of its weakest link, and since the container is for the most part vastly more impressive to behold than to protect (it was possible to cut a hole through the sides of several of the early types with a sharp penknife!) the seal had but to be broken and made to appear unbroken for the whole operation to be potentially abortive.

The early seals were made of a metal so slight that a gloved hand could easily rip one end of the linked loop from its little catch and afterwards push the torn end back into the seal so that in default of a sharp tug it gave no sign of having been tampered with. And of course containers had often to stand, loaded and ready, for many days and nights before loading or after discharge. To the average criminal, the entire system was a gift. And if he intended to remove a complete container, contents and all, this entailed only well-forged documentation.

Early security measures involved the replacement of metal seals with plastic ones, preventing a ripped seal end being replaced so effectively. But the criminal soon realised that these plastic seals were made up of an assembly of several parts, making it possible for whole seals to be acquired and cannibalised – fresh, identical, but illegal seals being constructed ready for replacement. At one stage, what was publicly described as a "wonderful new system of checking containers" involved no more than a platform constructed on castors enabling the gate policeman quickly to reach a level at which he could give the seal a sharp tug!

But one thought did give rise to a valuable development within the Authority. The opportunity for theft exists from the very first act of loading, and it was felt likely that many thefts were being laid at the Authority's door which had in fact taken place long before the goods in their container ever reached the docks for dispatch. The solution – obvious only in hindsight – was spotted and applied. The gate policeman examines the seal of the container on entry to the docks and spends a moment affixing an additional one, distinctive in colour and design. This brought an immediate drop in alleged and formerly unanswerable thefts from containers as they passed through the docks. The measure was initiated during Mr. Gannon's reign, it must be added. Under Mr. Ellen, however, it received fresh consideration by himself in company with his Operations Superintendent, Kenneth Luck. What they devised has now spread around the world through the good offices of the International Association mentioned earlier. It will have to undergo several years of full operation before it is as useful as it can be, but it is already starting to bear fruit.

In essence, it is what might be described as a 'Container C.11' – the cypher there referring to the department at Scotland Yard also known as Criminal Intelligence, and recognised as possibly the most significant development in detection since the finger-print. Applied to container traffic, it involves the detailed analysis in a pre-set and essentially unvarying form of the whole journey from start to finish of any container ultimately discovered to have been deprived of its contents on arrival. Questionnaires have been devised and circulated so that today every single theft from a container that has passed through London is logged – every single person or body who has been in touch with it even remotely, from first moment to last is carefully logged and charted. And already patterns are beginning to emerge which show points of importance in common – a certain man, here – a certain place, there. This is Criminal Intelligence. It is also a classic example of lateral, as opposed to tunnel thinking. It could, of course, never work at all, save for the existence of just such an International Association as is available. Moreover, it is not the slightest reflection upon an incomparable organisation to say that this is a gap which Interpol, for all its merits, simply could not fill. And as a matter of interest for those who are ever keen to appreciate the dangers inherent in a 'computer society' – this is an operation which cannot be processed by a computer which, for example, could not distinguish between 'Brown' and 'Browne', apart from its involving moments and items of personal judgment such as the question of the degree of weight which should be given to any factor, as well as other talents of which from its nature a computer is incapable.

So much, then, for containers and the way a very important problem is being dealt with. It is just one example of the approach currently being adopted by the Force. And sometimes, problems of a more internal nature can cause as much trouble as anything from outside the Force. Above all, there are those concerns which one may nowadays find under the heading Industrial Relations.

One factor which has the ability to check, or to maintain, even to cause strife in this field is the contemporary power of the Trades Union. Long before there is any question of 'taking sides' one must acknowledge that there are few causes where 'sides' are not operative today, in one way or another. Now as has been noted, all members of the Crown Police Forces are forbidden by law to be members of any Trades Union. They have their Federation – but they lack the power to strike, for policemen, from the unique nature of their service as professional citizens, cannot be seen to ally themselves with or against any government whether national or local, any party, any congress or any faction. On the job, a policeman has, and must retain, a total lack of concern with whether or not the law is fair. His duty is solely to see that everybody in the land obeys it. Off duty and privately, of course he may have his own opinion on the merits and demerits of this law or that. On the job, those views must be wholly irrelevant to his actions. On the other hand, in view of the special nature of their calling, it takes a particularly unwise or cruel Home Secretary not to champion in all ways the service for which he bears some measure of political responsibility. It is almost unthinkable to exercise such firmness in opposition to them that they are driven to call for the political muscle that is the Union, and its exercise, which is the right to strike. Constitutionally, the case for such power is untenable, because every policeman knows before entry that he has not got that power, joining the service is not compulsory, and if a man joins a body of others, even perhaps a club, he has no right to cavil if the rules he knew about prevent him acting as he wishes. One hesitates to raise the point because the answer is obvious. It lies not even in acquiring the power to threaten to strike. It lies in resignation. And if resignation *en masse*, which is legal, were threatened, let alone operated, the effect would be no less devastating than that of a strike. On the other hand, to give that sort of advice to a man with a wife and three kids as he sets off for night duty – with unemployment as it stands today – is quite unthinkable.

This book reaches completion at a time of political turmoil and an impending General Election, and with Lord Edmund Davies having announced the major salary increases which he rightly insists all police deserve, even though the date of implementation may be for some time uncertain. Nevertheless, a personal view which I happen to hold most strongly is that the police service – possibly also the Armed Forces, in other words those who cannot in the public interest be permitted to strike – must be given by the State something outside all questions of salary – something directly in exchange for the renunciation of that right to strike which their recruitment itself acknowledges, and yet something which will not offend or be affected by fiscal 'guidlines' or like political devices. What they could, and in my view should, be given is quite simply exemption from all income tax. No doubt financial experts would think up ways to show that this would be expensive and impracticable. I suggest firmly that any expense would be worth the lives that we owe to these services, and that only direct successful impersonation involving forgery could possibly make it ineffective in practice. It is nothing to do with wages. It is a financial exchange for the lack of the right to strike.

It must by now be clear that in the financial field the P.L.A. policeman is no better off, nor worse off, than his colleagues in the Crown Forces. The trouble begins only with the realisation that for reasons of legislation, the total ban on striking is not without exception and moreover the exception lies among the specialised police forces of the ports. Unless executive legislation (making law by means of Harbour Revision Orders which never touch our elected legislators) can be controlled – and unless, for example, the Port of Bristol Authority Police is equated with the rest of the service of which it is otherwise a full and responsible part – this theme will continue to be Mr. Ellen's most persistent and unpleasant headache.

And the P.L.A. Police Federation, however reasonably and wisely it is operated, has another major bone it rightfully seeks to pick. At a time of economic depression and high unemployment, one of the greatest advantages thought to be universally enjoyed by policemen is security of employment. Under the Police Act, members of Crown Forces cannot be dismissed save with cause shown. Under the Port of London Acts, no such saving applies to the P.L.A. policeman, and its Federation therefore has continually to press that one be granted. Some 237 men, reasonable and calm men though they may be, are not going to rest until it is. Their Chief Constable knows and fully appreciates their cause.

Mention of one other topic – a far happier one – may serve to show that it is neither idle boast nor hollow platitude to say that London leads the world in port policing. There is a subsidiary company created some years ago now by P.L.A., under the title PLACON. Its original aim was the creation of a unit through which the Authority could promote commercialy, for reasonable fees, the expertise in which it abounds in many of its spheres of activity. One of these fields is policing. Over recent years and in increasing numbers, parties of men from many lands have come to the Port of London to be trained in the organisation and practice of a port police force. Sometimes a P.L.A. officer with a special aptitude has gone out to visit foreign ports and to teach and lecture there. Among the results already achieved Nigeria now enjoys the benefits of a National Ports Police Force, and Venezuela has part of her national service devoted expressly and solely to docks policing. This indicates one of several important future roles for the P.L.A. Police – the international instruction of many things learned over their long and honourable history.

The Front Door of the Kingdom

Our history is almost at an end, and it is time for the author to step out of the wings of the foot-notes and acknowledge himself to the unseen audience of his readers. May I begin by reminding each of them of something mentioned in my Introduction; the historian's belief: "It is only by the light of the past that we can hope to penetrate the infinite darkness of the future." Our story told, we have in our hands a beam which we may now direct into that infinite darkness. Let us see together what it illumines.

The "front door of the kingdom" to which Sir Gerald Dodson alluded is really that represented by the Thames between London Bridge and the sea. True, the Port of London Authority's functions extend from Teddington to the Tongue Lightship, but above the pool lies the social river – the people's river – after which the ceremonial river assumes a temporary control. In fact the men of the Thames Division, whose roots lie in Colquhoun's Marine Police Institution created in 1798 – the first force of organised professional preventive police the world ever knew, absorbed by the Metropolitan Police in 1839 – that Thames Division polices the river as far upstream as Staines, right through to Dartford, the downstream boundary of the Metropolitan Police District. The P.L.A. Police are responsible not for that river at all, save in matters of navigation and of oil pollution, nor for the many wharves, now mostly sad and derelict, but only for the docks and works which lie mostly on its northern bank. Downstream of Dartford, and until the arms of the estuary are lost in the sea, such policing as exists is given over to the Forces of Essex and Kent, one to each bank, each of whom have one launch and no criminal expertise, although the world of commerce is spreading currently seaward from its former centre in the Pool, floating (one trusts only figuratively) on the oil which dominates its existence from Tilbury downstream

Within this length of river, the essence of this front door – one might almost say its key-hole – lies roughly between London Bridge and Woolwich. Here on either side the wharves once flourished, the river swarmed with barges, tugs, with humanity, and thrummed with activity. Of recent years, these bustling centres have been quite calculatedly choked to death, or at least to what Lyall Watson would call "goth", as the Port Authority under its present management has decided that the vast ships by which today's goods are carried in quantities unimaginable to our forbears who founded those wharves and dug those draw-docks, cannot possibly make their way up the winding, be-shoaled reaches of the river – at least further up than Tilbury. And so they have set out to move the Port of London to where the super-tankers and the container-carriers can most conveniently go. It is all perfectly logical. The docks, after all, were conceived and built to accommodate ships which, placed alongside a super-tanker, would look like tugs! And if the ships are nowadays too big to make their way to the front door of the kingdom, then they feel that an extension must be constructed, the front door moved out to meet the ships. Thus has run the justification for the Authority's recent policies. It may be – it has been – criticised as ruthless, to which it may reply that life itself is ruthless, that time and tide wait for no man – and that the P.L.A. of 1979 is no longer a "public trust for public service", as it was when Winston Churchill created it, but a commercial entity, which must stand on its own financial feet, too proud to scrounge. And if a still, small voice is heard to murmur that it never did scrounge when it was concerned with public service – nor lost money, either – that voice could not be expected to be listened to above the roar of a super-tanker's engines at full speed.

But that keyhole is not yet quite dead. It may seem to be, and much of it is unconscious and the rest sorely wounded. It can utter little more than a painful whisper of its need – a bleat, lost on the winter wind almost as soon as it escapes the poor, bruised mouth – a sound too soft to catch any ear save possibly that of the trained observer, the acutely sensitive ear of the professional citizen. But by him that soft cry has been heard.

The Thames Division, for all its history, all its integrity, not to mention its willingness, its energy, is not what it was. It has no C.I.D. of its own now. The men with the special expertise for the idiosyncratic ways of the ancient river have gone, and have not been replaced. There is valuable work to be done – and it is being done by night and day, by the men who man the dark launches which can swoop dramatically, or nose quietly, into the quiet corners of the tideway. But from the standpoint of the wounded wharves, they feel they are approached mainly from land. And the Metropolitan Police, in whose domain their landward aspect lies, not only have more than enough on their plates – their men of today lack that strange, eclectic knowledge, that esoteric experience of ships and wharves and seamen, which are the very birthright of the P.L.A. Police. And so, whether the cry be heard or not, the need cannot nowadays be answered.

And just as the Thames Division and the Metropolitan Force generally cannot help, nor can the P.L.A. Police, but for a different reason. Their powers are geographically limited. True, s.158 of the Port of London Act, 1968 makes it possible for this to be extended to specified premises but, without reflection on the devoted Miss Novarra, it is all impossibly cumbersome and not really intended to be the key to fit such a keyhole. And yet it is nonsense to maintain – as objectors would surely maintain – that the Authority's expertise is confined to docks alone. It relates to ships and men and places where they go but especially to the Port of London.

But anyway, the P.L.A. police alone could not be the answer, even if the financial complications could be worked out satisfactorily. For this is a major problem in its own right – and one with which P.L.A. cannot deny all concern, because it is its logical policy to move the Port downstream that has caused the keyhole's state. It is a problem which no existing police force could deal with satisfactorily. What, then, is the answer?

I believe the answer lies in the creation of a totally new Police Force – one created expressly to tackle and to solve a problem that is above all a new, a contemporary one, as individual and unique as it is new. After all, the idea of creating a specialised task force is not only not new – it has been operated in the past two decades, when the criminal realised that he had but to flee, when pursued, up or along the motorway as far as the boundary of a fresh Force to put the police service at a disadvantage. To answer this, we have today the Motorway Police – not in this instance a Force with its own Police Authority, but a separate and specialised group of men unified and united in a single task. In a not dissimilar way, I put forward my considered opinion that the only effective thing to prevent London's river and its dockland from deteriorating into the kind of state it was in before Colquhoun came and saw and conquered its villainy, would be to create a specialised and complete Police Force made up of the Port of London and the Thames Division of the Metropolitan Police, but with its jurisdiction limited to, say, the Thames from Blackfriars downstream to the open sea, together with the wharves and all that lie along both banks, including of course the Docks. Such a Force would be neither the Metropolitan Police, nor the P.L.A. Police, but under a specialised Police Authority all its own, financed of course from central public funds.

Among other things, herein would lie an acknowledgement that a Port is more than a dock's system – it is also the River that gave it its first life – in London which connects it even now that its trade has been shifted deliberately downstream. And it would be made up at base of the men who hold between them the history and traditions of the two first professional preventive police forces the world has ever known. The Port of London Authority, upon the creation of such a Force, would of course have no object in exercising any control over it, the new Force leasing police stations on its land where necessary, of course. And its name should be above question – it would be "The Port of London Police", carrying the torch into the future.

Nor is that all the light of the past may enable us to descry. If there is one lesson that history is never tired of repeating to her disciples, it is that life is but a series of phases which appear in embryo, grow sometimes to dominate, and which in time fade and ultimately vanish. I am personally quite convinced that the whole conception of "big is beautiful" which so fills the minds of so many today, will fade in the fullness of time. The enormity of today's marine commerce with which they seem to be obsessed will reveal itself in time to be merely unwieldy. The virtues of the small and manoeuvrable will reappear. Peering into the future by the light of the past, it is possible to discern the outline of a front door to the kingdom no longer tatty, covered with peeling paint. We shall come to see – or if we do not, our children shall – a Pool of London restored to busy, bustling, noisy vivid life, its wharves once more lined with ships – little ships – its docks thrumming with the life it once knew. Granted that certain methods of cargo-handling will never again return to general use – not all new ways are bad, by any means. But containers, for example, can be an economical advantage in themselves, without each one having to be almost as big as a Town Hall!

And whenever – even whether or not, if you like – we have a smart front door to our kingdom, with a keyhole burnished and gleaming proudly, there will be standing to attention at it, to guard it and to protect its people, the present members of the P.L.A. Police, that Force both ancient and honourable. Because the history that we have traced will be part of them, and they will be part of it.

It is not without a very special glory.

THE END

APPENDIX

1. Police Department Killed on Military Service (Alphabetical Order).

Alderson, H.	Constable	Corporal	Coldstream Guards
Amor, A. E.	Constable	Bombardier	R. Horse Artillery
Andrews, W. A.	Constable	Corporal	Royal Fusiliers (C. of London Regiment)
Arnold, A. E.	Constable	Private	Highland L. Infantry
Atley, F. J.	Extra Constable	Corporal	R. F. Artillery
Attwell, G. A.	Constable	Gunner	R. F. Artillery
Badkin, A. L.	Constable	Private	Essex Regiment
Batchelor, W. J.	Constable	Private	Coldstream Guards
Bates, J. G.	Constable	Private	Glos. Regiment
Begley, D. F.	Constable	Gunner	R. Fleet Reserve
Berry, B.	Constable	Private	Yorks. & Lancs. Regt.
Bilby, T. J.	Constable	Gunner	R. F. Artillery
Bull, W. S.	Constable	Gunner	R. Garrison Artillery
Burch, S.	Constable	Corporal	Essex Regiment
Bygrave, J. C.	Constable	Private	Middlesex Regiment
Caddy, W. T.	Constable	Sergeant	Durham L. Infantry
Copple, J. T.	Constable	Rifleman	Rifle Brigade (P.C.)
Cox, F. J.	Constable	Gunner	R. F. Artillery
Crickett, W. R.	Constable	Private	12th Lancers
Crook, W. S.	Constable	Gunner	R. F. Artillery
Day, A.	Constable	L/Corporal	Middlesex Regiment
Faber, J.	Constable	Private	Suffolk Regiment
Fox, E.	Constable	Private	Grenadier Guards
Gale, G. S.	Constable	Private	Grenadier Guards
Griffiths, W. T.	Constable	Labourer	R. A. Ordnance Corps.
Grist, A. G.	Constable	Gunner	R. Garrison Artillery
Groome, A. W.	Constable	Private	Essex Regiment
Hancox, W. J.	Extra Constable	L/Corporal	Scots Guards
Hinves, A. E.	Constable	A.B.	R. Fleet Reserve
Humphrey, T.	Constable	Private	Irish Guards
Kennedy, A. T.	Constable	Rifleman	The Rifle Brigade
Kennet, W. C.	Constable	Private	Scots Guards
Langston, B. W.	Constable	Bombardier	R. F. Artillery
Lloyd, G.	Constable	Sapper	R. Engineers
Lyons, E. E.	Constable	Gunner	R. F. Artillery
Makin, A. R.	Constable	Gunner	R. Garrison Artillery
Maser, C. D.	Constable	Sergeant	Middlesex Regiment
Masters, E. G.	Constable	Private	Grenadier Guards
Merritt, J.	Constable	Private	Royal Marines
Merritt, S. J.	Constable	Private	Grenadier Guards
Moran, A. (M.M.)	Constable	Bombardier	R. G. Artillery
Musto, J. H. G.	Constable	Private	Middlesex Regiment
O'Connell, D.	Constable	Private	R. Munster Fusiliers

Appendix—*continued*

Osterberg, C. T.	Constable	Gunner	R. F. Artillery
Palfrey, E. G. (M.M.)	Constable	L/Sergeant	Grenadier Guards
Parry, T.	P. Sergeant	Gunner	R. F. Artillery
Phillips, E. E.	Constable	L/Corporal	Ox. & Bucks. L. Infantry
Powter, F. A.	Constable	Private	Scots Guards
Prickett, J. W.	Constable	Private	Royal Marines
Ritchie, W. J.	Constable	Sergeant	Grenadier Guards
Roberts, C.	Constable	L/Corporal	Dorsetshire Regiment
Ryan, J.	Extra Constable	L/Corporal	R. West Kent Regiment
Smith, H. S.	Extra Constable	A.B.	R. Fleet Reserve
Stagg, C. E.	Constable	Private	Cheshire Regiment
Turner, W. H.	Constable	Private	Essex Regiment
Walton, G. W.	Pol. Fireman	Private	Royal Marines
Ward, F. H.	Det. Constable	Corporal	Yorkshire Regiment
Wesley, J.	Constable	Private	Grenadier Guards
White, W.	Constable	Private	Grenadier Guards
Williamson, A. J.	Constable	Instructor	Grenade School, Aldershot
Woodley, F. W.	Extra Constable	Private	R. F. City of L. Regiment

---

2. Police Department Decorations and Awards.

MILITARY CROSS

Clack, F.	Det. Constable	C.S.M.	Conspicuous gallantry at all times especially when leading raiding parties.
Shaw, H. V.	Pol. Sergeant	2nd Lt.	Commanding daylight patrol visited 3 hostile posts, rushing 3rd, taking 6 prisoners gaining inf'n. bringing patrol back without casualties. Determined leadership, high courage.

DISTINGUISHED CONDUCT MEDAL
(Seven out of Eight Awarded)

Blunt, W. H.	Constable	Corporal, R.W. Kent Regiment	Conspicuous gallantry in action. Wounded and alone he brought enemy m/gun into use until battle won.
Coe, G. H.	Constable	Sgt. Goldstream Guards	On 18/10/14 nr. Illies, out from trench under fire recovered wounded man lying exposed in open.

Marchant, C. J.	Constable	L/Sgt. Yorks. L. I.	On 21/10/14 at St. Julien rescuing badly wounded man under heavy fire.
Robinson, H.	Pol. Sgt.	C.S.M. R. Dublin Fus.	Devotion to duty. Stayed behind line with small party under heavy fire to collect wounded.
Seaman, A. J.	Constable	Gunner R.F.A.	20/5/15 at Rue du Bois, repairing vital comm'n wires under heavy fire, despite wounds.
Webb, E. J. C.	Constable	Sgt. R.G. Artillery	Gallantry and Dist. service in the field.
Woodhead, S. O.	Constable	A/Sgt. C. of L. Regiment	When enemy shell started mortar shell burning in amm. dump, dismantled it saving many lives thereby.

MILITARY MEDAL

Berry, T. A.	Constable	Sgt. R.F. Arty.	Bravery in the field (**Bar** for f'r same).
Bell, W.	Constable	Cpl. R.H. Arty.	Bravery in the field.
Bouverie, C.	Constable	Sgt. London Rifle Brigade	Bravery in the field.
Brereton, R. G.	Constable	Sgt. R.F. Arty	Bravery in the field.
Bullen, F. J. S.	Constable	Sgt. 4th Hussars	Bravery in the field.
Frost, G. A.	Constable	Sgt. C. of L. Regiment	Bravery in the field.
Martin, W. J.	Constable	C.S.M., K.Af. Rif.	Bravery in the field.
Maxwell, G. W.	Constable	Sgt. M.G. Corps.	Bravery in the field.
Moran, A.	Constable	Bombdr. R.G.A.	Bravery in the field.
Palfrey, E. G.	Constable	Cpl. Grenadier Guards	Bravery in the field.
Potterell, S.	Constable	Sgt. R.H. Arty	Bravery in the field.
Richardson, A. F.	Bge. Schr.	Gunner, R.G.A.	Bravery in the field.
Turner, J. W. G.	Constable	Cpl. R.G.A.	Bravery in the field.
Wren, H.	Constable	Trooper 12th Lancers	Conspicuous gallantry.

Appendix—*continued*

MERITORIOUS SERVICE MEDAL

Baldry, W. A. H.	Det. Insp.	B.Q.M.S., R.F.A.	Val. services with Army of Black Sea.
Major, J. W.	Det. Con.	L/Cpl. Mil. Pol.	Val. services with Forces in France.
Speller, T.	Constable	Private Mil. Pol.	Val. service in France and Flanders.
Tompkins, W. C.	Constable	Sgt. R.F.A.	Val. services with Forces in Italy.

FRENCH MEDAILLE MILITAIRE

Law, W. C.	Constable	Bombdr. R.G.A.	Distinguished services.

ITALIAN BRONZE MEDAL FOR VALOUR

Woodhead, S. O.	Constable	A/Sgt. C. Lond. Regt.	For distinguished service to King of Italy.

ORDER OF BRITISH EMPIRE (Civil)

Baker, E. C. Stuart	Chief Police Officer	O.B.E. 1/1/20
Seaton, J.	Superintendent	M.B.E. 1/1/20
Bower, E.	Chief Insp., C.I.D.	M.B.E. 1/1/20

INDEX